JEWISH
BASEBALL
STARS

JEWISH BASEBALL STARS

Harold U. Ribalow

&

Meir Z. Ribalow

Hippocrene Books
New York, New York

For information, address: Hippocrene Books, Inc.,
171 Madison Avenue, New York, N.Y. 10016

ISBN 0-88254-898-0

Printed in the United States of America

Contents

Acknowledgments

This book has grown out of many sources. Many of the facts and background material were culled from record books, daily newspaper accounts, magazine stories, sports books, personal interviews whenever possible and, now that this edition has been written by two writers, talks with personal friends who follow sports closely and have offered valuable insights into individuals and events.

Our gratitude goes to:

Frank Slocum of the National League, who made available all records, data and personal stories he had about the Jewish baseball players who starred in the National League. Without his help, the stories on Johnny Kling, Harry Danning, Morrie Arnovich and Dolly Stark would have been less complete than they are;

Bill Klem (still alive when the first edition of this volume was being prepared, but who has died since), great National League umpire, who helped track down some of the facts and stories about Dolly Stark and Johnny Kling;

Andy Cohen, whose long detailed letters have been tremendous aids in putting down a more complete story about him than could otherwise have been published;

Morrie Arnovich, whose cooperation was both necessary and welcome and who is no longer with us;

Larry Klein of *Sport* magazine, who provided background material on Ken Holtzman;

Arthur J. Horton of Princeton University, who made available records on Moe Berg, one of that university's most unusual graduates;

Dr. Edward Craig and Stephen J. Spaulding for sharing insights on baseball;

Tilden G. Edelstein for his informative article on Andy and Syd Cohen, "Cohen at the Bat," in the November, 1983 issue of *Commentary* magazine.

And to the various people and organizations who helped in the gathering of the hard-to-get photographs of the sports personalities included in this book.

Most of the sources used and quoted appear within the pages of this study and it would be repetitious to name them again, except that some of the books have been of special meaning and importance in organizing and writing a book of this kind. Let us, then, offer our special thanks to the following sports books:

The Jew in Sports by Stanley Frank, for historical surveys and overviews;

Moe Berg: Athlete, Scholar, Spy by Louis Kaufman, Barbara Fitzgerald and Tom Sewell, an original and exciting study of the Princeton scholar and baseball catcher, and spy;

Morris Berg: The Real Moe by Ethel Berg, an interesting collection of memorabilia about the author's brother;

The Great No-Hitters by Glenn Dickey, for its accounts of Sandy Koufax and Ken Holtzman;

How the Weather Was by Roger Kahn, for its special insight into the baseball career of Al Rosen;

Famous American Athletes of Today, Twelfth Series by Frank Waldman, for its interesting story on Sid Gordon;

Koufax by Sandy Koufax and Ed Linn;

ACKNOWLEDGMENTS ix

The Summer Game and *Five Seasons* by Roger Angell, for their general excellence and brilliant accounts of some of Sandy Koufax' feats;

Dock Ellis in the Country of Baseball by Donald Hall.

Encyclopedia of Jews in Sports by Bernard Postal, Jesse Silver and Roy Silver, an absolutely invaluable book for *all* sports fans, and particularly for historical information on old-time baseball player Erskine Mayer;

as well as reference volumes like *Current Biography,*

and librarians at the New York Public Library at 42nd Street and the Donnell Branch and at the Firestone Library at Princeton University.

Other credits are strewn throughout this work.

The footnotes "H.U.R." and "M.Z.R." that appear from time to time in personal eye-witness passages, indicate which of the two authors was the "witness" at the moment.

JEWISH
BASEBALL
STARS

Why *Jewish* Athletes?

"Why," a well-meaning friend asked, "are you writing this book? Does it really make a difference that Al Rosen and Sandy Koufax were Jewish, Joe Louis or Joe Morgan black or John McGraw an Irishman?"

The best answer would be that it shouldn't make any difference, but the sports fan, like the average citizen (who is the sports fan in another guise) likes to know all about his idols; he wants to know their history; he wants to be able to attach himself to them. Sports lovers are really dreamers. One of the attractions of sports is that the spectator can and does project himself into the shape of his heroes and makes believe that it is he, and not they, who are performing the great deeds which make all America cheer wildly. Therefore, the Negro, or black, fan feels closer to the black athlete than he does to the white one. Italian fans have a tendency to root for Italian ball players and Jewish fans take a special interest in Jewish players. It is hard to deny this conclusion, for life is not an isolated thing and neither is the sports world. The tie between the individual and his society is strong and so is the tie between the sports fan and his hero.

All men are gregarious. They are proud of their relatives, of their townsfolk, of their co-religionists, if these people do something outstanding. And because the world of sports is a great leveller, because there is a greater degree of equality between contestants in sports than in most battles in life, the sports world is, in a very true sense, one of the best of all possible worlds.

The sports world is a simple place in which to live. There are few complexities in that universe. There is the hero — and there is the villain. There is the champion — and there is the challenger. There is the big guy — and the little guy. There are drama and tragedy and disillusion and passion and hysteria, but they are starkly simple. Few sports heroes are contemplative people. And the fans, complex as they may be, shed their worries, their phobias, their complexes as they enter the sports arena. Games are fast and physically skilful. The cleverness of a boxer, the grace of a baseball player, the keen analytical mind of a football quarterback are unlike the cleverness, grace and keen analysis necessary in other spheres. There have been some exceptionally clever baseball players — unlettered men who never threw to the wrong base — who were rather stupid in other fields. Conversely, there have been intelligent, educated men who, playing a game, have been slow-witted.

So in considering the sports world, one must realize that it is a world entire unto itself. And the sports personalities described here are placed in their sports niche and are compared on a sports level.

Thus it must be realized that in the sports world the fan and the athlete are sometimes aware of bonds which would be overlooked by those who are not sports lovers. When there was a swelling of black pride upon the accomplishments of Jackie Robinson and the hundreds of black ball players who followed him; when Jews took pride in Benny

Leonard, or Hank Greenberg, or Sandy Koufax, it is to be taken seriously.

Here is why.

In the simple world of sports, victory is all-important. The word "champion" has wonderful connotations. It means just that, "champion," the one man at the head of the class. The "champion of the world" in boxing means that the champion can beat any other fighter in the world at his weight. It is a thrilling and all-embracing thought.

Therefore, when a Jewish prize fighter wins a title, as Benny Leonard, Barney Ross and Abe Attell did, it means to sports fans that Jews can fight. They don't need lengthy, scientific treatises to show them that Jews have guts; they don't need long histories to show them that Jews have participated in national wars; Israel has given enough evidence of that. But if they see a Jewish fighter wearing the Star of David and showing courage in the ring, they have proof enough of bravery.

And when they see a Jewish baseball catcher stand up to flying spikes and tag out a desperate runner, they know it is a lie to call Jews cowards.

Hank Greenberg, hitting the pennant-winning home run in the last game of the season in 1945, taught baseball followers that a Greenberg is as dangerous in a pinch as Babe Ruth or any super-star.

Larry Sherry, coming into a World Series, game after game, and stopping his opponents in their tracks, personified grace under pressure.

Sandy Koufax, pitching a perfect game while suffering from arthritis, demonstrated a remarkable degree of courage as well as skill.

Al Rosen, who grew up fighting Jew-baiters with a combative tenacity and fierce spirit that forced even his opponents to regard the tough ballplayer with respect and admiration, summed it up this way: "I wanted it to be, Here comes one Jewish kid that every Jew in the world can be proud of."

And so it goes.

The sports world is a spectacular world, an interesting world, and always a dramatic world.

That it and its followers are, in essence, tolerant and basically democratic, is proved by the very success of the headliners included in this volume.

The National Game

In the reams and reams of paper written about baseball, the sport's basic attraction is seldom stressed. It is this: baseball is America's most democratic game. The ball park is where everyone comes with his hair down, so to speak. The fans take off their jackets, roll up their sleeves, jeer or cheer at the players and forget their outside troubles, worries and tensions. In a sense, the same could be said for any sport, with this difference: one of the main attractions of baseball is to be part of the crowd. That is to say, it is not only the game itself which attracts the fan; it is the comforting knowledge that you know your neighbor, like you, is interested in the game itself and that he is, if only for a few hours, your buddy.

The fight crowd is, generally speaking, a pretty cynical body of fans. The gamblers, the people with primitive instincts and willing to display them, go to the fights, which cost more than baseball seats. One can pay hundreds of dollars for a seat at a prize fight and only a few dollars for a baseball seat. The football crowd is mainly a young group, especially collegians at the college games, and perennial collegians at the professional games, although in recent years pro football has grizzled fans as well. Here, as at baseball games, you get a cross-section of the nation, but somehow the camaraderie of baseball is lacking. The tempo is different; there is no time element in baseball.

Perhaps, also, the reason is that football is played once a week and too many people try to squeeze all their thrills into a short period of time.

Some of the best sports writing in recent years has been about baseball and its unique fascination. Donald Hall, a distinguished poet, happens to be a baseball follower and he published a book on the pitcher Dock Ellis, entitled *Dock Ellis in the Country of Baseball.* Hall phrases with eloquence the magic of the sport: "In the country of baseball, time is the air we breathe, and the wind swirls us backward and forward, until we seem so reckoned in time and seasons that all time and all seasons become the same." Hall continues: "Baseball is a country all to itself. It is an old country, like Ruritania, northwest of Bohemia and its seacoast ... It is a wrong-end-of-the-telescope country, like the landscape people build for model trains, miniature with distance and old age. The citizens wear baggy pinstripes, knickers and caps. Seasons and teams shift, blur into each other, change radically or appear to change, and restore themselves to old ways again. Citizens retire to farms, in the country of baseball, smoke cigars and reminisce, and all at once they are young players again, lean and intense, running the base paths with filled spikes ... In the country of baseball, men rise to glory in their twenties and their early thirties — a garland briefer than a girl's or at least briefer than a young woman's — with an abrupt rise, like scaling a cliff, and then the long meadow slopes downward. Citizens of the country of baseball retire and yet they never retire."

Probably the best of all baseball writers is Roger Angell, author of two classic volumes, *The Summer Game* and *Five Seasons.* He describes games in careful and loving detail;

he devotes a remarkable chapter to the baseball itself; to a
baseball scout scouring the country for talent; to upcoming
players, to stars on the decline, on the exhibition games, on
key games, on the World Series and, from time to time, on
the beauty and poetry of the game itself.

Read this magnificent passage and you will begin to understand the attraction of the game to an intelligent, sensitive, cultured man:

"Always, it seems, there is something more to be discovered about this game. Sit quietly in the upper stand and
look at the field. Half close your eyes against the sun, so
that the players recede a little, and watch the movements of
baseball. The pitcher, immobile on the mound, holds the
inert white ball, his little lump of physics. Now with abrupt
gestures he gives it enormous speed and direction, converting it suddenly into a line, a moving line. The batter,
wielding a plane, attempts to intercept the line and acutely
alter it, but he fails; the ball, a line again, is redrawn to the
pitcher, in the center of this square, the diamond . . . In
time, these and other lines are drawn on the field; the batter and the fielders are also transformed into fluidity, moving and converting, and we see now that all movement in
the baseball is a convergence toward fixed points — the
pitched ball toward the plate, the thrown ball toward the
right angle of the bases, the batted ball toward the as yet
undrawn but already visible point of congruence with
either the ground or a glove."

Angell remarks, after further descriptions of batting and
fielding, "It is neat, it is pretty, it is satisfying." Then, like
Donald Hall, he also notices the element of time. "The last
dimension," he writes, "is time. Within the ball park, time
moves differently, marked by no clock except the events of

the game. This is the unique, unchangeable feature of baseball, and perhaps explains why this sport . . . remains somehow rustic, unviolent, and introspective. Baseball's time is seamless and invisible, a bubble within which players move at exactly the same pace and rhythms as all their predecessors . . . Since baseball time is measured only in outs, all you have to do is succeed utterly; keep hitting, keep the rally alive, and you have defeated time."

Baseball is a pastoral sport, a leisurely game. To the uninitiated it is slow-moving. The non-baseball fan does not appreciate the background of the game. He cannot understand the struggle between a pitcher and a batter because he doesn't know, for example, that the pitcher may be striving for a strikeout record and that the batter is swinging for, say, his fiftieth two-base hit of the season. In a word, the person who comes to a ball game for the spectacle value alone, misses the backbone of the game: the facts and figures, the statistics, which make every single play an important one in the overall context of the single game and the overall season and the entire career of the athlete.

It is this understanding which brings baseball fans together. You can root for any one of some fifty players on the two squads during the course of a game. You can quote the batting averages of your favorites and a loud-mouthed fan can come back with statistics about his own men. The fan pays his money, yells at the players, the umpire, at his heroes. He argues with the guy sitting next to him, he buys a cold drink, a hot dog and a score card and for a few hours he is transported into another world. The weather is good (baseball games are not played in heavy rains or in the snow or in zero temperature, like football games), the game is played outdoors (not in a smoke-filled arena, like basketball or hockey) and time stands still (none of this two minutes left to play, as is the case with football, hockey, basketball and other sports).

Unfortunately, comparatively few Jews have made the major leagues. It is an outdoor game and the Jews in America have lived in the large cities. If you were to read about most major leaguers, you would discover that they come from small towns and hamlets of the United States. Amazingly few come from the crowded urban areas. Nevertheless, there have been a substantial number of Jewish baseball players. Some rank with the top stars in the game; others were mediocre; some lasted a very brief time in the big leagues.

The stories of the players in this volume are self-explanatory. It was impossible to write full-length stories about every Jewish ball player to hit the big time and somewhere a line had to be drawn. It is entirely likely that some better players were omitted and that some inferior players have been given too much space. For example, Benny Kauff, who led the Federal League two years in a row and then played good ball for the New York Giants, was undoubtedly a better athlete than some of the baseball players here included. The same may hold true for Lipman Pike who, according to the authors of *Encyclopedia of Jews in Sports*, was baseball's first professional player. Or take Barney Pelty, a teammate of George Stone. But these men played a very long time ago and their feats and personalities somehow have not carried down through the years. Others moved into and out of the major leagues so rapidly that they require hardly more than a passing glance, unless one can read a moral or an example into their careers, as one can into the professional baseball life of Andy Cohen, who represented a search for a Jewish star. Harry Eisenstat knocked around the big leagues for a long time as a southpaw pitcher, but never really made his mark. Phil Weintraub was a hitter but not much of a defensive player and he could not hold on. Fred Sington, a fine gridiron player as well as a baseball player, could not hit the curve ball and he came and went rapidly. Jimmy Reese of the Yankees, Joe Ginsburg of the Tigers, Barry Latman of the White Sox — the names come to mind, and vanish.

There also is the problem of who is and who is not a Jewish player. There has been an ongoing debate about Johnny Kling. Years after he was included in Jewish all-star teams, his family said that he was not Jewish. But I remember checking the National League records as long ago as 1947 and he was even then listed as Jewish. On the other hand, there are those who would include Rod Carew in a book of this kind because the Jamaican-born baseball player, who has been a great hitter and American Leauge batting champion for seven seasons, is studying, at this writing to convert to Judaism. He was the subject of cover stories in many national magazines when it appeared he might bat .400 in 1977 (He ended up hitting .338). At the time, however, he was not a Jew and thus had not "qualifed" for admission.

Baseball is a hard profession. A man has to be exceptionally talented to reach the big leagues and then a combination of skill and luck keeps him there long enough for him to win recognition as a star. Not many Jews went in for professional sports, because there was not much encouragement at home. Baseball did not become "respectable" until after Babe Ruth's homeric feats with the bat attracted all elements of American life to the ball parks of the nation. It is also clear that in the early, pioneering days of the game, Jewish players were given a hard time. Some changed their name. Others had to fight their way, literally, into the lineup. Al Rosen said as much. Saul Rogovin felt the lash of anti-Semitism. It is possible the same happened with Ken Holtzman in a more recent period, as the reader can discover in reading the chapter on Holtzman's career. Yet Jewish players were looked for in the 1920's and when Andy Cohen broke into the Giant lineup, he won publicity throughout the United States. A Jewish star, it was obvious, would draw additional fans in the big cities where Jews lived. But baseball was prejudiced for a very long time. Black players did not come into the game until Jackie Robinson broke the color bar, and then the gates were opened and now it is almost impossible to keep with the constant flow of black players.

Jews have had other options. Constantly seeking an education, Jews in the United States preferred medicine, the law, other professions, teaching, business, to the athletic field. This is why the number of Jewish basketball players diminished. It is why there are scarcely any Jews in professional football.

But history remains and looking to the past and even the immediate past, we find that Jews have made a significant contribution to baseball. It is the national game and the Jew is part and parcel of the national life of the United States. To that extent, Jews and baseball are tied together.

A RARE PHOTOGRAPH OF JOHNNY KLING

Johnny Kling
The Matchless Catcher

Until Babe Ruth placed baseball in the high income brackets, the game suffered in a social sense as well. The sport was played by men who were not acceptable everywhere. It was possible for illiterates like Joe Jackson to get by on their tremendous talent alone. Eccentrics like "Bugs" Raymond were permitted to pitch even if they did take too many drinks. In those "good old days," which were not really so good, the teams travelled in buses and slept in poor hotels. Today the men are set up at the finest hotels in every major league city, and they are taught the niceties of life.

For example, fellows like Ted Williams, who were brash and confident, were taught to behave. When Williams first broke into the big time, he refused to wear a tie in the hotel. Because he was still young and perhaps over-confident, his manager sent him back to the bush leagues, with the admonition that he'd have to learn to wear a tie.

The day of the Ring Lardner type of player, dumb, un-educated but talented, is nearly gone. Of course now and then a wise-guy player may break in. His ability brings him up. But within a season or two he is taught to behave not like a foolish athlete, but like a public figure, a man who has his own sort of dignity and position to uphold.

Back in 1900, when baseball was fairly old in years alone, but not well accepted by the masses of people, the game was harsh. Men played hard. They were paid little and they were drawn to the game mainly because they loved it. Today, one can safely say that every player considers his finances in the game. But in 1900, when pay was small, when crowds were meager and when the more decent elements of American life opposed the game, it took a lot of passion for the game to keep a player in it.

According to baseball historians, baseball was first played in 1836. Perhaps it was. But baseball became really national in the twenties, when Ruth hit his home runs and everybody, sports fan or not, came to see the Babe do his stuff. Before that time it was a catch-as-catch-can proposition. The players were a bit too casual; drinking was usual among players and managers and statistics of baseball, really the life-blood of the game, were virtually unknown. The newspapers gave baseball some space, but not near the society sections.

All this leads up to the story of Johnny Kling. Johnny was one of the greatest catchers baseball ever knew. According to Grantland Rice, who observed the game for years and years, Kling was one of the smartest men who ever handled a catcher's mitt.

In an interesting magazine article, Rice said that it was amazing how many men who were brilliant in school were not particularly bright on the ball field, while untutored men sometimes were geniuses on the diamond. Babe Ruth, for example, is known never to have made a mental mistake in baseball. He never threw to the wrong base; he never ran foolishly. Everyone makes automatic errors, like bobbling a ball, but some men know instinctively what to do in a split second. These men are born that way, and no college degree gives them that extra sense.

Johnny Kling, whose real name was Kline, and who was born in Kansas City, November 13, 1875, was a born ball player.

Catching has always been a thankless job. It is physically wearing. Crouching all day takes the spring out of a man's legs. The catcher is part of every play. He calls every pitch. He must be aware of the weakness of every single batter who steps into the hitter's box. He is always in danger of a split finger. Foul balls bounce off his chest. Runners slide high into home plate, the base which every batter aims to cross. At other positions a man can relax momentarily. A catcher is the brains of the game. Even the leading base stealers say that they steal off the catcher, not the pitcher.

In the rich and fascinating history of baseball, there has never been a better catcher than Johnny Kling. And he caught in a day when pitchers were permitted to throw spit balls and other sorts of dangerous pitches which are now outlawed.

Unfortunately, the baseball days of Johnny Kling were not modern. Kling never had an audience of 50,000 or 60,000 to watch him catch. He held the great Ty Cobb a whole World Series without allowing the great outfielder to steal a base, but fewer people knew it then than know the batting average of today's current stars.

National picture magazines did not splash Johnny's squatting figure on its front page. Johnny Kling played baseball in a hard day. From 1893 through 1895 and from 1897 through 1898, Kling played semi-professional baseball. And that was tougher than any other kind. It is nearly impossible to trace records back to those days, but it is obvious that Kling went to a good school, for when he joined the Houston club in 1899 and the St. Joseph team in 1900, he was a great player. In the Texas League he used his Jewish name of Kline.

In 1901 Johnny Kling became a member of the Chicago Cubs, the Cubs who are a legendary team today. This was the Cub team of Tinker-to-Evers-to-Chance. It was this club which won many flags. This was the team with Three-Finger Brown. This was the Cub team which made baseball fans glow with pride. Each man was a real player, and the best of them all was Johnny Kling.

And in this whirl of hard baseball, among these men trained in a hard school, a tough Jewish player from Kansas City showed them all how the national game was to be played.

Because baseball was not fully recorded in those days it is hard to get facts and figures about Johnny Kling. The bare statistics are to be found, but the color stories, the interviews, the detailed stories of the man's life are hidden in the fog of time.

It is easy to follow Kling's career in the World Series. For somewhere along the line, a sports fan can always get the history of the Series. In 1906, Johnny played against the White Sox. In a day when hitting .300 was a tremendous feat, Kling batted .312. And a Series historian, writing at that time, called him "the matchless Kling".

Baseball before Ruth was a different game from modern baseball. It was a thinking game. One run meant a lot. Home runs were rare. "Home Run" Baker, who won this famous name with the Philadelphia A's, did not hit more than nine homers the year he won his appellation. One run often meant a game. The ball was dead. The infielders were shrewd and the pitchers were strong, crafty men who knew more about their art than seems possible.

All this placed a heavier burden on a catcher than the catcher carries today. The game is so well organized now that no rookie is completely unknown to a complete team. When a new man breaks in against the Yankees, some Yankee played in the minors with the new man, or played against him. Baseball today is a continuous chain, and no player can get away from it. In Kling's day, each time at bat was a struggle between the catcher and the batter, with the pitcher as the puppet in between.

For Kling to lead his club to a flag and hit .312, was nearly incredible. But he became even better later in his career.

In 1907, the Cubs won another pennant and this time they met the Detroit Tigers, headed by the immortal Ty Cobb. It is impossible today to realize how good Cobb was. Not only did he lead the American League in batting twelve times, but he stole more bases than any player in baseball. He is the top man insofar as dynamite in baseball is concerned. Cobb lived baseball. He went to bed at night and thought of a flaw he found in a pitcher and in his mind he replayed the game. And when he discovered what he wanted, he planned to pull a play against the same pitcher three months later! Cobb was a master of the game. He studied it the way a Heifetz studies the violin. He was the most feared player baseball ever knew, because he was hard and cruel when he wanted to do something on the diamond. He flew into a base with spikes high. He sneered at rookies and tried to frighten them. He lorded over the field and when he quit he was acknowledged as the greatest outfielder in baseball. Ruth was more spectacular and hit a longer ball, but Cobb did everything else better than anyone else in history.

It was against Ty Cobb and his team that Johnny Kling did his best work. The first game ended in a thrilling 3-3 tie. Kling drove in one of the Cub runs with a single in the fourth inning. The Cubs won the second game 3-1. Kling singled in the second inning to start a rally. But he stopped Ty Cobb cold on the base paths and taught every other Tiger that it was death to run against Mr. Kling. The Series went five games, and the historian of the classic put it this way: "Kling was one of the bright stars of the Series and his superiority in his position gave the Cubs a decided advantage."

In 1909, Kling was a holdout. But it was not at all like the modern day stuff. He really meant it, and when the Cubs refused to see things his way, Johnny played semi-professional ball and a few games with Jimmy Callahan's Logan Square Club of Chicago. In 1910, he rejoined the Cubs and led them to another pennant. His value was obvious, now that he was back. But there was bad blood between the management and Johnny, and in 1911 Kling was sold to the Boston Braves. In 1913, the Braves sold him to the Cincinnati Reds and from there Kling slipped out of the big leagues. He died on February 1, 1947 at the age of seventy-one; at his death he was a wealthy man, due to his wise real estate investments.

In his day baseball was a passion to those who played it. Today it is a business. But the fans are never fooled, and if Johnny Kling's name and accomplishments are alive today, you can bet that he was all he was cracked up to be.

To the modern fan, Kling is remote and means only that he was an old-time great. They look at the players of today and think they are the best. But memories are long and baseball history is persistent. The name of Johnny Kling will always symbolize the best in the game.

ERSKINE MAYER, A WINNING PITCHER

Erskine Mayer

Twenty-Game Winner

Of the vast numbers of men who have played major league baseball, few have had more experiences than Erskine Mayer, the ace righthanded hurler of the Philadelphia Phillies during the second decade of the 1900's. During the course of his career, he became a star on a pennant-winning team with the legendary Grover Cleveland Alexander, moved on to a second team where he was involved in one of the great marathon pitcher's duels in history, and while with a third team became an innocent participant in one of the greatest scandals in the history of sports.

From the very beginning, "Erk" had a most unusual background. In an interview with the authors of the *Encyclopedia of Jews in Sports*, Erskine's brother, Mark, said, "My mother's mother converted to the Jewish religion. She traced her ancestry back to the Mayflower. That branch of the family was given tracts of land in what was then Virginia Territory and is Kentucky today. My grandmother's brother, Captain James Allen, ran a boat from Hannibal, Missouri, to New Orleans. Samuel Clemens received his name of 'Mark Twain' from marking twain on Captain Allen's boat.

"My grandparents on my father's side came from Germany. They were musicians. My father, Morris Mayer, wrote an opera in Hebrew. Grandmother's father was a

21

buyer for Bismarck and was murdered. His body was found years later buried in a stable."

Erskine's parents moved from Ohio to Georgia, and Erskine was born in Atlanta. His father, a concert pianist and music teacher, enjoyed baseball and played catch with his three sons. It wasn't long before Erskine's talent for throwing the ball became evident. After Georgia Military Academy, he attended Georgia Tech to study engineering. But he was known in college primarily as a baseball star. He was so good that while still an undergraduate, he was offered a contract with the Atlanta Crackers. In 1910, his senior year, he dropped out of college and went to Fayetteville of the East Carolina League, where he pitched in twenty games and racked up an amazing 15-2 won-lost record. It was clear that the slender righthander was meant for bigger and better things than the Southern minor league level of competition.

After winning fourteen games for Albany, Georgia, Erskine hurled twenty-six victories for Portsmouth while losing only nine; he also fanned two hundred twenty-six batters. That same year, the Phillies called him up to the major leagues. Mayer only got into seven games that season, with a 6-1 record, and he was 9-9 in 1913, his first year in the big leagues. But in 1914, he hit his stride and emerged as one of the finest pitchers in the National League. Hurling for a weak ballclub, Erskine won twenty-one games while losing nineteen, and chalked up· an impressive E.R.A. of 2.58.

He won the respect and admiration of baseball men all around the league. Although he had good speed on his fastball, he didn't depend on "smoke" as a primary weapon; he relied on superb control, a tricky delivery that was alternately underhand and sidearm, and a curveball so formidable that Dodger skipper Wilbert Robinson called Erskine "Eelskine" because the sharp-breaking curve was "so slippery."

To accurately measure Mayer's accomplishment, one need only consider that while he was winning twenty-one games for Philadelphia, the entire team could only manage seventy wins for the entire season!

But however good Mayer was, he had the misfortune to be the pitching partner — indeed, the roommate — of one of the greatest pitchers in the history of the game. Immortal hurler Grover Cleveland "Pete" Alexander, later elected to the Hall of Fame, toiled for the same hapless Phillie team, and Erskine was always in his shadow. The fine righty was seemingly always surpassed by his great partner. "Every time I pitched well, Alexander topped me," Erskine conceded.

In 1914, when Erskine won his twenty-one games, Pete won twenty-seven. In 1915, Mayer had an even finer season. Again he won twenty-one, but this time lost only fifteen. His E.R.A. was reduced to a paltry 2.36. But once again, his efforts were outshone by Alexander, whose phenomenal season included thirty-one victories. Between the two of them, they led the Phillies to the National League pennant, one of the few flags the Phillies have ever won.

Ironically, one area in which Erskine far outstripped Alex was at the plate. While Philadelphia's team batting average was a miserable .247, an historic low for a pennant-winning team, Mayer cracked out twenty-one hits in forty-three games for a .239 average, including two doubles, a triple and a home run!

The first Jewish pitcher in history to win twenty games in consecutive seasons, Mayer had tough luck in the World Series. He lost the second game of the Series to the Red Sox, 2-1. Although Boston managed ten hits off Erskine, the wily righthander continuously shut them off when it counted, and it wasn't until the ninth inning that Boston managed to squeeze out a victory. His teammates simply could not provide Mayer with any batting support. In the fifth game of the Series, Alexander was supposed to pitch, but just before the game Alex came down with an arm injury. The Phillies desperately rushed Mayer into the game, unrested and unprepared as he was; the Red Sox hit him hard, winning the game and the Series.

In 1916, Mayer could only manage a 7-7 record, but he returned to form the following year with an 11-6 mark and 2.75 E.R.A. in twenty-eight games. Midway through the 1918 season, he was 7-4 for Philadelphia when they sent him to Pittsburgh; he quickly showed that they had acted hastily when he attained a 9-3 mark with a distinguished record of 16-7, with seventeen complete games out of twenty-eight appearances, and an E.R.A. of 2.65.

It was during that season, shortly after he had joined Pittsburgh, that Mayer was a principal in one of the most remarkable games in big league history. He started a game against the Boston Braves, who sent Art Nehf to the mound. For inning after inning, Mayer and Nehf engaged in an awesome pitching duel. After nine innings, the game was still a scoreless deadlock, and both hurlers continued on into extra innings, as untouchable as ever. Unbelievably, the contest was still scoreless after sixteen innings, when Wilbur Cooper finally relieved the exhausted Erskine. Cooper continued where the slim righthander had left off, and finally, in the twenty-first inning, Pittsburgh eked a pair of runs out of Nehf and won the classic, 2-0.

In 1919, Mayer was 5-3 with the Pirates when they traded him to the Chicago White Sox of the American League, who were driving for the pennant and sorely needed the experienced winner that Erskine had proven himself. The White Sox won the pennant, but that was the World Series in which it was later revealed that several Chicago stars had deliberately thrown the games so as to assure a Cincinnati victory and secret gambling winnings. It was the worst scandal in baseball history. Several players were barred from the game for life, and the team is historically known as the "Black Sox." Erskine, who had made two appearances in the Series with an 0-1 record, had been completely ignorant of the dishonesty. When he found out, he was shattered by the revelation that his teammates had lost on purpose.

Mayer never played another major league game. He returned to Atlanta, pitched one game for that minor league team in 1920, and then retired from baseball. Stanley Frank writes in *The Jew in Sports* that Mayer had pitched out his arm and quit because he was physically worn out. But Mayer's wife offers a more convincing explanation: "Erk loved baseball for the true sport it afforded, and he felt if a game had been thrown he was through with baseball."

Erskine Mayer left the game with a lifetime mark of 91-70, a winning percentage of .559 that would be the envy of many a pitcher. The Jewish star will be remembered as a fine all-around ball player, a man of honor and one of the best righthanded hurlers of his time.

ANDY COHEN IN HIS HEYDAY

Andy Cohen

Morning Glory

There never has been a baseball player quite like Andy Cohen, the Jewish second baseman who replaced Rogers Hornsby at the keystone sack for the New York Giants in the fabulous twenties.

No player of his time got more reams of publicity than Andy. At no time in baseball annals (until the sudden emergence of Negroes in the big leagues) did the race and religious angle receive more prominence. In his era Andy Cohen was more than just a rookie trying to make good; he was all Jewry trying to make a mark in baseball.

Boxing and other major sports had their outstanding Jewish personalities; but could the Jew play baseball? Only Johnny Kling had proved that he could, and Johnny was the sole exception, though his name was not Cohen and his heyday was the pre-Babe Ruth era, when baseball was a rough sport, not exactly admired in the widest circles.

It is a matter of record that Andy Cohen did not develop into the finest Jewish baseball player of all time. But for a while he had the entire sports world agog with excitement. National magazines splashed his life story throughout their pages. Leading sports columnists called him a good replacement for Hornsby, and Rogers was one of the best right-handed hitters the game has known.

It was wrong to compare Andy Cohen with Rogers Hornsby. It was not fair to the Jewish boy and Hornsby was generous about it. When a New York paper ran a daily box score on both Hornsby and Cohen — to show that Andy was outshining the veteran — Hornsby said, "That's a lousy trick to play on the kid. I ain't hittin' now, but when I start I'll lose him." And Frank Graham, who told this story, added, "Which, of course, he did."

But the hysteria over a potentially great Jewish ball player was tremendous. Here is Grantland Rice's story in the *New York Herald Tribune* the day after Cohen made his debut with the Giants. To add to the drama, the Giants were facing the Boston Braves, with whom Hornsby was playing.

"It was Andy Cohen, the young Jewish ball player from Alabama University, who stepped into Hornsby's job at second for the Giants and lifted 30,000 frozen spectators to their frostbitten feet at the season's formal opening by taking full charge of a wild attack that beat Boston, 5 to 2.

"It was Andy Cohen, the Tuscaloosa Terror, who drove in two Giant runs, scored two more on his own hook, and covered the infield sod of the Polo Grounds, like a ball-playing centipede, to send the Giants spinning along to victory through a wind that came sweeping down from the Barren Lands with a rush and a roar.

"You may have heard of the Cohens and Kellys in the halls of the cinema, but it was the Cohen of Coogan's Bluff who took over the pictorial lead and kept the crowd from freezing stiffer than a Lapland iceberg...

"One old-timer became so excited that he stood up near the close of the game and begun to recite:

" 'And when he cracked another hit
And left big Hornsby flat
Not a tooter in the crowd could doubt
'Twas Cohen at the bat.' "

Rice, the dean of sports writers, was not the only one to wax so lyrical over the exploits of Cohen. James R. Harrison of the *New York Times* wrote as follows:

"It was, by far, the greatest demonstration to an individual player that we have ever seen — at least to a player who a year ago was an unknown minor leaguer and had never set foot on the Giant home field."

In the wave of enthusiasm for the Jewish hero, more than one parody of Ernest L. Thayer's immortal baseball poem "Casey at the Bat" was composed and printed in Cohen's honor. One of these variations of "Cohen at the Bat," while ostensibly celebrating Andy's opening-day feats, contains in its "praise" the kind of embarrassingly stereotypical references that suggest the kind of prejudice that Andy and other Jewish ballplayers had to fight during their careers. Included in this poem were the following lines:

And from the stands and bleachers
    the cry of "Oy, Oy" rose,
And up came Andy Cohen half a
    foot behind his nose.

and:

It was make or break for Andy,
    while the fans cried "Oy, Oy, Oy."
And it wasn't any soft spot for a
    little Jewish boy.

As Tilden G. Edelstein notes in an article in *Commentary,* Andy's debut was considered an event of such importance that the *New York Times* noted it not just in the sports section, but in an editorial as well. "Hogans," claimed the *Times,* "have always played good baseball; so have the Kellys and the Caseys, the Delehantys and the Bresnehans, so have the Wagners and the Zimmers. And the Lazzeris, the Lajoies, and the Chances have contributed stars for many years. But the Cohens . . .? None of their kinfolk has ornamented the professional diamond in New York." When a Cohen succeeds, continued the editorial, there is "much more than just a baseball game at stake."

Andy's own version of the story, a bit blurred by the years, mixes up some of the facts, but he admits that it was a thrilling day for him. This is what Andy told me.*

"In 1928 'opening day' against Boston was a thrilling day. We beat them 5-3 (the score was 5-2) and I believe I scored and knocked in either four or all the runs (he did). After the game McGraw shook my hand and said, 'Good game, kid, and now you have only 153 more to go.' "

In the early hysteria, many stories were passed around. One enthusiast wanted to change the name of Coogan's Bluff, which overlooked the Polo Grounds, to Cohen's Bluff. And Harry Stevens, who made a fortune selling drinks, hot dogs and peanuts to sports fans in parks all over the nation, was supposed to have told his boys, "Remember, in the Polo Grounds you are no longer selling ice cream cones, but ice cream Cohens."

Andy's performance reminded sports fans of John

*H.U.R.

McGraw's dream of a lifetime: "If there was only a Jewish baseball player who could fill the park." McGraw was good to Andy, who told me, "As far as I am concerned, McGraw was the greatest man in baseball. Although I have profound admiration for others, including Tris Speaker, Donnie Bush, Dave Bancroft, Mike Kelly of Minneapolis, John Ogden, former owner of Elmira, all of whom I have played for."

Andy Cohen was a natural athlete. At the age of sixteen he was a high school star on his team in El Paso, Texas. He was so good that he could have started as a professional even then. But he wanted an education. So he went to the University of Alabama. Andy tells me that "I was a three-letter man — football, basketball and baseball. I was elected captain of the baseball team, the first Jew to be captain of any varsity sport at Alabama." His exploits won him so much fame and so many offers that he succumbed after three years at Alabama and signed up to play baseball for pay. He joined Waco of the Texas League in 1925 and in less than two months was sold to the New York Giants for $25,000 and another player.

Andy's debut was an amusing one and is worth retelling. Here is the story as Andy Cohen told it to me: "My first appearance as a Giant was as pinch-hitter for Frank Frisch, in Philadelphia in 1926. I singled to center on the first pitch. I was so surprised when McGraw called me off the bench (Frisch had a sore foot) that I couldn't open any of the buttons on my jacket. There were no zippers at that time. So I jerked with both hands and buttons flew to the left and right. McGraw remarked, 'What does he care for expenses?' "

But McGraw wanted Andy to get real experience. He

couldn't very well break in with the great Frisch on the team. Andy, at this point, showed a lot of common sense. He showed himself willing to go to the minors to gain experience. Many players would have remained with the parent club, but Andy was looking for work, not obscurity. So he chose Buffalo, while Frisch and then Hornsby covered second for the Giants.

Andy never regretted the decision he made. With the Bisons he was a star and one of the most popular men on the club. He showed his appreciation by hitting .353. In 1928, the next season, Andy started the season at second for the Giants.

While at his peak, Andy told reporters that he had three handicaps to overcome before attaining his post as Giant second baseman. First, he said, was his name. "It is hard for fans to believe that a guy named Cohen can play ball," he said. He admitted that this sometimes made him sore. But he overcame this attitude as well as what he called his second "handicap," his "Jewish nose." Although there is no "Jewish nose" just as there is no "Jewish face" or "Jewish blood," baseball players made it fairly rough for Andy. But he finally overcame this attitude, too. He could not hurdle the third handicap: that of succeeding a great player.

In a friendly and detailed letter to me,* Andy Cohen discussed the anti-Jewish attitude in baseball. This is what he wrote:

"I was treated by fans and other players just as any other player. Good plays were cheered and bad ones jeered. At first the going was tough. I remember reading some years

*H.U.R.

back where Hank Greenberg appealed to the umpire over a
certain amount of 'riding' he was taking from the Cub
bench when he came to bat and the umpire stopped them, I
believe. But did you ever hear of an umpire appealing to
the player that he didn't have to take such a riding? When
the Cubs rode me and the ump told me I didn't have to
take it I told the ump to suit himself. He went to the Cub
bench (the same outfit that rode Greenberg later) and stopped them. When I came to bat next time, all was silent on
the Cub bench. So I shouted, 'What's the matter with you
blankety-blanks? Lost your guts?' And, boy, did they let
me have it then. But I asked for it — and got it good. But
they all accepted me as one of the boys after that. Beans
Reardon was the umpire and a swell guy is he."

After his brilliant beginning with the Giants, Cohen
played in 129 games in 1928 and batted .273, which isn't
bad for an infielder. He got nine homers, twenty-four doubles in 138 hits. He was fine. But Hornsby batted .400 three
different seasons and generally got twice as many hits as
Andy. Andy improved in 1929 and batted a respectable
.294, but obviously McGraw wasn't as happy with this performance as he was with what he thought was Cohen's
potential form.

Nevertheless, Andy had his good times. Jesting about his
Giant career, Cohen told me, "Shanty Hogan and I were
pals. We spent one winter in vaudeville. We were lousy but
had lots of fun. It was always 'Cohen and Hogan' till we
got to Boston. And with all those South Boston Irishmen
pouring in, it became 'Hogan and Cohen.' Hogan was
famous for his appetite. It was never a piece of chicken, but
always a whole one, or two whole ones. It was never a
pickle or two; it was a jar of pickles. Never a piece of pie;

but a whole pie. He visited me in El Paso and I spent time with him in his home in Somerville, Mass."

From this story, the reader can see that the fact that Andy was Jewish certainly did not harm his relations with his teammates. And although Andy left the Giants at the end of the 1929 season, he had plenty of good memories.

"Mel Ott and I," he recalled, "joined the club about the same time. He was a fuzzy-faced kid, kinda small, who came up as a catcher." And he remembered "Phil Weintraub, Goody Rosen (who used to be batboy for Toronto when I was with Buffalo in 1927), Al Cohen, Harry Rosenberg and others."

After he left the Giants, Andy drifted around the minors. He played with Minneapolis for a good many years, from 1932 to 1939. With the experience he had obtained as a long-time player, Andy was asked by Larry MacPhail to join the Brooklyn organization as a manager. He moved to Pine Bluff in the Cotton States League and the following year he managed the Brooklyn farm in Dayton. In 1941 Andy led Elmira in the Eastern League, which was owned by his friend John Ogden. It was during this season that Andy had marked managerial success. His club won the Governor's Cup, emblematic of baseball success in this circuit.

In 1942, like millions of other Americans, Andy Cohen joined the Army. A first sergeant with the 21st Engineers, he took part in the invasion of North Africa in November of 1942. He was one of the GI's who landed at Casablanca and he participated in the Tunisian campaign. He spent a year in Africa and a year in Italy.

Returning from Army service in 1944, Andy married an Elmira girl and became the playing manager of the El Paso

Club of the Mexican National League in 1945. A year later the league was accepted into Organized Ball as a Class B league, so that Andy retained his job as a playing manager in a recognized circuit. A few years later Andy progressed as a manager and handled the Denver club in the New York Yankee chain. But he quit within a season and faded out again. Apparently his experiences here and at Indianapolis earlier had convinced him that managing was not for him.

One of the many Jewish ballplayers who followed Andy into the major leagues was his own brother, Syd. Ironically, by the time that Syd Cohen reached the Washington Senators in 1934, major stars like Hank Greenberg and Buddy Myer had firmly established that ballplayers who were Jewish could be just as good as those who weren't; and Syd's arrival on the scene, unlike his brother Andy's, caused no great fuss. Syd hung around the Senators for three seasons as a marginal pitcher; but perhaps the most ironic aspect of his career was an incident that illustrates just how ridiculous racial prejudice can be.

Three years before he reached the major leagues, Syd went to Mexico to pitch for the Nogales team in that league. The hot-blooded local fans were so desperate for a Mexican player on the team — which was composed of non-Mexicans — that soldiers literally patrolled the field with bayonets to discourage rioting. The team had one mediocre Mexican pitcher, but they wanted at least one quality Mexican standout. So the management did something as outrageous as it was inventive. Syd, with his dark skin and fluent command of Spanish ("he could '*habla espanol* like a bullfighter,'" notes Edelstein), was brought to Nogales and introduced to the fans as the left-handed pitching ace Pablo Garcia. So accepted was he that twenty years later, when he returned as Syd Cohen to manage the Juarez Indios to their first league championship, many Mexicans continued to refer to him as Pablo.

Today Andy Cohen is not well remembered. In a sport where you have to be outstanding for a decade to win any sort of real fame, Cohen lasted less than three years in the majors. Although he wasn't equal to all his publicity, he was the first Jewish player in the big leagues who was aware that he was carrying on his shoulders the reputation of his people. He opened the gates to others. Hank Greenberg, Goody Rosen, Sid Gordon, Al Rosen, and Sandy Koufax would have made the majors anyway, but things were made easier for them because there had been an Andy Cohen to blaze the way.

Andy had a lot of people rooting for him and when he failed, thousands of fans were disappointed. John McGraw kept looking for a Jewish star but never found him. Harry Danning came along after McGraw's death, as did Sid Gordon. But Andy Cohen, a meteor on the baseball firmament, had his day of glory and will always be remembered because of it.

HANK GREENBERG IN HIS TOP TIGER FORM

Hank Greenberg

Bomber from the Bronx

It was the last game of the 1945 pennant race and the whole
baseball world was waiting tensely to see what would happen. The Detroit Tigers had to win this game from the
pestiferous St. Louis Browns, the 1944 American League
champions. The Tigers were not far enough ahead of the
Washington Senators, and here it was, the last game of the
season and Nels Potter, the ace of the Brown staff, was
twirling.

The score was deadlocked and it was the last of the ninth
inning. Somehow the Tigers had filled the bases on infield
hits and a bit of wildness on the part of Potter, a smart old
campaigner.

And the batter was Hank Greenberg, the mightiest right-
handed slugger in baseball. But Hank was rusty after a
long hitch in the Army. Fans turned to one another, some
in hope, some wishing that Greenberg had suddenly grown
blind in the Army.

And then, with a count of one ball, Potter grooved a
medium-fast pitch. Greenberg swung hard. The ball began
to climb towards left field. Because it was two out every
Tiger on the base paths ran with the crack of the bat. But
they didn't have to. The ball grew smaller and smaller as it
rose and when it disappeared among the patrons in left
field 351 feet away, the Tigers had won another American

League flag, Hank Greenberg had re-established his reputation as a great money player and once again the city of Detroit went quietly mad.

*   *   *   *   *

It was the fifth game of the 1940 World Series. The Detroit Tigers and the Cincinnati Reds were tied at two games apiece. Gene Thompson, right-hander, was pitching for the National League champions. There were two runners on the bases. It was a crucial moment.

Swinging three heavy bats, a husky figure emerged from the Tiger dugout. A roar like the pound of surf greeted the tall player who took his careful stance at the plate, after having dropped two of the bats. Thompson looked at the base runners. He wound up and blazed one in there. It was a strike. The count went to two strikes. The Redlegs pitcher measured his opponent. He breathed deeply, took a long windup and pitched. The batter swung. Bang! The ball took wings and disappeared over the left field wall. Pandemonium reigned. The noise shook the park.

Hank Greenberg had hit another home run.

For hitting home runs at such times, Hank Greenberg was paid more money than any other player in baseball in 1940, again in 1941 and in 1946, his next complete year in baseball. The reason for this is obvious. Hank Greenberg, a Jewish boy from the Bronx, had become the favorite of millions of baseball fans all over the country. Hank was unable to play as many years as he could have, because in 1941 he became one of the first major leaguers to join the Army and play the grim game of war.

Leaving one of the most lucrative spots in sports, handsome Hank Greenberg shouldered a rifle instead of a bat and trained as a private instead of a $60,000-a-year baseball star. Within six months he became a sergeant, and then, because he was nearing the age limit, was given his military release and placed on the reserve lists. But Pearl Harbor made history and Greenberg immediately returned to service before the Army called him. The war years dragged on and Greenberg became an officer, finally being sent to the China-Burma-India theater, where he was placed in charge of a Headquarters squadron of the 20th Bomber Command.

When the war ended Greenberg was discharged and returned to the Tigers. He was older than thirty-four, which is generally the beginning of the road down for a major league ball player. But Hank showed that his eye was still deadly when he began to swing his mighty bat. In half a season, rusty from lack of work, Hank hit .311, slammed thirteen home runs and, from the day he came back, led to victory after victory.

Henry Greenberg was born January 1, 1911, in the Bronx, the son of Orthodox Jewish parents from Rumania. They were ordinary, simple people, to whom the idea of a famous son was strange at first. But they must have sensed years ago that Hank would be something special, for he grew into a huge young man, six feet four inches tall. Even though Hank loved baseball, he had the good sense to turn down many cheapening, but financially good, offers after he became a star. He never took show bookings. He lived quietly and, unlike many other ball players, he never spent the winter hunting, which never was a Jewish way to spend free time. Instead Hank played handball, lived with his folks and did not marry until he was nearly thirty-six.

Hank attended James Monroe High School in the Bronx

and became a four-letter man. He was especially adept at baseball, for his big frame carried a lot of power. True, he was awkward, but he hit the ball tremendous distances. Then Hank began to play for the Bay Parkways. One day, when Paul Krichell, clever New York Yankee scout, watched a game in which Hank hit three home runs, the big Jewish player was given a offer by Krichell to join the Yankee organization.

"I'll give you $1,000 if you come with us," Krichell told the eager young man.

But Hank had New York University in mind, for he wanted an education.

"No," he said, "I want to go to college."

Krichell wanted Hank badly, and so he said, "I'll give you $1,000 down and $500 a year while you go to school, $3,000 all together. What do you say?"

And before Hank could say anything definite, the wily Krichell had Hank see Ed Barrow, the Yankee general manager, who lunched with Greenberg and tried to talk him into joining the Yankee system. Hank's parents liked the idea and they told him to go ahead and sign with the Yankees. But Hank remembered that Lou Gehrig, the great and powerful first sacker on the Yankees, would be impossible to replace. So he did not give Barrow a definite answer.

Then Hank began to play with a baseball team in East Douglas, Mass., a mill town. He grew homesick and after doing no work for three weeks he announced that he was going home after the next game; this was July, 1929. Hank played that day. He slammed a home run and a double. Joe Engel, Washington Senator scout, was impressed with what he saw and offered Greenberg a $10,000 bonus for signing up with his club plus a salary of $800 a month, immediately. Hank still had NYU in mind and said "No." But the Detroit Tigers played it smarter. They offered Greenberg $9,000, $3,000 immediately and the rest after he left NYU.

Realizing that he could go to college, Hank said, "I'll take it." And so he signed up with the Tigers.

*   *   *   *   *

But after one semester at NYU Greenberg became uneasy and unhappy when the spring training season started. He dreamed of playing ball, and the lure became too strong. He wired the Tigers that he would like to join them at once. He was given the rest of his money and got $500 a month to play with Raleigh, in North Carolina. So far all the breaks were going his way. Major league scouts had been fighting for him and Greenberg was getting lots of money. Now the grind began. Up and down the minor league circuits, in bad hotels, travelling on poor roads in rumbling buses, Greenberg followed the hard trail taken by anyone who wants to be a star in baseball. The big crowds, the big money and the cheers and headlines look good but they don't come easily. First there is the training in the minors, the day-by-day sweating it out, the bad breaks, and the good ones, learning how to hit the good pitchers and how to evade the wild pitches of the tyros just breaking in. With Raleigh in the Piedmont League, Hank began to learn. He hit .314 and he felt better because a bit earlier he had played seventeen games with Hartford in the Eastern League and had done badly. But Hank had power. He weighed more than 200 and his lumbering awkwardness at first base was overlooked. He was learning.

Then, in 1932, Greenberg's coordination and power and ability began to crystallize. With Beaumont in the Texas League Hank hit well. He drove in one hundred and thirty-one runs, drove thirty-nine home runs out of the park and was voted the most valuable player in the league. He could no longer be overlooked. He was on his way. The Tigers brought him up and in 1933 he was a rookie trying to make the majors.

*   *   *   *   *

Hank had a hard time in his first season. He happened to break into the lineup in the face of obstacles few talked about after Greenberg made the grade. Baseball is a peculiar game. There are always personal struggles and prejudices, even if they don't appear in the box scores. Bucky Harris, then the Detroit Tiger manager, had been nursing along a promising first baseman named Harry Davis to play first for the Tigers. Davis cost the club $50,000. And when a player costs that much a manager must stick with him, even if a tall, lumbering player with a lot of power stumbles into the training camp. So Harris paid no attention to Greenberg. He moved big Hank to third base. Hank was never what can be called a natural player. He worked hard to master a position. He slaved and practiced and worked in his mind as well as his body. He did not expect to be moved to a new and strange post as he worked his way up. He looked very bad at third.

Than one day Harris had to leave the club and Del Baker, a coach and later a manager at Detroit, ran the team for a while. He saw that Greenberg was no third

sacker and he moved Hank to first in an exhibition game
against the Giants. Eager to prove that Baker was doing
the right thing, Hank got three hits that day, a single, double and triple. He felt better. He thought he had proved
where he belonged. But when Harris rejoined the team,
Davis returned to first. At this stage Greenberg grew mor-
bid and decided to see Frank Navin, the popular and fair
owner of the Tigers.

"I am a first baseman," Greenberg told him, "And I
want to play there."

"Wait," Navin advised him. "We'll use you against lef-
ties and Davis against right-handers."

But when the season began and the Tigers faced their
first southpaw, Lloyd Brown, Davis was announced by
Harris as the starting first sacker.

But he had not reckoned with Navin. As soon as he read
off the batting order, Harris got a phone call. Then he
returned to the dressing room.

"There is a change in the batting order. Greenberg will
play first base," the manager said.

Nervous, upset and tense, Greenberg had a hitless day at
the plate. Grimly, Harris replaced him with Davis and for
three weeks Hank sat on the bench as he watched the
graceful but light-hitting Davis play first. Then, in Boston,
Hank got a break. Brown, who had been traded to the
Red Sox, was pitching. Greenberg got into the batting
order. This time the story was different. Hank got two hits.
That year he played 117 games, despite Harris' attempt to
install Davis as his first baseman and justify the $50,000
price tag for the Fancy Dan. Greenberg batted .301 in his
first full season, breaking into the charmed circle of .300
batters. He hit twelve homers, showing potential power

and, more significant, he batted in eighty-seven runs, which is the true sign of the valuable player.

*   *   *   *   *

But Hank did not find it all easy. Davis was smooth around first base. Greenberg was clumsy. The fans booed his lack of grace. They liked his batting, but they were critical and their chatter drove Greenberg to morning sessions at the ball park. He came to the park at ten o'clock and practiced spearing grounders. He learned how to stretch for wide throws. He became death on pops to the infield. He learned how to make the double-play and how to move his feet smoothly. He became a real major leaguer, and only through hard work and the knowledge that his own manager did not think much of him.

But in 1934 Harris was replaced by popular Mickey Cochrane, a great catcher and fine leader of men. Hank and Mickey hit it off from the beginning. Cochrane showed his confidence in Greenberg by selling Davis. Hank had the first base job to himself. He relaxed and played better ball. He had a tremendous year and began to assert himself as one of the top sluggers in the game. Hank batted .339 and led the league in doubles with sixty-three. He more than doubled his homer total of the previous year by slamming twenty-six. He batted in 139 runs. He was a baseball star, and no longer "promising." Hank Greenberg had arrived.

Nevertheless, he was aware of his Jewishness all along. The Tiger infield was setting a record of having played all season long without a substitution. But when Rosh Hashanah came Hank refused to play. The *Detroit Free Press* printed Hank's picture with Happy New Year

Greetings in Hebrew captioned above the photo. And nine days later Yom Kippur came. The day before Yom Kippur Hank hit a home run to beat the Yankees 2-0 in a tense pennant race. He did not play on Yom Kippur and the Tigers lost. When he returned to the lineup the club perked up and took the flag. The entire city respected Hank for his attitude. Edgar Guest, America's most popular verse-maker, devoted a long poem to Greenberg's action. Hank was acclaimed not only as a fine player but as a sober, religious citizen who was setting a fine sportsmanlike example for everyone to follow.

* * * * *

In the World Series that year Greenberg tried his best against the Deans and the Cardinals, even though the Tigers couldn't win. He batted .321, drove in seven runs and showed that he did not tighten up in such an important sports event as the World Series. Many players do. The great Ty Cobb did badly in his first Series. But in the first game, in which the Tigers lost to Dizzy Dean by an 8-3 score, Hank hit a long home run in the eighth inning and got one other hit besides. In the fourth game, which the Tigers won to tie up the Series at 2-all, Hank was the batting star. Here's why:

In the third inning with a rally going, Dazzy Vance, onetime great pitcher, came in to relieve for the Cards. Greenberg singled and drove in a run. This was only one of his hits. He found Card pitchers for four hits that afternoon.

In the sixth game he drove in the tying run against Paul Dean and the Tigers went ahead to win it.

*   *   *   *   *

Greenberg's power developed as the years moved along. He discovered that his seriousness about baseball was paying off. In 1935 Hank was voted the most valuable player in the American League, one of the highest honors paid to a baseball player. And no wonder! He hit .328, led the league in homers with thirty-six and led in runs batted in with one hundred seventy, which was an amazing figure. And for the second year in a row he connected for more than two hundred hits, a feat usually reserved for light hitters, not sluggers like Greenberg.

Hank did not try for home runs, even if he did hit them. A line drive hitter, he said that "I am tall, heavy and reasonably strong," when asked about his power. He was also modest. After his fine 1935 year he was compared with the great players of the game. Naturally enough he was placed against players like Foxx and Gehrig, two phenomenal sluggers.

"It's a mistake to compare me with either Foxx or Gehrig," Hank said. "They are veterans with years of service. I am only a beginner."

Perhaps he sensed something, for when the World Series came that year, Greenberg had a tough break. He played in only two games, for he broke a wrist sliding into the plate. In the second game, however, Hank pulled his famous home run act. Facing Charlie Root, the Tigers teed off quickly. After the first three batters hit safely, Greenberg drove Root out of the box with a long home run. Happily, the Tigers won the Series.

*   *   *   *   *

The 1936 season was one of the worst Greenberg ever
had. After twelve games he collided with Jake Powell in a
base-line scuffle, and hurt his wrist again. The wrist gives
leverage to a slugger and it meant the end of Greenberg in
that pennant race. Hank seemed to be on his way out.
Word spread that he was brittle, in spite of his fine body.
But then one day, in an exhibition game the next spring,
Greenberg got five hits in five times at bat. He was ready.
And the fans knew it. That year Greenberg drove in one
hundred eighty-three runs, the second highest in the entire
history of the American League. Only Gehrig in the
American and Hack Wilson in the National League ever
bettered that. Babe Ruth and other legendary sluggers
never came close to this figure. On top of that Hank hit
.337, nearly the highest he had ever soared in his attacks
against major league pitching.

From here on in Greenberg was considered the best of
all the right-handed sluggers in the game. And if there was
any doubt at all, it vanished the next year when Hank
again battered at established records.

In 1938 he hit fifty-eight home runs.

Babe Ruth made baseball what it is today when he slammed sixty homers in one season. That mark intrigued all
America. Men and women who never showed any interest
in the game started to come to baseball parks to see the
Babe. As a personality he transcended the game itself. He
became a great figure in American life. No one else ever
approached his home run rampages. But Greenberg came
mighty close; he hit nine homers in one week and was sixteen days ahead of Ruth's schedule. He worked hard. During a batting slump he paid some kids a few cents to prac-

tice with him on a sandlot, at a time when he was the
greatest slugger in the game. Instead of choking up with
tension toward the end of the season, as some baseball
writers said he did, Greenberg did nothing of the sort. The
facts are these: in his last twenty-four games he hit twelve
homers, an average of one every two games. And if he
would have maintained this pace all year he would have hit
seventy-seven home runs! It must also be remembered that
Ruth was left-handed and aimed at a 296-foot wall at the
Yankee Stadium most of the time. The park was built for
him. Greenberg, right-handed, aimed at a fence 340 feet
away. And despite this handicap he fell only two shy of
Ruth's record! Years later, in 1961, Roger Maris
managed to hit sixty-one homers in a lengthier schedule of
games.

Hank did shatter one Ruthian mark, when he hit two
homers in one game eleven times. All but one of the games
ended in a Tiger victory, which is another indication of
Greenberg's value to his team.

*   *   *   *   *

The 1938 season was Greenberg's peak year, even if he
did hit .340 two years later and win the most valuable
player award for the second time and lead the league in
home runs for the third time. In 1940 he led the team in
doubles, with fifty, in homers with forty-one and in runs
batted in with one hundred fifty. In the World Series that
year he batted .357. In the fifth game he hit a home run off
Gene Thompson, the home run described earlier in this
story. But when a man drives fifty-eight homers in one year
no accomplishments can dim them. That was Hank's year,
the one which established him in the immortal class with

Babe Ruth and Jimmy Foxx, who also hit fifty-eight one
year.

*   *   *   *   *

Normally statistics are uninteresting, but they are the
lifeblood of baseball. The fans at the park always talk in
figures. Educated and illiterate voices roll off statistics with
equal glibness. And even if figures do not always tell the
entire story, they are the best proof of accomplishments in
baseball. To those who are casual ball fans, the mysterious
figures in the box scores, the record books and the sports
columns do not mean much. To the dyed-in-the-wool fan,
they mean nearly everything. To them the way to prove
Greenberg's greatness is to show that his one hundred and
eighty-three runs batted in in one season was only one
behind the record; that after his first year with the Tigers
he drove in more than one hundred a year every full year
he played; that day-in-day-out he has been a great performer. His records and accomplishments mark him as
perhaps the greatest Jewish baseball player in the history of
the sport and a star who ranks with the greatest simply
through his deeds on the diamond.

And toward the end of the 1946 season of play, in the
hot climate of August and the dog days of September,
Hank Greenberg accomplished some startling deeds, all
with the stamp of greatness. Grantland Rice declared that,
"In my opinion Greenberg's September surge was one of
baseball's greatest achievements when you consider all the
angles involved."

In 1946 Greenberg, flushed with his remarkable comeback of 1945, knew that the season was going to be a hard
one. He was thirty-five, and his legs were beginning to go

back on him. He wasn't able to unwind himself until August, a month in which most old players begin to feel the years. In September his home run bat began to flail. Within a short time he was again the Hammering Hank of old. He hit sixteen homers in September and batted .345 that month. He ended the season with the title he most coveted — that of runs-batted-in leader. He smacked across one hundred twenty-seven runs, four more than the highly-publicized Ted Williams and sixteen more than Nick Etten drove in to lead the league a year earlier. It was the eighth time in his career that he had knocked in 100 runs or more a season, and the fourth time that he led the league in RBI's. His homer splurge netted him forty-four, to lead the majors in homers. He slammed six more than Ted Williams, although for most of the year Williams held a wide lead over Hank. On August 31, Hank had hit twenty-eight homers, most of them early in the season. Within less than a month he had his forty-four.

And then the 1946 season ended and on January 18, 1947 one of the most surprising deals in major league baseball was completed. Hank Greenberg, a top Tiger for a long, long time, was sold out of the league, to the Pittsburgh Pirates in the National League.

When the deal was first announced, the entire sports world was aghast. And for weeks the sports pages were loaded with stories about the Tiger management, Greenberg's reaction, the attempts of the new owner in Pittsburgh to inject power into a fading team.

General Manager Billy Evans of Detroit said that the seven other American League clubs had declined to claim the slugger at the $10,000 waiver price — but later it developed that the Yankees wanted Hank, and passed him up only because the Tigers had sworn that they would withdraw their waivers on Hank if New York claimed him.

Upon hearing the sudden news of his sale, Hank was deeply shaken. He issued many statements and debated retiring. But finally, he decided to go along with his new owners.

When he was asked whether he would play for Pittsburgh, following his shock over leaving the Tigers, Hank declared: "Playing baseball just for what financial returns there may be in it for me does not interest me. I've been around a long time and anyone who knows me knows I'm not that kind."

And then came his official statement:

"The news that I was sold to Pittsburgh which I heard over the radio, came as a complete surprise. I signed with the Detroit Baseball Club immediately upon graduation from high school and played for them continuously for fourteen years, excepting the four years I served in the Army.

"When discharged from the Army in 1945, I returned to Detroit and have been with them ever since. My whole major league career has been spent in a Detroit uniform. I have always given the Detroit club and the fans my best efforts and my record speaks for itself. I am deeply grateful to the Detroit fans — the finest in the world — for their loyalty and encouragement and to the members of the press and radio for their fairness and support.

"I also regret leaving my teammates, many of whom are my close friends. Naturally, after this long and pleasant relationship, I am disappointed to be traded from the Detroit club and waived out of the American League."

This statement reveals how deeply hurt and disap-

pointed Hank was when the Tigers released him. And
Hank's following action showed that he was willing to give
up the game. He informed the Pirate management that he
was retiring.

"This decision," he said, "is not easy to make. I love the
game and feel there is yet much good baseball in me as a
player and executive. But after seventeen years and 1,150
games in a Tiger uniform, I always expected to finish my
career in Detroit. Since it was decided for me that this
could not be, I do not desire to start anew in a strange environment."

Frank McKinney, Pirate owner, expressed his chagrin,
but never gave up hope that Greenberg would change his
mind. The pain, however, was fresh in Hank's mind — and
for a while he did nothing.

Meanwhile, the sports writers had a field day and they
all praised Hank to the skies. Arthur Daley of the *New
York Times* wrote that "the baseball writers will resent bitterly the way Greenberg presumably is getting pushed
around in this latest switch in clubs. Big Hank has no
firmer supporters than among the typewriter pounders. He
always has been gracious and nice to everyone of them;
talks intelligently and interestingly on every occasion; has
always been overpoweringly friendly and has been a colorful personality down through the years — well, they're all
in his corner to the very last man."

Other writers went to town on Hank. Dan Daniel, the
New York World-Telegram baseball expert, pointed out
that "the records at Briggs Stadium say that without
Greenberg the Tigers have not been a big draw."

And Hal Newhouser, the Tiger ace southpaw pitcher,
upon hearing of Greenberg's departure from Detroit, said,

"Hank's a great guy and it's tough to see him leave with that big bat of his. Those forty-four home runs last year meant a lot to all our pitchers, including myself, and I hate to see him go." Hal added: "I figured he'd get awfully tired as the 1946 season wore on, but as the weather got hotter, so did Hank."

Newhouser, without Greenberg's 1947 bat, experienced his worst season in four years and won less than twenty games.

Greenberg, in time, decided against quitting, and played with the Pirates in 1947. While talking to reporters one day after he joined the Pirates, Hank said: "I really meant it when I said I didn't want to play ball any more. It had been hard enough, getting into shape and playing last year. Being sold to the Pirates meant I had to start all over again. A new club, a new league and a new manager. It seemed too much. I didn't even want to try it. So I quit, but they came to me and said:

" 'Look. We need you in Pittsburgh. We have sound plans for the future. We're going to rebuild the club, bring in the best players we can get and give the town a real ball club. We want you. We don't care if you don't hit at all.' "

Than Hank laughed a little. "Well, that was stretching it a little far, I thought. But, anyway, they convinced me that the fans in Pittsburgh were counting on me to — what? Lead them out of the wilderness? I don't know what I'm supposed to do, but I would like to have a good year."

And here is the lead of the Associated Press story on the opening game between the Pirates and the Cubs:

"Big Hank Greenberg belted only one hit in his National League debut, but it was a screaming double that enabled the Pirates to nip the Cubs, 1-0, and settled a stirring mound duel between Truett Sewell and Hank Borowy before 29,427 thoroughly chilled fans."

In the second game of the season Hank hit his first National League home run off Hank Wyse — and he was off. But then he slowed up and although he had fifteen home runs in July, he asked to be benched after a protracted slump.

Throughout the rest of the season, Greenberg played in spurts. He ended the year with twenty-five home runs, plus a painful chip in his elbow which kept him inactive toward the last weeks of the season. During the heated Yankee-Dodger World Series, the Pirates announced that Hank had been given his unconditional release. Declaring he would first submit to an elbow operation, Hank said he would seek a job in baseball for the 1948 season.

He found one shortly, as the general manager of the Cleveland Indians. Within a brief period, Greenberg became one of the leading executives in the game, running, in effect, the Cleveland organization. He became a stockholder and a controversial personality because he continually came in second to the Yankees. In 1958 he finally sold his shares in the club and left the Cleveland organization after being ousted as general manager, and later became a stockholder in the Chicago White Sox.

It was almost inevitable that Greenberg should have been elected to the Hall of Fame for his impressive accomplishments during a brilliant major league career.

But the true sports fan remembers a player not for his statistical achievements alone, but for the kind of a job the player did when the fan watched him. Apart from the record books, what kind of a man was Hank Greenberg?

In the many years I* have been watching sports,
Greenberg seemed a fine performer and equally fine
person. Of course, as a New Yorker, I saw Hank most
often in the Yankee Stadium, playing against great Yankee
teams before his own home crowd. He pressed because he
wanted to show the home folks that he was good enough to
play in the Stadium as well as in Detroit. And when he was
not relaxed, he did not hit. No one does.

It is good to remember that tall, husky figure, wiggling a
bat, standing quietly while waiting for the pitch. Each time
he came to bat, he was a potential homer. The pitchers suddenly screwed up their eyes and watched for the catcher's
signs. Somehow, Greenberg at bat meant something more
than just a hitter at the plate. He was power personified. I
have seen him strike out vigorously. Later, in the same
game, against the same pitcher he would send a screaming
liner booming into the distant stands.

Once I saw Charlie Ruffing of the Yankees fan him twice
in a row and the next two times at bat Hank drove the ball
out of the park. I saw Joe DiMaggio rob him of a homer
when he nabbed a 450-foot Greenberg drive. Yet later in
the game Hank drove in the winning Tiger run.

To those men who were in the Army, baseball meant a
lot because it was a symbol of home. When, in 1945, I
found myself in Ceylon, serving with the Air Force, I
listened to every World Series game on the radio. And
when the boys got together and heard that Hank
Greenberg was still walloping homers, they felt better
because they knew that "home" was still the same.
Greenberg was part of American life and a significant part
of the national game.

*H.U.R.

CHARLES "BUDDY" MYER, AT THE HEIGHT OF HIS CAREER

"Buddy" Myer

Second-Sack Slicker

In 1935, when Hank Greenberg was voted the most valuable player in the American League and led the league in nearly everything, the batting champion of the American circuit was another Jewish boy. His name was Charles Solomon "Buddy" Myer.

"Buddy" Myer was one of those under-rated, unpublicized baseball players whose talents are appreciated by the sports writers and the studious baseball fans. But he seldom won headlines, and the fans paid little attention to him. It was not until 1935, after ten years in the big time, that Myer was accepted as a star. That year he hit .349 and came in second in total hits, with 215. That winter Clark Griffith, wise owner of the Washington Senators, told reporters that he would not sell Myer for less than $500,-000. Perhaps this was only talk, but it was a slight indication of the value of the silent keystone sacker of the Washington club.

Charles Myer was born in Ellisville, Mississippi, a small Southern town. If you ride through the Southland you will find there are more Jewish families in such towns than you think there are. "Buddy" was a quiet kid whose folks sent him to college, just as many Jewish families dream of sending their growing children to college. "Buddy" was graduated from Mississippi A and M in 1925. He played such good college baseball that he received many major league offers. Eventually, he accepted the bid of the Cleveland Indians.

But early in his career, Myer showed a stubborn streak. When the Indians sent him to Dallas in the Texas League, he refused to report. He wanted to begin in the majors. Not knowing quite how to handle the confident young man, the Indians did bring him up to the majors. But angered over his attitude, the parent club released "Buddy." As a free agent Myer signed up with New Orleans.

From the start, Myer showed that he was a real player. He batted .336 and drove in forty-four runs. Before the year was out, the Washington Senators bought him. And there is a story attached to that purchase.

Joe Engel, Washington's chief scout, had been tipped off that "Buddy" was quite a ball player but Engel wasn't the only major league scout on the lookout for Myer. Old Jack Doyle of the Cubs was also trying to buy Myer from New Orleans.

One day Engel was sitting in the stands, watching Myer, and decided that he wanted to buy him for Washington. But Doyle managed to see Engel and asked him what he was doing around this part of the country.

"Not a thing, Jack," Engel said. But he realized that Doyle might attempt to sign up this promising player, so he said, "Hey, Jack, you want a coke?"

Jack looked at him suspiciously and said, "No."

"Well, I do," Engel said, and ran off to the office of the New Orleans owner and bought Myer.

Then Engel returned to the stands, sat down next to Doyle and began to enjoy the game. In the first inning Myer singled cleanly to left and then stole second. Doyle looked at Engel; Engel looked at Doyle. Both were silent and peered ahead at the diamond. When New Orleans took the field, Myer made some spectacular catches and a fine throw. The next time he batted he pulled the ball down the right-field line for a two-base hit. But Doyle and Engel maintained their silence.

When the inning ended, however, Doyle turned to Engel and said carelessly, "I think I'll go out and get that coke, after all." But, Engel, in telling the story, added that "I knew Doyle never drank a coke in his life." And here's the punch ending, as told by Engel:

"Five minutes later Doyle is back and he starts lacing into me. 'Nothing here worth looking at, eh? You double-crosser! You so-and-so!' It was music to my ears, because I knew that if Jack was that mad about me signing Myer, I'd got myself a real star."

"Buddy" proved to be just that. He came to the Senators that year, in 1925, and remained with them for fifteen seasons, having a brief whirl with the Red Sox in 1927 and 1928. He returned to Washington in 1929 and remained until he was given his release in 1941. A persistent stomach ailment cut short the Myer career, but even so, "Buddy" lasted a longer time than most ball players.

"Buddy" Myer was a money player. When the chips were down, he played his best. He broke in with the Senators in 1925, the year the club won the pennant. He was in the lineup only for four games, but in the World Series that year he played third base for three games. Although he got only two hits in eight times at bat, he indicated, with his looseness, that he was capable of his top play at any infield position at any time. As a small man who never weighed more than 165, Myer could not have made a very good first baseman, but throughout his career he batted well enough to make anyone proud of his record.

A lifetime average of .303 made Myer a really good hitter for a second baseman. Just stop to consider that Joe Gordon of the Yankees and the Indians, one of the top men at his position, was only a .275 hitter and that Bobby Doerr, the Red Sox star, was a .290 batter. Compared with them, Myer was tops. As a matter of fact, he was second to Charlie Gehringer for a decade, and Charlie was ranked as the greatest of all modern second basemen, or at least the best in twenty years.

When Myer won his crown, he did it the hard way. On the last day of the season he had to hit well to get that honor. But Myer was always aggressive. He was the steadiest major leaguer in the game for many a year. The fact that he batted between .279 and .313 in a ten-year period is a good indication of his capabilities. Myer was notorious for seldom hitting at a bad ball. But his quietness did not mean he was meek.

He got into a fight with Ben Chapman, later manager of the Philadelphia Phillies, for two days running, and was fined $100 for his fisticuffs. Although both men were Southerners, Chapman coming from Birmingham, Alabama, Myer was Jewish and the Alabamian was alleged to have been anti-Jewish in feeling. The fiery Chapman must have been shocked to see the slight Jewish infielder take off against him. Perhaps it made him reconsider his idea of Jews. Whatever the case may have been, Myer showed that he took dirt from no one. He played his game and did the best he could, but he never let anyone step over him.

Chapman was, potentially, a great player, but his temper

always got the better of him, and when he blasted out against a group of fans one day in Yankee Stadium, the Irish manager of the Yankees, Joe McCarthy, got rid of Chapman in a hurry.

"Buddy" Myer may have had a hard time with anti-Semitic ball players, although there were never many of them on the record, but his play on the diamond never revealed it, except for that flare-up against Chapman.

In the 1933 World Series, when the Giants ran roughshod over the Senators, Myer shone for the American Leaguers. He batted .300 and out-starred most of the Giant infielders. When the Senators dropped the opening game of the Series to Carl Hubbell, 4-2, Myer scored one of the two Senator runs. In the third game he singled and scored one run and later doubled in another run. He got a third hit in that game, the only one the Senators won in the Series.

Because he was seldom domineering and tended to the business at hand, "Buddy" Myer never won the plaudits he deserved for his seventeen years work as a major leaguer. When he was forced to quit in 1941, he got just a few lines in the papers. But the Southern Jewish boy who played second for the Senators was one of the finest keystoners in the game, and deserves a spot in Jewish sports history because he was the best Jewish second baseman in the annals of baseball.

HARRY DANNING POSES IN THE POLO GROUNDS

Harry Danning

The Man Behind the Mask

In his fine biography of John McGraw, Frank Graham overlooked one baseball phase of the pugnacious manager's career. Nowhere did he mention McGraw's desperate search for a Jewish ball player to attract the vast New York Jewish population to the Polo Grounds. If McGraw was anything, he was an outstanding showman. He signed up the great Indian Jim Thorpe, even when that versatile athlete proved unable to solve major league pitching. The Giant manager knew that Thorpe would draw the crowds, and so he was willing to go along with the Indian.

In much the same spirit, McGraw looked far and wide for an outstanding Jewish baseball star. The story of Andy Cohen, his brilliant beginning, the hysteria surrounding his career and his rapid decline, is told elsewhere in these pages. This is the story of one of the best Jewish players who wore a Giant uniform, and it is ironic that McGraw never really saw his potentialities and that Harry Danning of Los Angeles became a star catcher under the leadership of the sometimes hardbitten Bill Terry who succeeded John McGraw as manager of the New York Giants.

Oddly, one of the greatest of all Jewish baseball players was also a catcher, Johnny Kling of the Chicago Cubs, when the team boasted of Tinker and Evers and Chance.

Although Danning could not compare with Kling — few players in all history could — Harry was one of the best backstops of his time. He was a very dangerous hitter, a steady receiver and a hard competitor. Never fast afoot, Danning made up for his slowness (which is a common ailment among big league catchers) with a blazing spirit which McGraw would have loved.

Harry Danning was born in Los Angeles on September 6, 1911, and after he retired from the game following a hitch in the Army during the war he went into the auto business there. He later returned to the game as a coach on a Pacific Coast League team. He loved baseball from his early youth and his brother's success as a professional ball player sparked Harry's own ambition. It is a matter of record that Ike Danning, a fine player in his own right, was never as good as younger brother Harry.

Like any ambitious young man, Harry Danning went into business as soon as he could. He worked as a rug salesman before the baseball bug really bit him. And when it bit, Harry found himself doing some unusual things. Because his brother was doing well in Mexican semi-pro ball, Harry masqueraded as a Mexican ball player and started to lambast the ball hard. He was thankful that he had always caught instead of played the outfield. When asked why he was always a catcher, Harry said, "The kids wouldn't let me play with them unless I caught." This is an interesting statement. It reveals that catching is, actually, the toughest of all positions. And it is the position in which one can most easily get hurt. In 1946 Walker Cooper was sold to the New York Giants by the St. Louis Cardinals, for the heavy sum of $175,000. And Cooper, who was one of the best and shrewdest catchers in the game as well as one of baseball's most dangerous batters, continually split fingers on his catching hand and on his bare hand, thus minimizing his value to the team which had spent so much money for his services. And if a veteran catcher can break his fingers, what can one say about a young kid with no experience but with plenty of ambition?

Danning had a hard time of it in his baseball career. After he starred in Mexico he entered organized ball by signing up with the Bridgeport team in the Eastern League. He was lucky that Pancho Snyder, a clever old-time catcher, took time out to teach him the tricks of the complicated catching trade. Harry's own natural ability took care of the other necessary elements of good catching. In his first year in Bridgeport, Danning batted .324 and he drove a long ball. Sometimes he was used in the outfield when his punch was needed. But he proved above all else that his strong six-foot one-inch frame had plenty of power to carry him to the majors.

The next year, which was 1932, Harry started the season with Bridgeport but after a fast start which saw him blast Eastern League pitching for a .320 mark, he moved to Winston-Salem of the Piedmont League, this time as a full-fledged catcher. Again he stayed over the .300 mark, working his average up to .313. Apparently he was now on his way up. He jumped to a higher league, the International, and became the starting catcher with the Buffalo Bisons. This time the New York Giants, who owned him, decided to put him on the official club roster. This marked a sort of victory for the young man, because for a couple of years now he had been going south with the Giants for their spring training and each year the club sent him to one of its farms. After his performance with the Bisons, where he hit

a good .349 in less than half a season, Harry finally wore a
Giant uniform, and he was not to take it off until Uncle
Sam asked him to don another kind of uniform.

But Harry did not become a star right away. He faced a
difficult situation. The Giant first-string catcher was Gus
Mancuso, a heavy-footed backstop who did not hit hard
but who was an exceptionally clever receiver. In the big
leagues a man who knows the batters, who can win the
confidence of his pitchers is sometimes more valuable than
the hardest hitting catcher in the game. A catcher is often
the key to the success of a pitcher, especially a young, inex-
perienced pitcher. In 1933, when Danning broke in with
the Giants, the team won its first National League pennant
under Bill Terry and the catchers were Gus Mancuso and
Paul Richards, both veterans, both valuable to a team
much beyond their batting averages. Richards was also a
cog in the pennant winning Detroit Tigers of 1945, later
manager of the Chicago White Sox. Danning could not
break through this duo and he sat on the bench throughout
the rest of the 1933 season and also observed the World
Series from a bench. No doubt he learned by observing.
And the following year he was used a bit more often. Now
and then he would catch the great Carl Hubbell. Even then
Harry showed his ability to hit major league pitching. In
the fifty-three games in which he played he batted .330. But
he was unhappy playing second-string catcher to Mancuso.

After two more years of bench-warming, Harry approached Bill Terry in 1937 and asked him for a real
chance to catch. Luckily he found Terry in a receptive
mood. Bill was irked over the turn of his baseball fortunes.
He had won a pennant in 1933 and then watched the flag
slip from his grasp in the last days of 1934, as a rampaging

St. Louis Cardinal team swept past the Giants in September. And in 1935 his club gave way to the Cubs. Terry had a winning temperament and, when losing, was willing to try anything. Yes, Mancuso was good and reliable, but perhaps this younger man, this harder hitter, would help. Besides, the Giant pitching staff was loaded with veterans, men like Hal Schumacher, Fred Fitzsimmons and, of course, Carl Hubbell. These men could pitch to anyone, especially a fellow like Danning, who had been around. Terry decided to give Harry his chance.

And it was on June 9, 1937 before 55,577 fans jamming the Polo Grounds, that Danning proved himself. I* was among those fans, and it must be admitted that Harry Danning was not the main attraction. The magnet was the incomparable Jerome Herman "Dizzy" Dean, by far the most voluble and talented right-handed pitcher the National League possessed in many generations. This was the background to the doubleheader between the Giants and the Cardinals and an understanding of it will give a deeper appreciation of Danning's feat. Dean had got into a fight a month or so earlier with the Giant team when the Giants, behind Hubbell, had beaten him in St. Louis. The riot which he started was not overlooked by National League chief Ford Frick, who suspended Dean for his activities. He also asked Dizzy to apologize for his actions. There was nothing Dean could do about the suspension but Dizzy was the No. 1 personality in baseball and his fight with Frick (later baseball's High Commissioner) was the top subject in baseball. And on this day, Dizzy was making his first start since the suspension was lifted.

*H.U.R.

The thousands of fans who crowded the Polo Grounds came to see Dizzy, and they were not disappointed in what he accomplished. Pitching wonderfully well against the brilliant Hubbell, Dizzy tossed a three-hitter as he held the Giants hitless for seven full innings. Hubbell was knocked out of the box and the fans were nearly ready to go home and talk about the expert tossing of Dizzy. But there was a second game to be played. More than that, this was really top baseball drama. The Giants were pennant-bound and they had to beat the always-dangerous Cardinals to make sure of their dreams.

Bob Weiland did the pitching for the Cardinals in the nightcap and he had a 2-1 victory in his grasp as he entered the ninth inning. Weiland had given up only two hits so far and a sweep of the twin bill would constitute a heavy blow to Giant chances for the flag. In the ninth Ott walked. One man made out. And then Terry called on Harry Danning to bat. Few of the fans paid much attention to the announcement. Weiland was pitching well and with a slow runner batting it looked like a double play was in the offing, and that would mean the end of the game. Harry came up and took a called strike. He watched a wide one go by. Then he put his shoulders behind a fat one and blasted the pitch into the right field stands. It was a home run and gave the Giants two runs. The final score was 3-2 and Weiland slumped his shoulders as he trotted sadly from the mound.

A new star was born that afternoon. The homer gave Danning a chance to play regularly. And he made the most of it. On top of that, Mancuso was hurt and Harry really took over the catching chores in earnest. On July 13 he again revealed his power when he hit a homer in each game of a doubleheader. He dropped five home runs into the stands. He hit a peak on August 20 when he got five hits in a single game, four singles and a triple. And then he just about sewed up the flag for the Giants on August 25. It was one of those crucial, seesaw games with the Chicago Cubs, which could so easily have gone the other way. The score changed many times but at the end of nine innings, it was all tied up, 7-7. The game carried into the eleventh frame. And then Harry Danning drove in the winning run and gave his team another victory.

The sudden spark added to the attack of the Giants by the insertion of Harry Danning into the lineup gave fire to the club. And it swept to the flag. In the World Series against the New York Yankees, Harry split the receiving chores with Mancuso. The powerful Yankees were too strong for the National Leaguers, but Danning starred in at least one game, and that was Carl Hubbell's winning effort in the fourth game. Harry got three hits and caught Hubbell's slants well enough to stifle the Yankees.

After this season, Danning became the top catcher for the club. For the next four years he caught at least 120 games each season. In 1938 he batted .306, the following year he hit .313 and in 1940 he batted an even .300 .It was at this time that baseball experts realized that here was a new catching ace, and the Jewish fans all over America knew that even if Danning was no Kling, he was one of the best backstops of modern times. There were arguments throughout the hot stove league, where ball fans discussed the virtues of baseball players, about Danning and Hartnett, Danning and Dickey and Danning and any other good catcher.

When Harry went into the Army, his career was nearly at an end. He had slowed up and was hitting much less powerfully than ever before. In service his legs went back on him and as soon as he was discharged he announced that he was retiring. And so he vanished from the baseball limelight with hardly any fanfare. Even at his best Harry was not colorful. He caught well, hit hard, handled some of the finest pitchers in the game with no difficulty at all, and then left baseball when he could no longer play. He took with him the good wishes of thousands of fans, and he also left with the nickname of "Harry the Horse," which was given to him by the sports announcer Ted Husing, who was a reader of Damon Runyon. And it was Runyon who created a character named "Harry the Horse."

Danning, in four top-grade catching years, set a standard for all catchers of his era, and particularly fellow Jews who were to follow in his footsteps. There are few really good receivers — and Harry was one of them. Perhaps the future will produce mask-and-mitt men who will supersede Danning in this history. Thus far, he and Kling stand alone.

MORRIE ARNOVICH, IN HIS PHILLIE DAYS

Morrie Arnovich

Spring Hitter

There is a baseball phenomenon called "the spring hitter." He is a mystery to the ball fan and a headache to the baseball manager. There is no apparent reason for it, but he hits exceptionally well during the months of April, May, June and sometimes July. Then, in the important months, in the dog days of the baseball chase, he wilts badly and nowhere resembles the hustling, hard-hitting player he used to be in the early months of the season.

Thus, whenever a player does well from the opening "Play Ball!" command of the umpire, the wise fan says, "Let's wait until July, and then we'll see if he can hold up." Generally, the hero in question falls apart, but his average is so good during his hot streak that at the end of the year, he still seems to be a good athlete.

One of the best spring hitters in modern baseball was a hustling Jewish boy from Superior, Wisconsin, named Morris Arnovich. Affectionately called "Morrie" by his followers, Arnovich looked like a Ty Cobb each spring; generally he cooled off late in the pennant chase. But nearly every June he was the National League's star batter, only to fade away rapidly as the season progressed.

Arnovich did not last very long in the majors. He played five full seasons before the Army grabbed him. Most of his career was spent with the cellar-dwelling Phillies. He played part of a season with the 1939 champion Reds and his last year in baseball was spent with the New York Giants. In the Army he played and managed a pretty good service team, but when the war was over and Morrie won his release, he found himself unable to make the grade with the sub-standard Giant team of 1946 and was even released by Jersey City in the International League. There was deep-felt regret all around the circuit when Arnovich dropped out of the picture for he was always popular and the fans appreciated his valiant hustling spirit.

Never a really classy outfielder, Arnovich was the kind of player who can be the making of an ambitious team. He always tried and never slacked up for a minute. He was a small man for a baseball player, five-ten, and never weighed much. He was heavy at 170 pounds. He was not much of a slugger either; he hit fewer than twenty-five home runs in his entire major league career. But he hit fair-ly often, had one very good year, in 1939, and generally made himself a valuable member to his team.

Morrie was the son of Orthodox Jewish parents and his background is obvious in his actions. He was one of the few major leaguers to abide by the Jewish dietary laws and he was proud of his family which includes two cousins who are rabbis. Arnovich, after his career was over, spent his off-season time in coaching a Catholic high school basket-ball team in his home town.

Like many a small town Jewish boy, Morrie was eager to obtain a thorough education, even if he did reveal athletic ability which was good enough to help him make his own way in life. Then he decided not to devote himself to com-munal life. He did not become a rabbi, despite his family's closeness to the rabbinate. He did get a good Jewish education and studied Hebrew. But he wanted to devote himself to baseball. So he did the natural thing. He signed up with the local club in his home town and played for the Superior team in the Northern League in 1933 and 1934. From the very beginning Morrie was brilliant. Even though the records kept in the Northern League were not complete, it was evident from the available records that Arnovich was much too good for this circuit. In his first year he batted .331 and pounded out fourteen home runs in a league where fences were distant. In 1934 Morrie really grew hot and slammed Northern League pitching for the sky-high mark of .374. This time he added twenty-one homers to his record and connected for 182 hits of all assortments.

This type of work won for Arnovich a promotion to Hazleton in the New York-Penn League. He proved the hurling there was not good enough to mystify him, and he hit .305, fielded fast and otherwise pepped up his club with his dynamic spirit. In 1936, his last season in the minors, he led the same league in total bases and tied with another player in home run leadership with nineteen. It was one of his best performances and nearly ranked with his major thrill in baseball.

In answering the question of what was his premier thrill, Morrie said, "When I was playing ball for Superior in 1934, I had a wonderful day against Fargo, in the same league. One hot day I slammed out three home runs in succession, and I will never forget it when I think of thrills in baseball."

After his work in the minors, Morrie was ready for big time play. Unfortunately, he was picked up by the Philadelphia Phillies, who were then doormats for the more ambitious, better-stocked teams. And a second division club has more than bad players. It suffers from poor spirit. Players don't hustle for a team that from opening day isn't going anywhere. The fans never fill the park, there is seldom a holiday spirit in the stands and even the most hustling players succumb to second-division spiritual ailments.

It is to Morrie's credit that he always gave his best to the fans and his club. He had a touch of major league play in 1936 when he played in thirteen games and came to bat forty-eight times. He batted .313, but it was the end of the season and Morrie was readying himself for the next season, his first full year in the majors.

In spring training in 1937 Morrie clinched a starting spot in the Phillie outfield. This would seem to be no great accomplishment to cynics who knew how many talentless players hooked up with the Phillies that year. Morrie, however, clicked from the beginning. He began the season auspiciously. On Patriot's Day in Boston, which was opening day in Beantown, Morrie was in the starting lineup against Guy Bush, who was one of the good pitchers of his time. The final score was 2-1, in favor of the Phils. Arnovich's home run was the margin of victory.

This gave Morrie the confidence he needed. He played regularly all year and the low position of his team made no difference to his spirit. He batted a fair .290, was alert on the bases, fielded flashily and otherwise comported himself like a big leaguer. With only a few years of professional ball behind him, he was doing well.

In 1938, Morrie slumped, although he solved major league tossers for more hits than the previous year. He managed to get 138 safe blows and drove in seventy-two runs, more than he knocked across the plate the previous year. He was pegged as a hard worker without much punch. And the final averages do not reveal the damage he wreaked during the early months. Each year his mark soared during the spring, only to stagger down to the .270's or .280's later on. Thus Morrie was a valuable man in the spring, and just about managed to hold on as the season wore along. Some critics pointed to his slight weight and said that his stamina slipped in the hot days of August. Whatever it was, Morrie never stopped trying, even if the hits eluded him.

In 1939, he had his best year, by far. His final mark was .324, but that hardly covers it all. For more than two-thirds of the season he led the league in batting. Through June he slammed National League pitching for more than a sensational .400 average. He was the talk of the league and his manager, Doc Prothro, stated flatly that he would not trade Arnovich for Joe Medwick, then of the Cardinals and one of the most feared sluggers in the game. When Morrie was kept off the All-Star team, fans all over the country complained bitterly in newspaper columns and in telegrams to the League. And he was typical of the sort of ace produced by the National Leaguers. He was smallish, fast on his feet, a sure fielder and a batter who managed to get on base often. Besides, his eagerness to play won him the admiration of many fans and, in his own way, Morrie became a drawing card. In Philadelphia, where indifference was common, a fighting player was a novelty.

From here on in, Arnovich began to fade. Early in 1940 Morrie was traded by the Phillies to the pennant-bound Cincinnati Reds. For years the Reds were plagued with the need for a decent left-fielder. During a few short seasons they bought, or brought up from their farm teams, more than thirty men. Most of them failed to make the grade. In the large garden of the Reds, Morrie's drives refused to fall safe. He did his best and undoubtedly he helped the team to the pennant with his drive and his spirit. But his batting average fell to its all-time major league low. He hit a puny .250 and did not hit a single home run.

The reputation that Morrie had made for himself, however, was paying off, for at the end of the year, Arnovich was sold by the Reds to the New York Giants for a reported price of $25,000. In the one year he played with the Giants, Arnovich lifted his average to the .280's but that wasn't really good enough for a star major league outfielder. The club was disappointed in him and at the end of the season Arnovich found himself ready for the Army. When he came back to the Giants, his legs were gone. Four years were too many to miss and whatever top caliber was left in the courageous man vanished in the service. Reluctantly, the management released Arnovich to Jersey City, and there, too, he could not make the grade. His career was ended.

Arnovich's career brought to mind the other Jewish players who had a whirl at the game, the men like Phil Weintraub, and Freddy Sington, and Jimmy Reese and Moe Solomon. They did not stick around long, for they didn't have the stuff to last. But for players like Arnovich, who lasted for years in the majors, had a couple of good seasons and offered a few thrills, there is room in a book like this.

GOODY ROSEN WAITS FOR A TURN AT BAT

Goody Rosen

Canadian Clubber

Because baseball players are a proud race of men, Goodwin Rosen, diminutive New York Giant outfielder, was full of the wrathful spirit one day in April, during the 1946 pennant race. He had belonged to the Brooklyn Dodgers in 1945, a year in which he attained his highest major league batting mark of .325. But the Dogers had cast him aside this April and had sold him, a move which Goody could interpret only as contempt, toward the Giants, the hated interborough rivals.

Generally a quiet fellow, without fire but with plenty of hustle, Goody decided to show his old mates that they would regret the move of the Brooklyn front office, which was responsible for the trade.

So, the first time Rosen faced his old companions, the two teams were locked in a double-header, with the Dodgers the heavy favorites, for the Giants were destined to have a poor season and the Brooks a very good one.

Rosen, trying hard to please his new fans and to show his old ones that he was still a potent player, was the outstanding hero of the day, as the Giants swept the twin bill. Goody hit a three-run homer in the nightcap to give his new club the margin of victory and generally strutted about like the sudden big shot he had become. When the afternoon was over Rosen was batting .714!

Two weeks later the Giants were playing the Pittsburgh Pirates in Pittsburgh, enmeshed in a brilliant pitching duel between Dave Koslo and Fritz Ostermueller. With a 0-0 score and two Pirates on the bases in the fifth inning, Frank Gustine, a Pirate, hit a ball to left center which looked like an extra-base drive. Rosen, who always played hard, dove for the ball after a long run, pulled it down and plunged heavily to the ground — but held the ball for the out. He was helped from the field, writhing in agony, but when he left the Giants were not losing and then went on to win a 1-0 shutout. At the time he was hurt Goody was batting .306, one of the top averages on his club.

The rest of the season Rosen was downright poison to all enemy teams, especially the Dodgers. Like all ball players, Rosen played beyond his capacities to wrest victories from the team which had discarded him. It is an old baseball custom for a player to ruin the team with which he used to play.

And Goody Rosen was a real ball player, a professional. He was the kind of fellow whose average never really gave a true indication of his value.

A small man in a game which is loaded with giants, Rosen managed to hold on, to hustle hard and to keep his team in the fight each day of the season. He never gave up and when his club was in the doldrums, he gave it whatever spark it could boast of. Yet for many years Rosen was an underrated player whose abilities were scorned by managers and players alike.

Perhaps it was because Goody was only five feet ten inches tall. With his 160 pounds he did not look like a real major leaguer. But after six years in the big time, Rosen showed that he had what it took to play ball under the big tent.

Born in Toronto, Canada, Rosen was quite a high school athlete. Small though he was, he was a daring football player. Among his mementos was a broken nose, a football gift from his high school foes. But Goody was made of rough stuff. In a land where hockey is the prime sport and where baseball has sneaked in, so to speak, Rosen swore to himself that he would become a baseball star. It took him a long time, but he finally made it.

He spent five seasons with Louisville in the American Association before he could get a look-in with a major league club. It did not seem to matter to the scouts that this little hustler always batted better than .300, which placed him in the charmed circle of hitters. Except for one season with Louisville, Goody rapped the ball for better than .310 as an average. He never hit many homers, but he made himself felt in a ball game. Finally, at the end of 1937, the Brooklyn Dodgers called him up.

In those days the Dodgers were easy prey for most National League clubs. They were a second-division team, without spark or talent. Goody, who had hit .312 with Louisville that year, showed the Dodgers that the big time was not too fast for him. In a little more than twenty games, he batted exactly the same for his new team. The wise heads on the Dodgers decided to give Rosen a try at a permanent position. In 1938 he was one of the regular Dodger outfielders. He never made bad plays and he was not one of those boys who added to the loony legend which surrounded Brooklyn ball players. Consequently, he seldom made news. All he knew was how to play ball.

He did well enough in 1938, but after an indifferent start

the next season, Goody was shipped back to the minors, this time to Montreal, a Canadian team in the International League. He revealed that he was not discouraged when he slammed the horsehide for a better than .300 mark. But he did not intrigue the scouts any longer. To begin with, baseball scouts are always on the look-out for husky sluggers; Goody was a small fellow who could not slug. He was a singles hitter, a guy who tried but could not compete with men like Jimmy Foxx or Mel Ott. From 1940 through all of 1943 Rosen played with Syracuse, except for a brief whirl with Columbus, in the American Association. With Syracuse he held an amazing record: he never batted as high as .300 with the minor league club, and yet stuck with it and was one of its most popular players.

Of course it became evident at this stage that Rosen was not much of a batter. But Rosen had something. It must have been the fighting spark which does not reveal itself in the cold statistics.

Despite his poor record, the Dodgers brought him up again in 1944. He did badly again, batting only .261. There was little reason to believe that he would stick around. However the war years gave added baseball life to many a player, Rosen included. In 1945 Goody was a star. For the first time since 1939 he batted over .300. He connected for a .325 mark, higher than any average he had ever garnered in his life, either in the minors or the majors.

He was a winning player, a spark-plug. The Dodgers did not regret their move to keep him, even though he had a poor average the previous year.

Until 1945, Goody had only one distinction: he had ruined a no-hit game being tossed by Hal Schumacher of the Giants in 1938. His was the only safe blow made by the

Brooks. But now he was a star in his own right, for he was the third leading batter in the senior circuit.

But it only seemed that he was a real star. In the early stage of the 1946 season Brooklyn let go of him. What happened after that is fairly well known. Rosen showed that he could play major league ball. This is what he did:

In July, in an ordinary game against the Chicago Cubs, who beat the Giants regularly in 1946, Rosen came to bat as a pinch-hitter in the ninth inning of a 2-2 tie game. The Giants had filled the bases with two out. Goody hit the first pitch into right field — and that was the ball game.

A month later in Cincinnati, Rosen, who seldom hit homers, drove a prodigious wallop over the right-field wall to win for his team, 4-3.

That's how it went most of the season. He played in over 100 games and batted .281. He probably would have batted .300, had he not sustained that injury in Pittsburgh.

Here is Goody's version of it, and it indicates the pressure under which a major leaguer sometimes has to play.

"I remember," Rosen declared, "that after six weeks on the sidelines, Mel Ott came to me and asked me when I would be ready to get back into the lineup. I told him I could hardly comb my hair, the shoulder was that stiff, and he said: 'Well, the front office is beginning to holler. You'd better get back anyway.' "

Rosen wasn't the same player the rest of the year, although it is apparent that when Brooklyn traded him to the Giants, the Dodgers lost the 1946 flag. Remember, the season ended with Brooklyn and St. Louis in a deadlock and a playoff was necessary to determine the winner. And Rosen, by himself, won three games from the Dodgers while wearing a Giant uniform.

At the end of the 1946 season, the Giants sold Rosen back to the minors, where for a number of years he continued to play hard in the International League.

Never a great player, Rosen always got by on hustle, on utilizing his limited ability to the utmost and on his genial personality which adds much to the morale of a club. He belongs in this book because he exemplified the everyday ball player who is the backbone of baseball. He won the admiration of both the fans and his fellow players, and for a man like Rosen, that was reward enough.

SID GORDON CONNECTS

Sid Gordon

The Brooklyn Giant

When the original edition of this volume went to the press, Sid Gordon was only twenty-nine years of age and just beginning to flex his big league muscles. "His big thrills," it was predicted, "are still ahead of him and in time he may rank with the top Jewish players of history."

That was one of the most solid predictions made, for before Sid Gordon reached the end of the big league line he had become one of baseball's great players and one of its most feared sluggers. He starred with the New York Giants and the Boston Braves (later the Milwaukee Braves). When he was traded to the Pittsburgh Pirates, it was obvious that his advanced baseball years had placed him in the expendable veteran category; nonetheless, he was traded with reluctance. Soon after the trade, he left the game.

A Jewish kid from Brooklyn, where baseball fever ran high, Gordon always wanted to be a major leaguer. He had the power and hitting ability to give it a whirl. He began doing well in high school, and realized that sports was a way to fame and comfortable living. His father, Morris, came to this country from Russia, and met and married his wife Rose Meyerson in Brooklyn. The family moved from Brownsville to Flatbush — a step up the social ladder —

and Sid was able, when he was old enough, to attend Samuel Tilden High school.

Sid was what the game called a "natural" hitter. He needed little coaching to give him the leverage and the smoothness which mark a slugger. Joe Solomon, the astute baseball coach at Tilden, was cautious with Gordon. He taught Sid what he knew but was careful not to tamper with the normal form of the youngster. He knew that no matter how much a coach may be able to impart to a young hopeful he cannot teach him the God-given gift of timing and coordination which differentiates a great hitter from a mediocre hitter.

Like many baseball men he remembered the story of Al Simmons, the temperamental Pole from Milwaukee who came up to the Philadelphia Athletics with a "one-foot-in-the-bucket" stance. This meant that Simmons drew his body away from the ball when he swung, instead of stepping into it. Ordinarily this means a loss of power so great that a potentially good hitter can get too little power to realize his potentialities. But Simmons was a born hitter. He pulled away from the ball, yes; but he drove it a mile when he connected. Within a few years he became one of the most dangerous sluggers in baseball, and this happened because shrewd old Connie Mack never altered his stance. "Anyone who can hit .390 in Milwaukee with this form," Mack said, "can hit for me this way, too."

This is important to remember because many a young fellow is ruined by an over-eager coach who wishes to impose his own ways on a talented player. Solomon let Gordon develop on his own. But they played only two games a week at Tilden and Gordon was anxious to get in more and more practice. So he played semi-professional ball as well. He joined the Bushwicks and a club called the Brooklyn Pirates. In brief, he was taking this game of baseball with real seriousness. But he was no burden to his parents during this period. His father, who had been in the plumbing trade, gave it up for the coal business and Sid spent his summers driving a coal truck for his father. This saved his father the expense of adding a driver's wages to his costs and it helped Sid develop his muscles. A good deal, all around.

In 1936, Sid was graduated from high school and received an opportunity to try out for the Brooklyn Dodgers, then managed by Casey Stengel. Gordon's ability attracted the eye of the veteran manager, who proved in later years that he was an expert at handling diamond talent. But Stengel, while encouraging, was unwilling to commit himself to offering Sid a contract. "Casey was real nice," Gordon said years later. "He told me I had good possibilities and that he'd let me know as soon as an opening came in the Brooklyn system." But Stengel was soon fired by the Dodgers and so Gordon never heard from Brooklyn again!

A year later, in 1937, Sid played ball with the Queens Alliance League, where he caught the eye of a New York Giant scout. The Giants thereupon made Gordon a peculiar offer. They asked him to pay his own way for a tryout with the Giant farm in Milford, Delaware in the Class D Eastern Shore League. If he could make the team, they would refund him his money. If not, he would have to get home as best he could. In his eagerness to play ball, Gordon agreed to these terms. All winter long, he worked from nine to five-thirty selling pajamas in a New York department store. He managed to play ball, too, for the store had a team. Then, winter ended and Gordon was beginning to dream of Milford — when his father died. Sid realized that he had other responsibilities now, and he prepared to tell the Giants that he would not report to Milford, when his mother, knowing how much the chance meant to him, persuaded him that he had to give himself the opportunity to try out in the minors and that she would run the coal business left behind by the father. She gave him thirty-two dollars for the trip and Sid Gordon was on his way to fortune.

The manager gave him a chance at third base, where Sid made good. He was paid seventeen dollars and thirty-two cents a week, but at last he was a professional ball player. In one game he hit two home runs in a row. They were unusual homers because one was slammed with the bases full and the other with two men on base. In other words, Sid took two swings and drove in seven runs in a game! He played in every one of the team's 112 games and hit .352. He hit twenty-five home runs, led the league in total hits with 135, in total bases and in triples, with nine. Of course, this sort of performance did not go unnoticed. The Giants, hungry for talent, shifted Sid to Clinton, in the Three-I League. This was a faster circuit but it did not stop him, either. Such promotions never stop men who are headed for the majors, and that was where Sid Gordon was obviously going to play ball. With Clinton, Gordon batted .327 and again led his circuit in three-baggers, this time with twenty-four, which is an amazing number of triples in any league. At the end of the season, he was brought up to the Jersey City Giants, and managed to get into three games before the race ended in that circuit.

During the winter, Sid returned to work as a coal truck

driver and in 1940 he made his bid to win a real job in the International League. This was a top minor league, which meant that the brand of ball played there was just below the major league standard. If you made good in this league, you received a shot at the big time. Sid played two years with the "Little Giants" and hit over .300 in his second season. He was on his way. Late in 1940 he married Mary Goldberg and knew that he had to make good in order to support a wife and family. His performance in 1941 was a convincing one. He hit .304 and stole fifteen bases. The Giants yanked him up for a look at the end of the season. For the first time in his life he played the outfield in a major league game, after having played the infield most of his career. The Jersey City Giants had given him a brief whirl at the outfield, but to break into the majors in a strange position was a double handicap. Yet his debut was successful. In a game against the Cincinnati Reds, Gordon started in left field. He snagged eight fly balls, which are a lot of chances for an outfielder in one game, and showed commendable patience by driving in his first run when he waited out Johnny Vander Meer for a walk with the bases loaded.

Another unusual aspect of Gordon's career was that when he made his debut in the Polo Grounds, he was one of four Jewish players on the field that day, all wearing the uniform of the New York Giants! Morrie Arnovich was another outfielder and the battery starred Hank Feldman and Harry Danning. Sid celebrated his Polo Grounds debut by slamming a triple and a single.

Sid's single came in his very first major league time at bat, against Boston hurler Art Johnson. In the stands that day were Sid's mother and two sisters. Having heard over the radio that he was to play that afternoon, they had rushed to the Polo Grounds by taxicab.

Ironically, Sid's adaptability and willingness to play anywhere were the cause of his being sent back to the minors. He started at third base for the Giants in 1942, but after a few games, in which he hit .316, he was sent back to Jersey City. Manager Bill Terry told Gordon that he was needed as an outfielder, and should work on mastering that position.

Obediently, Sid returned to the little Giants, where he played the outfield (and the occasional third base) and hit an even .300. On his afternoons off, he would go to the Polo Grounds and study the play of Joe Moore, the Giants' smooth left fielder. When the conscientious Gordon reported to the Giant training camp in the spring of 1943, he had made himself into a solid outfielder. But Mel Ott, the new Giant manager, told the startled rookie that he was going to play third base. He ended up playing in the outfield and even at first base as well. As always, Sid uncomplainingly did his best, even though having to play a number of unfamiliar positions might have distracted his concentration at the plate.

Playing all over the infield and outfield, Sid hit a long ball and made his presence felt on the team. True, it was a wartime team, and if the regulars had been playing Sid would not have made the grade. He hit a mere .251, which is not good. And when the year ended and Sid went into the Coast Guard, it seemed that he had had his chance and had flubbed it. Surely, a few years in the Coast Guard were not going to improve the caliber of his game.

But in 1946 Gordon returned to the Giants. In spring training Gordon played brilliantly and wrested the left field job from a couple of veterans. On opening day he was a starting outfielder.

The opener was played in New York against the Phillies. Oscar Judd was the starter for the Phils and for the Giants it was Bill Voiselle. Early in the game, Gordon was hit in the thigh by a medium fast ball. He limped to first base and then was replaced by Johnny Rucker, one of the men he had beaten out for a position in the outer garden. Rucker played the rest of the game and helped the Giants win with a far-flung triple. It looked as though the breaks had gone against Sid, especially when it was announced that he had a blood clot and would be out for a few weeks.

Here, however, is where Gordon received a good break. The outfielders, who on past records were supposed to be good hitters, showed an inability to cope with major league hurling. Their averages began to drop and Gordon was pushed back in as soon as possible. As soon as he returned, the team perked up. In a dozen games, Sid did the top slugging. He hit the extra-base blows that break up ball games. The Giants, who had dropped into the cellar, soon moved back into the fight for a first-division berth. The *Sporting News* gave Gordon a big spread and called him the solution to the Giant outfield problem. He gave the outfield its punch. He learned how to do things in the majors: to bunt and to knock the ball over the fence. He had hit only .251 in 1943; now, in 1946, he ended the season with a mark of .293. He thought he had clinched a job on the Giants.

But in 1947, Gordon once again found himself forced to fight for a position, in spite of his solid 1946 record. A lot of spring flashes were vying for outfield posts and Mel Ott, the manager, was eager to try them all out. So Gordon started the season at third base. Unsteady at that post, Sid was benched a few days after the race started. It seemed that Ott was interested in seeing how his rookies could play, for with a cellar team in 1946, he was anxious to discover new talent. But soon he returned Gordon to the outfield. Sid was ostensibly filling in for Whitey Lockman, a highly-touted rookie at the time, who had broken a leg in spring training and was due back in July. Lockman did not make it; but even if he had, it was doubtful if he could have displaced Gordon, for Sid had become a master at outfield play in the Polo Grounds, having learned to play the rebounds like Mel Ott himself. He hit .272 and hit thirteen home runs, an immense improvement over the five he hit the previous year.

It was in 1948, however, that Gordon really bloomed, and thanks were due to a Giant coach named Red Kress. Kress noticed, in spring training, that Gordon, who was powerfully built, could improve himself by pulling the ball to left field. This was how Gordon related the change that led him from a total of thirteen home runs to thirty in one season:

"Before 1948 I could hit a fairly long ball but it always went to right or right-center. At the Polo Grounds right-center is just a big out. Red Kress, a coach on the Giants, used to get me to pull the ball to left. He started out by moving my right-hand grip on the bat around a little and he opened up my stance — I now put my left foot toward third when I hit. I learned to roll my wrists more and to step into the ball. Pretty soon I was dropping them in left. Red spent hours working with me on it. I can't give him enough credit."

But when the 1948 season began, Gordon had a tough time breaking into the Giant starting lineup. But after the

race got under way, one of the Giant flashes, Bobby
Thomson, hurt himself — and in came reliable Sid. When
Thomson regained his full health, Gordon returned to the
bench until another regular was injured. That was how it
remained until May 22, when he got back in the lineup and
hit a home run with the bases full. That was the beginning
and he stayed in the lineup for the rest of the season. The
Dodgers that year saw a most astonishing event occur, for
Sid's Brooklyn friends tendered a "hated" Giant —
Gordon himself — a day at Ebbets Field. Sid thanked
them by hitting two homers that afternoon. Leo Durocher
replaced Mel Ott in mid-season, but Gordon kept going
like a fire-cracker and when the season ended, he had hit
.299, had driven in 107 runs and accounted for thirty home
runs.

By this time, he was a regular with the Giants but not at
any one position. In 1949, he played the outfield, first base
and third base. In all, he got into 141 games, hit .284 and
showed that he was a steady long-ball hitter when he connected for twenty-six home runs.

Nevertheless, the popular Sid Gordon, after becoming
one of the finest Jewish baseball players ever to wear a
New York uniform, was traded in the winter of 1949 to the
Boston Braves. It was a six-player trade and Gordon was
the key man in the deal. As soon as details of the trade
were made public, Giant manager Durocher called
Gordon and told him that he personally had opposed losing him but that he could not have got the men he wanted
unless he yielded Gordon. It was a nice — and honest —
gesture on the part of Durocher. A few minutes after
Durocher's call, Billy Southworth, his new manager, called
to say how happy he was to have Sid on his team. Ap-

parently, Gordon's last few seasons had convinced professional baseball men that the man was really good!

In 1950, Sid had a wonderful season. He batted .304, hit twenty-seven homers and drove in 103 runs. He also tied a major league mark for the most home runs with the bases loaded in a single season, when he pulled the trick four times. He hit his first two within a few days. During the last two weeks in May he nursed a swollen elbow, after having been hit by a pitcher. He returned to the lineup on June 1 against Mel Queen of the Pittsburgh Pirates. The bases were loaded — but a moment later they were all cleared as Sid drove the ball out of the park. Two days later, on June 3, Gordon faced Bill Werle of the same Pirates, and again with the bases full. Werle threw close to Gordon to keep him respectful. Sid hit the next pitch into the stands. One of the other homers with the bases full was a particularly satisfying one. It happened at the Polo Grounds, during the second game of the young season. The fans were showing their unhappiness at seeing Gordon in an enemy uniform. They cheered his every move and taunted the Giants on the field. Early in the contest, Gordon hit a home run and the fans went wild with glee. Then, in the sixth inning, he came to bat with the bases loaded and hit the very first pitch into the left field stands. It was a happy day for Gordon and an even happier one for his followers.

In 1951 and 1952 the Braves fell on bad days, but Gordon continued to play solid, steady ball for them. He batted .287 in 1951 and .289 in 1952. In 1953 he hit a good .274, drove in seventy-five runs and hit nineteen home runs. He was, at this point, thirty-five years old and one of the true pros of the sport. Then, after the Braves had moved to Milwaukee and Gordon had won new friends, the Braves traded him to the Pittsburgh Pirates when he and five other men were dealt away for a young infielder named Danny O'Connell. It was apparent that the veteran outfielder was considered to be on his way out. As Gordon said to a newspaperman, "You get old fast in baseball." Then he expressed an eagerness to get a job as a coach or a minor league manager when his playing days were over. Certainly, he proved — apart from his ability to play ball well — a patience and self-discipline necessary in men who would guide others.

In 1949, Gordon was involved in a case of Jew-baiting, but managed to emerge with dignity and without losing control of himself. In June of 1949, Gordon was playing very well and, during a game with the St. Louis Cardinals, who later became infamous for their treatment of Jackie Robinson, found himself the object of ridicule and scorn. New York newspapers attacked the Cardinals for their "personal comments on Sid Gordon's religion." Dan Parker of the *New York Mirror* said that "Sid Gordon of the Giants has been subjected to this despicable form of jockeying for some time."

Gordon refused to comment publicly on the attacks and was justified when Cardinal manager Eddie Dyer said to a newspaperman that Gordon was a friend of his and that Gordon had not been attacked verbally because he was a Jew, but simply because he was a good ball player and the good ones receive the attention of the "bench jockeys." "I do know," the reporter, J. Roy Stockton, said, "that the rank and file Cardinals admire Gordon as a player and like him personally."

Gordon took the abuse with the aplomb of a professional athlete, forced the bigots to respect and admire him

— and continued to play well. As a private citizen, he saw to it that his children received a Jewish education and he himself helped the Jewish Education Committee and other Jewish groups whenever he could, by lending his name to their projects.

On June 18, 1975, Sid Gordon, then an insurance underwriter, was playing softball in New York's Central Park. He collapsed on the field with a heart attack, and died before he could reach a hospital. His passing evoked a flood of admiring praise from sportswriters and ballplayers who had known and admired Sid.

"He was THE Jewish athlete in New York City," wrote John Piesen of the *New York Post* in an article entitled: "Sid Gordon: Always a Giant." Many others recalled the slugger's lifetime .283 average, his thirteen-homer contribution to the 1947 Giants' then major league record total of two hundred and twenty one, and his versatility in playing the infield, the outfield, and even catching for the Giants.

But most of all they remembered a fine ball player who was an equally fine human being. Sid Gordon was the consummate professional, willing to play anywhere that would help the team, and do anything that had to be done so long as he was able to play baseball.

After he had traded Gordon to the Braves, Horace Stoneham, Giant owner, told Sid that "It broke my heart to let you go. There are certain guys I like to have around me and you're one of them." His sentiments were echoed by almost everyone who knew Sid Gordon, one of the most admired ball players of his day.

"DOLLY" STARK, IN HIS UMPIRE'S UNIFORM

"Dolly" Stark

Man in Blue

In a moment of confession, a great umpire once said, "Our greatest reward is silence." This was his way of saying that in baseball, one of the finest spectator sports, the only real reward of the man in the blue suit comes when no one is aware of his presence, his work, his ability and his fairness.

But there was one umpire who in his own way made baseball history. He was lauded as one of the finest umps in a demanding profession. He was given a car by a group of admirers; he won a title as the "Best Umpire" of a particular year and he was not an anonymous figure on a ball field studded with stars, for he was a star in his own right.

His name was Albert Stark, better known to all baseball fans as "Dolly" Stark.

The man who calls the plays seems to the baseball fan to be above the crowd, a man who is mysterious. Little is known about the ump. What's more, hardly anyone cares about him. He is the fellow they scream at, work their emotions on. When a home town player gets a bad break, they scream, "Kill the ump!" When a favorite pitcher, though wild, hears the ump call balls instead of strikes, the fans roar in unison against the ump. The umpire is the whipping boy of all the dictators and evil rulers and people in the world.

And the chief whipping boy in the National League for

many a year was "Dolly" Stark, a Jewish umpire from the poverty-stricken East Side.

The story of "Dolly" Stark is loaded with human interest. Unlike most umpires, Stark was not a colorless man with the mask. He exuded as much class and as much color as the best players who heeded his decisions. And they all listened to "Dolly," because he was as hard as the toughest of them. He was raised in a rough school and when he was at the top of his profession his success was due to the character he forged in the furnaces of experience.

"Dolly" was born on the lower East Side, which was the New York version of the European ghetto. It was nothing to be ashamed of; some of America's outstanding men came from the picturesque and heart-breaking East Side. Certainly some of the greatest American sports figures did. So did "Dolly." But he suffered deeply for he knew almost from birth the pain of hunger and destitution. He was homeless at the age of seven and his father died when he was a child, leaving only a struggling mother to "Dolly." Recalling those bitter days, "Dolly" said, "Many times we went without our dinner. As far back as I can remember, I sold papers, ran errands for two cents and did any other jobs that came my way." One morning a good-hearted policeman found him slumped over in the cold street, sleeping the sleep of exhaustion. The cop woke him up, and tried to help him out. The result was that "Dolly" spent some time in a home for the homeless. But at the age of twelve he was on his own again. For three years he tried to make some money as an eager pushcart peddler. "I used to be up at three in the morning," he said, "no matter what the weather was." But "Dolly" Stark was made of tough material. Although he lived in the Bronx, in Schenectady, the East Side and wherever else he could earn a dollar, he always remembered that he had to have some kind of an education. Therefore, he managed to go to school whenever and wherever he could.

Of course, as the boy grew older, he became interested in baseball. He tried hard to make the big league grade. But his years of struggle, his nights of hard work, and his days of walking around in the cold streets took too much out of him. He was thin and not robust enough for the major leagues. He never weighed more than a puny 115 pounds when he tried to play ball. He had a trial with the New York Yankees and in 1920 the Washington Senators gave him a whirl at making the big time. These trials were a tribute to his courage and to his inherent ability. But even if his weight, or lack of it, kept him from the majors, Stark's love for baseball never dimmed. He took a job as an umpire in a college game in 1927 and found himself the recipient of an offer to do the same kind of work in the Eastern League. When he accepted this job, he found the way was open to the majors, even if he was not a player. He did such a spectacular bit of umpiring in the Eastern League that three weeks later the National League snapped him up!

From that day forward the fortunes of "Dolly" Stark improved. Not only was he a major league umpire, but he became the successful coach of the Dartmouth College basketball team, and held the job for twelve years. Little "Dolly" Stark, thin, underfed and from New York's East Side, was working for one of the high-tone American colleges and was, at the same time, holding down a post as one of the top umpires in America's national game. He had come a long way.

Noted for his speed afoot, his mobility and his alertness, "Dolly" Stark seemed to become a ranking umpire in hardly any time at all. But his own version of the job runs something like this. "I remember," he said, "how Hank Greenberg once said that he did not really feel like a big league ball player for a couple of years after he hit the majors. Whenever he followed the great Charlie Gehringer at bat he felt a bit of awe. And then one day it suddenly disappeared and he felt that he was as good as anyone." And then "Dolly" told this story about his own confidence.

"It was the ninth inning of the deciding game of the 1931 World Series between the St. Louis Cardinals and the Philadelphia Athletics. The Cards were ahead 4-0 and then the A's began to go to work." Stark chuckled and recalled that the Cardinal pitcher, Burleigh Grimes, was knocked out and Wild Bill Hallahan came in. It was a tense moment and Stark was calling them closely. Then he called a pitch on Max Bishop of the A's "and all of a sudden I relaxed and knew at that moment that I was calling them as I saw them and that as far as I was concerned I was calling them right. That moment made me a big league umpire."

It must have done that, because four years later an unprecedented thing happened in baseball. "Dolly" was riding the wave of popularity, and he was an umpire at that! The *Sporting News* ran a poll for umpires and Stark was an easy winner. The players and the managers and even the fans knew that they had a rare umpire in Stark. And they showed it.

Frank Slocum, one of the National League publicity chieftains, told me* unbelievingly, "The fans gave 'Dolly' a

*H.U.R.

car at the Polo Grounds, and if you refuse to believe it, you'd better, because I was a witness to it. There they were, thousands of fans, cheering an umpire!"

But the following year "Dolly" Stark won other kinds of headlines. He announced he was quitting the sport and in his complaints one could see what a sensitive man he was. In effect he said, "Umpiring is a hard business. You have no friends, you can't talk to and live with the players and the highest praise for an umpire is silence. I don't think I can take the jeering and the booing any more."

Even "Dolly" Stark, the man who won the applause of the crowds for his work, found himself unable to cope with the fickle fans. And there is where some new drama entered the scene. Bill Klem, the greatest umpire in the business, the man who nursed Stark along like a doting parent, took "Dolly" in hand. Although Stark went into radio for a year, Klem worked on him and in 1937 persuaded him to come back to the game. And Stark returned to baseball.

For a couple of years "Dolly" did the same wonderful job that had won him honors in the past. But in 1939 he developed a trick knee, probably a result of his speed afoot, his rapid turning and his eternal alertness during a game. Early in 1940 "Dolly" collapsed on the field and was carried away from the game. That marked the end of his career. But a man like Stark does not give up entirely. He was used to the bad breaks, the harshness of life, the struggle for existence. He went into the dress business and his originality of designs immediately won him a huge following. The "Dolly Stark" dress was eagerly sought after and "Dolly" became a successful businessman in an entirely new field. A few years later he re-entered the sports world when he became a radio and television commentator.

There were rumors spread about in 1935 that Stark was driven out of baseball because there were a lot of ball players who refused to take decisions from a little Jewish umpire from the East Side. I* was unable to discover if there was any truth in these tales. Of course it would seem completely unlikely. "Dolly" Stark won more adulation than any umpire, except Bill Klem, in National League history. He was firm on the field and lasted a long time. Only an injury forced him out of the game. True, there were moments when he was unhappy and blasted his job and the loneliness of it, but he was a sensitive man who never really had the temperament for his work. That he developed into a great umpire is a tremendous achievement and symbolic of Stark's strength of character.

Baseball, like most sports, is a highly democratic game. No matter who you are, or who your father was, the ability of the athlete counts more than anything else. And one of the most potent arguments in favor of sports is the fact that men like "Dolly" Stark are able to rise above their circumstances to win an honored place in the annals of a sport which is nearly a religion to millions of young Americans.

Throughout his baseball career "Dolly" Stark had been written about by all the leading sports writers in the country. In the storm of his 1936 activities, I* never read a slighting remark about "Dolly." Even when he had some vinegary things to say about baseball, the writers never forgot to call Stark one of the finest of all umpires and to praise him for his devotion to the game. Frank Graham, one of the best sports writers in America, devoted many a column to Stark. Each column was sentimental, full of ad-

*H.U.R.

miration and affection for one of America's finest personalities in baseball. This was the typical attitude. Everyone thought well of "Dolly" Stark, even the few magnates who squirmed under his attacks which implied that baseball was harsh to its men in blue.

The career of "Dolly" Stark, from his hungering days on the East Side to his moments of glory on the diamond and beyond them, is truly an American story.

SAUL ROGOVIN ON THE MOUND

Saul Rogovin

Power Pitcher

Since the season of 1915, when Erskine Mayer helped pitch the Philadelphia Phillies to a National League pennant, there was no other first-rate Jewish pitcher in the major leagues until the blossoming of huge Saul Rogovin with the 1951 Chicago White Sox. In that startlingly successful year, Rogovin led the majors in earned-run averages and won recognition as a coming star in the big leagues. That he never again attained the form that gained headlines for him in 1951 is one of the mysteries which makes baseball such a fascinating game.

Rogovin's sports career has been one of ups and downs, and so the 1951 season with the White Sox stands out even more vividly in his own life than it does in the record books. In 1951, Rogovin won only twelve games, not many for an ace twirler. Yet his 2.78 earned-run mark topped the majors and the dozen victories scarcely hint at the effectiveness of the tall Jewish lad. Rogovin lost eight times in 1951, and yet seven of the defeats were by the slim margin of a single run; the eighth was a 2-0 shutout at the hands of the Yankees, when Rogovin yielded only eight hits himself. His own victories were astonishing in their brilliance. In one four-day period he shut out the Detroit Tigers twice (the very team that had traded him to the White Sox!). Once he pitched a seventeen-inning game, two eleven in-

ning games and six complete games against the champion
New York Yankees, who seldom permitted any pitcher to
go the route against them more than once. Three of his victories were against these same pennant-headed Yankees.

It was obvious, when Saul Rogovin ended the 1951
season, that here was a star in the making. Nevertheless,
that year remained his peak season. Never again did he
come close to such pitching skill. A casual perusal of his
baseball record will indicate that he always had difficulties
and perhaps it is remarkable that he performed as well as
he did in 1951.

Saul Rogovin was born in Brooklyn, on October 10,
1923. The son of Jacob and Bessie Rogovin, Saul was an
only child, beloved and cared for by his parents with an
overwhelming and considerate love. When he showed an
interest in playing ball, his parents did not become angry.
Instead, they encouraged him, and when he attracted
Brooklyn Dodger scouts at an Ebbets Field tryout in 1941,
he signed with the Dodger organization and was sent to
Valdosta of the Class D Georgia-Florida League as a slugging first baseman. At the very outset of his baseball life,
Rogovin revealed himself to be an independent individual.
He discovered that Valdosta had another first baseman
who had been given a $2,500 bonus for signing with the
Dodgers. "I asked for a $500 bonus," Rogovin recalled
after he had reached the majors, "because I felt I was at
least one-fifth as good as he was." He did not get it, so he
quit and then signed with Beaver Falls, in the Penn State
Association. During the war, Rogovin took a job with the
Brewster Aeronautical Corporation and played the game
only intermittently. Here he received his first good break.
"Dolly" Stark, the great umpire, saw him play and

recognized in him a coming baseball star. "Dolly wanted me to be another Hank Greenberg," Rogovin said. "I had a strong arm, but I could never hit like Greenberg. The only thing we have in common is we're both Jewish." But Stark's word carried weight, and on the strength of that word, Rogovin was accepted by the Jersey City Giants. He was given a chance to win an outfield job, failed and was sold to Chattanooga of the Southern Association, where he was a third baseman on the club's roster. It was 1945, and Rogovin began to realize that time was running out on him. He was helped again, this time by a former pitcher for Cincinnati, Red Lucas, who was a coach for Nashville and saw that the powerful young man had a tremendous arm. "You're wasting your time at third," Lucas informed him. "You can be a good pitcher." Rogovin, in turn, thought that perhaps pitching would be easier. "I thought all you had to do was throw the ball hard," he said.

Toward the end of the 1945 season, he was given a chance to pitch. In the second game of a double-header with Birmingham, Rogovin pitched a four-hit shutout, and was convinced that he had been working at the wrong positions all his life. From that point forward, he did nothing but pitch. In 1946, he worked for Pensacola, where he won eight games and lost five. His seasoning had begun. Then, in 1947, he met the man who, more than anyone else, was responsible for his successful career — Paul Richards, a former major league catcher and later a big league manager, who knew pitching well and what made a good pitcher. Rogovin has been free in crediting Richards with his effectiveness. "For the first time since I started playing ball," Rogovin said, "I began to learn what it actually meant to be a pitcher. And in order to learn, I had to forget all the mistakes I had picked up along the way. Until Paul took me over, I honestly didn't know the first thing about getting the side out."

In three seasons with Buffalo, Rogovin won thirty-two games and lost only seventeen. In 1949, he won sixteen games and struck out 163. This work earned him a call to Detroit, where he won only two games in 1950. Back to the minors he went and received a second crack at the majors in 1951, again with Detroit. He made an unfavorable impression on Red Rolfe, Tiger manager, and was traded to the Chicago White Sox, then being managed by Rogovin's old friend, Paul Richards. It was with Richards that Rogovin bloomed and became a star. Yet the inside story of how a man succeeds for one manager while failing for another indicates the importance of approach to a player as sensitive as Saul Rogovin. This is how Rogovin has told it.

"Red wanted to win that pennant badly in 1950 and I guess he thought I was alibiing when I told him I couldn't pitch." Rogovin was cursed with a chronic sore arm, a horrible fate for any pitcher, but Red Rolfe, the Tiger manager and a former New York Yankee star, had no interest in excuses. Rogovin's narrative points its own moral:

"I wanted to pitch more than he wanted me to, but my arm simply was shot. There's no worse feeling for a pitcher than when he has a bum hose. The whole trouble started, I guess, when we were coming north from Lakeland, Florida, 1950. Rolfe told me there was a chance to stay with the club as a relief pitcher. But I wanted to show him I could be a starter so I bore down extra hard. One night I got a chance to start against the White Sox in Memphis. It was very cold, below thirty degrees, I think. In fact it was so cold that Rolfe sent half the ball club back to the hotel. Billy Pierce was going against us and I decided to give it all I had. Everything went along okay until the seventh inning. Then I started to feel a twinge in my arm. Well, even though my arm hurt, I was a little timid about asking to be taken out. Finally, though, I said, 'Red, do you think I've had enough?'

" 'You can go another two innings,' he said. 'You can finish up.'

"That was the last time I pitched for two weeks. When the regular season started and I finally did get into a game against Philadelphia late in the month, I could hardly get the ball up to the plate."

Milton Richman, the sports writer to whom Rogovin told this story, wrote a sympathetic article on the Jewish pitcher and added another significant tale concerning Rolfe's handling of Rogovin and it is not unlikely that Rogovin's later woes were traceable to his mishandling by Red Rolfe.

When Rogovin's arm went dead after the "gentle" Rolfe treatment, the tall boy from Brooklyn was not much use to the Tigers through much of the 1950 season. Then, in late July, Rolfe suddenly called on Saul to pitch in an important game against the New York Yankees at Yankee Stadium.

"It was my life's ambition," Rogovin said. "I was brought up in New York and I always dreamed I'd be pitching in Yankee Stadium some day. I used to root for the Yankees and Joe DiMaggio was my idol. I could hardly believe it was happening to me."

For a while he did well. In the second inning, with the bases full, Saul caught a curve ball off the slants of Ed

Lopat and hit a grand-slam home run, sufficient indication that he was not frightened of the responsibility given him by Rolfe. Then the Yankees began to whittle away at the four-run Tiger lead and in the sixth inning Rogovin was ahead by 4-3 and his arm was tightening.

"My first impulse," he told sports writer Richman, "was to keep on pitching and say nothing. But that wouldn't have been fair to the others on the club. The game was too important, so I told Rolfe I didn't think I could go on. But he said, 'You're all right. Get in there and pitch!' "

When a pitcher is ordered to pitch, he simply does not walk off the mound. Rogovin returned to his work. On his first toss, DiMaggio hit a long home run. On the very next pitch, Yogi Berra hit another homer. Rolfe was convinced. But that was more or less the end of the "relationship" between the two men.

In 1951, Rogovin started with the Tigers but was soon sold to the White Sox and Paul Richards. "Everything changed when Paul Richards got me from Detroit," Saul said. When a big game came up with the Yankees and Richards asked Rogovin how he felt, Saul admitted that his arm was sore. Richards was not Rolfe. His reaction was radically different. "We have no heroes on this club," he said. "If your arm bothers you, I don't want to risk ruining it permanently." And Richards found himself another pitcher for the game. He knew that he had to move carefully with Rogovin for Saul had trouble with his arm after the 1950 season and when Richards bought him in 1951, the Rogovin arm was still sore.

Richards sent Rogovin to the bullpen and worked on him carefully. The result became apparent as the season progressed. From a sore-armed pitcher who had won only two games, he led the league in permitting fewer earned runs than any other pitcher. He was made, and it was Richards who had made him.

In 1952, Rogovin reported out of condition and had a difficult task getting into shape. Starting slowly, he nevertheless managed to improve on his wins for the previous year, when he chalked up fourteen victories against nine losses. But in 1953, the chronic sore arm of Rogovin began to plague him once again, and it became evident that Paul Richards, too, was losing patience with the man who had such outstanding possibilities. In mid-season, 1953, Richman quoted Richards as saying that "sheer laziness" kept Rogovin from being a twenty-game winner. Then the arm acted up and Rogovin was unable to win. By the end of July, he had lost eleven games and won only five. After taking a battering in an exhibition game, the White Sox placed Saul on the disabled list, as a club spokesman declared that Rogovin was suffering from a sore arm and was able only to lob the ball to the plate. Yet, earlier that year, Rogovin had pitched some brilliant games. In his first 1953 victory, for example, he tossed a six-hit shutout against the Tigers, his old club. He was, nevertheless, aware that there were those who believed that the sore arm was a figment of his imagination. But Rogovin always denied this. "After all," he said, "I'm not a complete dumbbell, nor am I a hypochondriac." But there it was, the arm plagued him continually.

In September of 1953, Rogovin went off the disabled list and in his first start shut out the Cleveland Indians with four hits. Certainly, when healthy, Rogovin was hot. But he ended the year with seven victories and Paul Richards finally gave up on him. On December 10, 1953, the White Sox traded Rogovin out of the American League to Cincinnati. The Sox got Willard Marshall and yielded, in addition to Rogovin, two utility infielders. Certainly, they had given up completely, and soon thereafter Rogovin was moved about to Baltimore and then to Philadelphia in the National League. In 1957 he slipped out of baseball.

In 1979, Rogovin, after years of silence, won some space in the *New York Times,* in an interesting column by Red Smith, who disclosed that Rogovin had become a teacher in a New York City high school.

"Being out of baseball hurt me," Rogovin told Smith, "hurt me so bad I couldn't go to a game for years. I wanted to visit my old team, keep up my baseball contacts, but I couldn't. I got to be a loner." He got a job with a liquor company, but it did not make him happy.

"Then," the former pitcher said, "I thought about going back to school. I was fifty-one or fifty-two. I enrolled in Manhattan Community College. After two years, I transferred to City College and took a degree. I had some friends who were teachers and I began to think about that. I enjoyed being with young people. I thought about phys. ed., but decided I was a little old for that. So I majored in literature with a minor in education. Last October I got a job here as a substitute teacher, and this term I'm a regular with four English classes and one is phys. ed. The emphasis is on reading because a lot of these kids are going on to college, and in college reading and writing are where it's at."

Rogovin loved the challenge of teaching, as he enjoyed the challenges of pitching.

Rogovin proved in 1951 that he was a strong pitcher with a powerful fast ball. As the personification of power on the mound, he won frequently and twirled brilliantly.

Even though he never measured up to his potentialities, Saul Rogovin had put his name into record books — and into the history of American Jewish sports.

AL ROSEN AND HIS STANCE

Al Rosen

Indian Chief

Of the many outstanding Jewish baseball headliners in the long history of the national game, few have ranked with the superstars of the sport. But in the winter of 1953 there occurred an event which indicated that a Jewish diamond ace named Al Rosen had the potentialities of becoming a legend in the game. On November 27, 1953 the American League announced that Al Rosen, slugging third baseman for the Cleveland Indians, had been named its most valuable player for 1953.

Other athletes had won a similar honor, so there was nothing extraordinary about the announcement. What made it remarkable was that all twenty-four members of the Baseball Writers Association, three from each American League city, had listed Rosen as the best player of the year. It was an unprecedented unanimous vote. Rosen received 336 points, highest in history — and in winning the award saw himself lifted to the ranks of the great players of his time.

It was no wonder that Rosen had been acclaimed in this fashion. He led the circuit with home runs — blasting forty-three; was first in runs batted in with 145 and missed winning the batting championship of the league by the proverbial hair. Casey Stengel, manager of the New York Yankees, called Rosen a great player. Marty Marion, once a slick major league shortstop, said that "As far as I'm concerned I have yet to see a better clutch hitter." Harry Brecheen, an astute veteran of the game, who had pitched successfully in both major leagues, said of Rosen, "He's the best hitter in the American League." After a pause, he added, "And there's none better in the other league." He amplified: "Rosen has no real weakness. Even when you get him out he usually hits the ball hard. I'd rather face any other player than Rosen in a clutch spot."

A former major leaguer named Buddy Blattner, who became a sports announcer, paid his tribute in this fashion: "If I wanted to try to teach a youngster how to hit I'd tell him to watch Rosen, day after day. Rosen has become a picture book hitter. Watch how he cradles the bat and how he never commits himself to the pitcher . . . and see how smart he is. He has very strong arms and quick wrists, yet he isn't afraid to choke up on his bat and make his stroke more flexible."

During the 1953 season, when Rosen was roaring along, leading the league in practically everything, he heard nothing but chimes of praise. His manager, Al Lopez, said "What I like about Al most of all is his determination. After a pitcher gets him out he'll come back to the bench and say, 'I'll get him next time.' And, by golly, he does. To him, each pitcher is a personal challenge."

Yet Rosen's rise was neither rapid nor expected. He was not the super-athlete all his life long. Instead, the peak he reached in 1953 was a tribute to his courage and his determination rather than to his innate ability. Blattner's remarks on Rosen's beautiful stance, Stengel's grim concession that Rosen was the best player in the game, and the chorus of applause from players and fans alike were the fruit of much hard labor. Rosen, like Hank Greenberg, had more ambitious spirit than skill and his emergence as a star proved that the will to succeed is often more compelling than any other element in sports.

Rosen had said that "everything about this game is a challenge to me. I don't want to accept mediocrity. I want to be as good as I possibly can in every phase of the game." Thus he concentrated on running and on fielding, as well as batting. A former teammate of his, Hank Bauer, who won headlines as a Yankee star, said, after watching Rosen perform in the majors, "The change in Rosen's fielding is amazing. I roomed with him at Kansas City and even Flip will admit he was a poor fielder in those days. Now the guy is polished. If you had seen him before, you wouldn't believe it's the same person."

The manner in which Rosen became a polished fielder was typical of his approach to the game. In the spring of 1952, the Cleveland Indians held a pre-season camp for rookies at Daytona Beach. Only the eager youngsters were expected, not the stars of the team. Nevertheless, one morning Rosen appeared as Hank Greenberg and Al Lopez were at the batting cage.

"You don't have to be there," Greenberg told Rosen.

"I know I don't," Rosen replied, "But I can use this time to work on what's bothering me."

"Go ahead," Greenberg said, "You might as well take your swings," thinking that, like all hitters, Rosen could hardly wait to get a bat in his hands. But Rosen was taking the long view. He had already improved with the bat. "That can wait," he replied. "There are some things I've got to do at third base first."

And Rosen, called "Flip" by his mates, practiced in the broiling sun with the Indian coaches and, in time, his work paid off. Between 1952 and 1953 he was the most improved man in the game — and that difference made him the best player in baseball in 1953. He lost the batting crown to Mickey Vernon by .001 of a percentage point, .336 to .337, but swept honors in homers, runs batted in and slugging (his percentage in this department was .613; Vernon's .518).

Even in the matter of batting, the story went beyond the statistics. Rosen refused to play ball on the High Holy Days. Had he done so, he might easily have made a few hits and, at season's end, attained a fatter average than Vernon. That, however, was only part of it. Going into the last day of the 1953 season, Rosen and Vernon were waging a close fight for the batting title. Rosen was aiming for the coveted triple championship: homers, runs batted in and batting. Two of the three already were his. He had only to beat out Vernon to make the sweep. But Rosen missed two ways: by a close play at first base and by the lack of sportsmanship of the teammates of Mickey Vernon.

This was how Arthur Daley of the *New York Times* described it (and it was told in substantially the same fashion by the correspondent for the *Sporting News*):

"It happened in Al's final time at bat. The prematurely gray-haired Clevelander dribbled a slow grounder to Gerry Priddy and scampered down the line toward first. He made a frantic lunge toward the bag. His foot fell inches short and he had to make a mincing half-step with his other foot to make it.

" 'You're out!' barked Umpire Hank Soar. The throw

from Priddy had beaten Rosen in the fraction it took him to switch steps.

"Down in Washington, meanwhile, Vernon was striving earnestly to hold fast to his lead. The Cleveland game finished ahead of the Washington game and Washington writers flashed word to the bench that Vernon was home free if he didn't get up to bat again.

" 'I was wondering if I should bench you, Mickey,' began Manager Bucky Harris. But he stopped and sighed. 'But I guess you wouldn't want to win the championship that way. Go ahead. And good luck.'

"That's when the Washington conspirators took over. Being good at arithmetic, they figured that Vernon would not get to bat if none of them reached base. Two were forgetful but they speedily made amends.

"Mickey Grasso, for instance, doubled in the eighth inning. So he promptly took so big a lead that the enemy pitcher couldn't resist. He picked Mickey off the bag. In the ninth, Kite Thomas, a pinch-hitter, singled, but compensated for it by trying to stretch a stretchless hit into a double. He was thrown out by a mile. Eddie Yost, possessed of the sharpest batting eye in the league, popped out by hitting a ball a foot over his head. Pete Runnels struck out and Vernon, who would have been the next hitter, never did get to bat."

That was Arthur Daley's account. The Associated Press, in another version, said that Rosen, in his race to the bag in his last time at bat, made it so close that "Most of the 9,579 fans thought Rosen was safe." Rosen himself declared, "I missed the bag. I had to take an extra step, and that did it. Soar called it right, and I'm glad he did. I don't want any gifts. Why, I wouldn't sleep at night all winter if I won the batting championship on a call I knew was wrong." Not only was this sportsmanship of the highest order; Rosen also played his heart out in that final game. In the first inning he singled, in the third, he doubled and in the seventh he bunted safely for a third hit, raising his average to .3355. If he had been safe on the final play (or Vernon would have come to bat and missed hitting safely), Al would have been the triple champ.

Still, his brilliant season did not go into the discard. The fans and the reporters knew that Rosen was top man of the game, and voted him just that.

Typical of the kind of ball Rosen played in 1953 were these games, chosen nearly at random. On August 21, 1953, in a double-header against the Browns, Al hit three home runs, driving in seven runs, helping his mates to two wins. His homer in the second game came with one man on base. The Indians won the game by a score of 3-2. On September 9, 1953, Rosen's fortieth home run of the year came in Boston against the Red Sox. It was a scoreless tie going into the top of the eighth inning, in a duel between Mike Garcia and Bill Henry. In that frame, Bill Glynn drew a base on balls. Rosen strode to the plate two batters later and lashed the game-winning homer off the left field light tower. In the final inning the Red Sox scored a run. Final tally: Indians the winners, 2-1. When Rosen hit homers forty-two and forty-three on September 25, 1953 against the Detroit Tigers, he broke a club record of forty-two originally set by Hal Trosky, and drove in four runs in the bargain, leading his mates to an overwhelming 12-3 victory.

That is why Al Rosen was the player of 1953.

As Milton Gross of the *New York Post* phrased it, in discussing the award Rosen won: "Against the background of provincialism usually shown in this voting, the landslide not only is unprecedented, but the most sincere sort of testimonial to the prematurely graying twenty-eight year old after only four full seasons of big league baseball."

The major league years, curiously enough, were the easy ones for Al Rosen. It was his fight up the ladder which was difficult for him. His sports career, like most others, had its ups and downs. His were rather complicated, however. Al was born on March 1, 1925, in Spartanburg, South Carolina. His mother and father were divorced when Al was a child and Al and his brother Jerry were brought up by the mother, who worked as a saleslady in a dress shop to support her family. While she worked, the boys' grandmother, Mrs. Gertrude Levine, originally from Poland, looked after them. Al's mother, unlike many Jewish mothers, encouraged her children to indulge in sports. When Al suffered from violent asthma attacks, his mother heeded the advice of the doctor that he be allowed to play outdoors as much and as long as possible.

His mother told Harry T. Paxton, who wrote an intriguing story about Al Rosen for the *Saturday Evening Post,* that "when he was little, I'd watch him playing with the other boys, gasping as if each breath would be his last. His grandmother was afraid he was going to drop dead on the spot. But he never would stop playing. He had those attacks from the time he was a year old until he was about sixteen, and finally cured himself."

The Rosen family had settled in Miami, Florida and Al was about fourteen when he was attached to a baseball school, which his grandmother permitted him to join. It was not a very happy experience, but Al's determination was already in evidence. He even earned some money playing semi-professional softball. When he was in Miami High School he became a pretty good player, winning a job at third base and being named to the all-city team.

That summer, the recreation director of the city of Miami asked Al if he would like to attend military school. Al was thrilled by the offer. He was accepted — with a full scholarship — at Florida Military Academy. At the school, Rosen was a four-sport man, excelling at football, basketball, boxing and baseball. He won the middleweight championship in the Florida high school tournament, but never gave professional boxing any serious thought. Baseball was his real love. At sixteen, he obtained a tryout with the Cleveland Indian Class A farm team at Wilkes-Barre. He did not show enough to stick with that team, but received an offer to play with Thomasville, a Class D Club in the North Carolina State League, at the munificent sum of seventy-five dollars a month. He was rather shocked at the small sum and decided to get some advanced schooling. He entered the University of Florida and later the University of Miami. In time, between baseball seasons, he continued to attend classes and managed to earn his degree.

With his characteristic aggressive determination, Rosen became an all-around college sports star. He played end on the football team, won the state intercollegiate boxing championship, and picked up his nickname "Flip" because of his talent in scoring with a basketball.

But in 1942, he thought once again of playing baseball. He connected himself with the Red Sox farm system, was eventually told he would never make a ball player, made contact again with Thomasville and there started his professional career. One day, however, that career nearly came to an abrupt finish. The manager said to him that he was planning to drop him. Rosen, amazed, asked why. The manager gave it to him straight. "I'll stick with anybody as long as he puts out, but you aren't putting out any more." Rosen begged for another chance, and got it. Years later he said, "Believe me, I know now that the real ball players are always hustlers. I've hustled ever since."

The war came and Rosen served in the U. S. Navy, emerging in 1946 as a full lieutenant. He returned to the Cleveland chain system, and moved around a great deal. He performed with Pittsfield, Mass., with Oklahoma City and with Kansas City. He hit with all these clubs, and with power. In 1947 he nearly tore open the Texas League when he starred with Oklahoma City. At one time, he hit seven doubles in a row and ended the year batting .349, being named the best player of the league. This won him a 1948 trial with the parent Indian club, but he did badly in the spring and was shipped to Kansas City. There he batted .327, hit twenty-five home runs and was voted the rookie of the year. In one game he got four hits in five times at bat. The last three were home runs. He drove in seven runs in that game. The very next night he hit two more home runs in his first two trips to the plate and a double later in the game, a hit which narrowly missed being another round-tripper. He drove in six runs, making it thirteen for two games. He naturally earned another Cleveland shot, but was unable to beat out the veteran Ken Keltner. He managed to get into twenty-odd games and hit practically nothing. This time, he was sent to the San Diego team in the Pacific Coast League. There, too, he blasted the ball well.

But when he came up to the Indians for his third attempt

in 1950, it appeared that this would be his last chance to make the big league grade. In spring training, Keltner showed that the years had caught up with him. But Lou Boudreau, the Indian manager, wanted to keep Keltner on the bag, hoping his aged legs would warm up in the sun. The Cleveland general manager, Hank Greenberg, argued Lou into giving Rosen a chance. He said that Al was ready. Perhaps Greenberg remembered how he was ready with the Tigers and Bucky Harris, then the Detroit manager, insisted on going along with the fancy-fielding Harry Davis at first base. In any case, Al was given his opportunity.

On opening day, before 65,744 Cleveland fans — a hard, tough bunch of baseball followers — Rosen came up in the eighth inning with a man on base and his club trailing, 6-4. He hit a home run to tie the score. He slipped soon thereafter, but then perked up again, hitting eight home runs in the first month of the season. Later, as the season progressed, Rosen gained confidence in himself and let his bat do his talking. By July 4 he had twenty-five home runs, an astonishing total for a rookie. In one stretch, he hit six home runs in eight games and then seven in another streak of nine games. But he was now a major cog in the Indian machine, and there was little doubt that his minor league record as a hitter was an authenic indication of his skills with the bat.

His thirty-seven home runs, and his 116 runs batted in made him the slugging king of the league, although he did not attain a mark of .300. In 1951, as in his first year, he drove in more than 100 runs, but his average slipped to .265 and his homers to twenty-four. In 1952 he was back in stride, batting .302, hitting twenty-eight home runs, and driving in 105 runs. He became known not only for his averages but his spirit.

Though a strong man, the big third baseman was no stranger to injury, and an accident ultimately shortened his brilliant career. One May day in 1954, with a baserunner screening his view of the ball, a hard line drive crashed into the fingers of his right hand. Unwilling to stay out of the lineup for long, he returned before the hand had fully recovered. Each time he hit an inside pitch, the contact further damaged the index finger. The injury never did heal, and today Rosen retains only half the use of that finger. But the fierce competitive nature of the man was such that in the 1954 All-Star game, with his right index finger stiff and useless, Rosen smashed consecutive home runs, and drove home five runs to lead his team to an 11-9 victory.

Al continued to perform well, with blazing spirit and with a hot bat. But during the 1956 season he slowed up considerably because of his physical pains. As the season was ending, Hank Greenberg stated that "I think he would be better off playing with another team." Rosen's reaction to the statement was, "I'm just a ball player. If those are his feelings then they're his feelings. He has a right to his own opinion."

This was a cruel twist to an unusual story. Al Rosen had been an enormous star for the Indians, appreciated by his foes on the field more than by anyone else. In 1956, however, the fans of Cleveland — famous for their violence generally — got "on" Al, and once they reacted in a disgraceful manner. Rosen had made a try for a difficult infield grounder, stumbled and hurt himself. As he lay on the ground, in agony, the fans cheered his misfortune.

Shocked, Al Lopez, the team manager, blew up and said that the Indian fans did not deserve to have a big league team. This act of theirs was the beginning of the campaign against Rosen in Cleveland.

Rosen chose his own way out. He quit baseball and said, "I've seen other players get to the end of the line with nothing in mind for the future. I didn't want that to happen to me." And it didn't, as he joined the investment house of Bache & Co., where he became a successful securities executive, and later a top executive with the New York Yankees and then the Houston Astros.

Rosen always was a fierce competitor, and friends of his continually stressed his willingness to take on foes of all sorts. Tim Cohane, writing in *Look* magazine, once said, "An opponent, now friendly with Rosen, slurred Al's religion — Al's a Jew. Rosen dropped his bat, stalked to the enemy dugout, invited the fellow under the stands — and everybody else who wanted to come along. Trouble was averted when a couple of the fellow's teammates, just as incensed as Rosen at the off-base crack, advised the offender to stow that stuff."

In 1951, the popular New York columnist and television star Ed Sullivan wrote that "Al Rosen, Cleveland third baseman, is a native of Miami, Fla. Of Jewish parentage, he is Catholic. At the plate, you'll notice he makes the sign of the cross with his bat."

Rosen entered a bitter denial of that story. He said that ever since he had been a kid he made an "x" mark on the plate before stepping up to bat, a superstitious gesture not uncommon to many players. He asked for a retraction of the Sullivan statement and insisted that he was a proud Jew. He told this writer that "I have belonged to a synagogue for most of my life." When Rosen was the recipient of a Bible from a Philadelphia congregation, he accepted it with humility and with pride and said as much in a telegram to the members of the congregation.

In an expressive interview with writer Roger Kahn in Kahn's excellent book *How the Weather Was,* Rosen explained that he first took boxing lessons in the gyms of his youth so that he would be able to defend himself against the anti-Semitic remarks that so often came to the athletic "Jewboy."

"I wanted to learn how to end things," he remarked tersely. "That was important. I wasn't starting trouble in those days, but when it came to me, I wanted to end it, and damn quick."

Once, when he went out for football at a Miami high school, the coach was curious as to why he had come out for the violent sport. When Rosen replied that he loved to play the game, the coach told him, "Rosen, you're different from most Jews. Most Jewboys are afraid of contact."

All of his career, Rosen fought against that image of the timid Jew. He observed to Kahn that when he was struggling to work his way up through the minor leagues, he sometimes wished his name was one less Jewish than Rosen. But once established as a star, he wished his name were more Jewish, "perhaps Rosenthal or Rosenstein," Kahn writes. "He wanted to make sure that there was no mistake about what he was."

Kahn then reflects that "One suspects that even now, as parent, businessman and tennis player, he would react to an anti-Semitic remark by shedding the tweed jacket, along with the broker's manner, and punching hard, to end it fast, the way he used to in Miami, Florida, so that whoever started this, and whoever was observing, would remember, next time they were inclined to pick on a Jew."

The career of Al Rosen, like that of Hank Greenberg, was created by hard work, for few things came to him without difficulty. Like Greenberg, Rosen overcame his flaws and developed into one of the finest stars of the game.

Moreover, his awareness of the name he bears and the faith he carries has made him a proudly self-aware American Jewish athlete. "When I was up there in the majors," the big slugger told Kahn, "I always knew how I wanted it to be about me.

"I wanted it to be, Here comes one Jewish kid that every Jew in the world can be proud of."

In the summer of 1980, Rosen was inducted into the Jewish Sports Hall of Fame in Beverly Hills, and told the audience what already had become typical of his thinking, "At no time have I been so deeply moved as I have been this evening to be recognized a Jew by Jews."

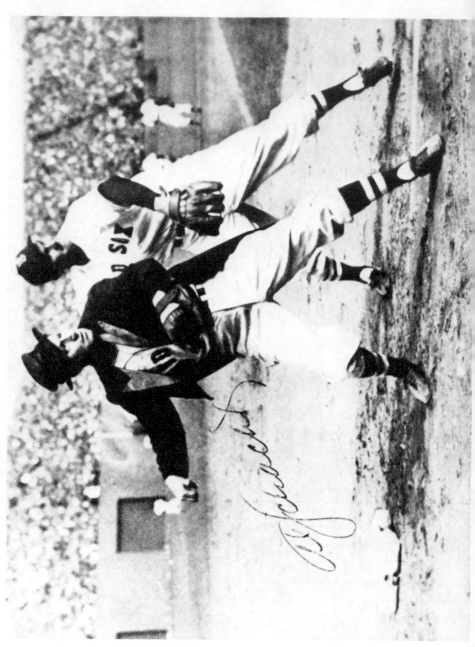

COMIC AL SCHACHT IN "WORKING CLOTHES," WITH PINKY HIGGINS

Al Schacht

Clown Prince of Baseball

Baseball fans are called "fanatics" for a very good reason. When they go to a ball game they like to see nothing but baseball. To the dyed-in-the-wool baseball fan beauty contests, potato races and other such trivia are out of place on the diamond. They come to see the squeeze play, the long triple, the thrilling slide into home plate, the home run, the curve ball and the blazing fast ball.

But there is one exception concerning showmanship on the diamond. There was one man who stepped out on the field who did not play ball, who did not pitch, hit homers or make spectacular fielding plays at shortstop. All he did was to come out there before thousands of baseball-hungry fans and proceed to act funny. He was a baseball clown, an artist in pantomime, a tremendous drawing attraction and one of the most popular men in all baseball. He was Al Schacht, the "Clown Prince of Baseball."

Al was known wherever baseball is played. He was its chief comic. His antics made the crowds howl with glee. He was the only man to hold up a game at a ball park and make the fans like it and yell for more. He played all over the majors; he hit the smallest bush leagues in America. His humor was sure-fire, for Al Schacht humored the fans about their favorite sport: baseball.

I* have sat in jampacked stadiums and watched Al go through his routine before as many as 65,000 fans. Yes, they came to see the great stars, but they seemed to have plenty of time to wait for them when Al walked out. He would come out in a uniform with a baseball cap worn askew on his head. His first act would be to emulate a pitcher who has just thrown a home run ball to the batter at the plate. Al would wind up carefully and the spectators would chuckle with glee, because more often than not Al would imitate one of the pitchers of that afternoon. After a hilarious windup, he would make believe he threw a ball. And then, pathetically, but wordlessly, he would turn around and watch the spheroid leave the park. Before the crowd was through laughing at that one, Al would offer another trick. He had nearly one hundred different pantomime burlesques. And the fact that he made more money travelling all over the country amusing fans than he ever made as a ball player proves that he had something the fans wanted. He was good enough to keep thousands laughing; he was good enough to make them forget for a long time that they originally came out to watch a ball game. For more than thirty years Al was baseball's No. 1 clown and he was loved wherever the game is known and played.

Al said that his religion was Jewish, that his politics were impartial and that his first love was baseball. This about sized him up because if you asked him where he was born he said, "In the Yankee Stadium." And this is one time when he was not kidding. For Al was born in the Bronx, in 1894, just about where the Yankee Stadium now stands. Al

*H.U.R.

was born with a love for baseball. As a kid he used to
haunt the Polo Grounds and follow his heroes about with
wide-eyed admiration. He was a poor kid, but his mother
used to give him fifty cents for piano lessons every week.
And Al tried to make some more money by running errands for the Giant ball players. This was no chore to him;
it was next to living in paradise. Jokingly, he recalled that
he used to be the "special sandwich bearer to Christy
Mathewson," one of the greatest pitchers in the game.

Al, however, didn't only carry sandwiches for the
athletes. He played ball himself. He was a winning pitcher
with the Commerce High School team in the Bronx and he
also played ball in the Catskills, with a team which toured
the famous "Borscht circuit." When the high school
authorities heard about his ball playing, they expelled him
from school, but Al bounced back and signed up to pitch
for a semi-professional team in New York. He immediately
proved himself to be a brilliant pitcher and the Cincinnati
Reds asked him to report to their camp, so that they could
take a look at him.

At this time Al Schacht weighed 130 pounds. He was
wiry and thin. Apparently, he did not weigh enough for
the major leaguers. After pitching in batting practice he
was told to go home and gain some poundage. But Al continued to support himself by playing ball for a couple of independent teams. And then he used his head. He met John
McGraw, the famous Giant manager, and persuaded
McGraw to let him work as a batting-practice pitcher with
the Giants. Al was so eager that he offered to work for the
Giants for nothing. It was during this period that he picked
up pitching wiles from Christy Mathewson and, armed
with this lore, he signed his first professional contract the

next season, which was 1912, with the Cleveland club in the new Federal League. Al said that he "set some kind of a record" in his first game, when he was called upon to pitch with the bases loaded. He struck out the next eight batters on twenty-five pitched balls, which means that he fanned them all, except with the slip of one pitch, on three straight strikes. When the game was over Al had struck out eleven of the fifteen batters he faced. But a week later the new league was dissolved. The ambitious youngster was never out of a job because he could always earn a living playing for independent clubs; and that's what he did.

After bumming around with a variety of teams, the Army grabbed him when World War I broke out. Al didn't do much to help win that war, for he spent his entire military career at Fort Slocum in New York, where he played baseball. In 1919, discharged from the service, he hooked up with a minor league team, pitched well, wrote letters to Clark Griffith, manager of the Washington Senators, saying how good a fellow named Al Schacht was. The letters helped. Griffith was convinced and signed him up.

For the next fifteen years Al Schacht was a major leaguer, with a few trips to the minors in between. His playing career was ended in 1924, when a knee injury benched him. But he remained with the Senators as a coach. It was said of Al that he was one of the best coaches in the game.

So what have we? A baseball clown who was a fair pitcher and a good coach. Is this enough to make him an outstanding character in baseball? Hardly. What really happened was that Al Schacht had teamed up with Nick Altrock, another Washington coach and a real funny fellow. They started to entertain fans before game time. The fans were hugely pleased. By 1921 Altrock and Schacht were good enough and well enough known to fans to amuse them before World Series games. The boys also made a thousand dollars out of this little job. Al played before nearly every World Series after that. Suddenly he found himself in great demand both in minor league ball parks, in the majors and on the vaudeville stage. Realizing that there were over thirty minor leagues, 7,000 independent clubs throughout the land and two major leagues, Al gave up coaching in 1937 and after that spent his time amusing the fans in baseball parks.

He helped break attendance records all over the country. He brought laughter to all fans. His acts of scooping up grounders, throwing wildly to bases, imitating silly players and making boners on the field, drew the laughter of all the fans. Al was tireless and limber. Lean and agile, he literally turned over backwards to give the fans a laugh.

But there was a serious side to Al Schacht. He related part of the story in his books, called *Clowning Through Baseball* and *GI Had Fun,* which tells of his career and of his experiences entertaining troops during the war. Al was a tremendous morale factor with the USO. He flew to Africa, Sicily, New Guinea, the Dutch East Indies and the Southwest Pacific, playing for the GI's. In a period of two months, he played 159 stage shows, seventy-two hospitals and 230 wards, spread over 40,000 miles. Then he went to Japan and the Philippines and performed 124 more times. He was in the front lines and under bombing. He played his heart out and as a result won more affection than most entertainers had ever known. Of his second book, *GI Had Fun,* Joe Williams, famous sports columnist, said: "He almost manages to achieve the Ernie Pyle touch." And in January 1946 the New York chapter of the Baseball Writers of America voted Al the twentieth annual Bill Slocum Memorial Award for high contribution to baseball over a long period, "with stress on his work during the war."

Al did not stop with these activities, however. He opened a successful restaurant in New York, which was modelled after a baseball park, and he acted on the stage. It is odd that a man like Al Schacht should have come from the sports world. He was the sort of character who fits well on Broadway. He had that Jewish kind of humor which is most effective when the comic scoffs at himself and makes fun of his own failings. A shrewd showman, Al must have been a wonderful psychologist to be able to hold entranced thousands of people at one time, without uttering a single word. He surely must have understood more than baseball; he knew the human heart, what makes it tick, why it laughs when it does and what brings tears to its possessor. Al Schacht stood alone in the sports world and in the entertainment world. He blended the two of them. From a Bronx home, this Jewish boy tried hard to reach the top of the baseball peaks. Failing that, he managed to win for himself a reputation as the finest entertainer in the game. Nothing held him down. And then, years later, he was loved and recognized by millions of fans. How many baseball stars have attained as much as he?

Al Schacht, the "Clown Prince of Baseball," was one of America's top humorists because in performing for millions upon millions of baseball fans and as many GI's all over the world, he offered a clean, fine brand of humor.

And to the stage he brought the baseball gags which have amused millions for decades.

Perhaps the finest thing that can be said of Al Schacht was that everyone who saw him loved to watch him. This made him one of the top personalities in the world of sports.

MOE BERG, BACKSTOPPING

Moe Berg

Diamond Scholar

One of the most fundamental attractions of sports are the personalities that get involved in the various games. In a very basic way, the endeavor of professional sport reduces all men to competing on terms of natural equality. A white second baseman from the Deep South can turn the double play with a black shortstop, and both men gain an understanding and a mutual respect new to both of them. A shy country hick like Mickey Mantle can become fast friends with a slick city sharpie like Whitey Ford, though the two might have never met were their talents not joined on the Yankee team.

Avid sports fans obtain rich enjoyment from the differentness of their athletic heroes. Devotees of the great New York Knickerbocker basketball team of 1969-73 delighted in the fact that the stars were so different in temperament and background: the muscular stockbroker DeBusschere, the stylish black clotheshorse Frazier, the studious Rhodes Scholar Bradley, the Louisiana country boy Reed. Yet all these men, once on the court, blended into a single, smoothly functioning unit of precision and intelligence.

The history of sports includes a great number of striking figures and unusual personalities, several notable for standing out in their chosen world. Gene Tunney was an intellectual who quoted Shakespeare in a sport, boxing, which was filled with tough, semi-literate brawlers, many with criminal records, who would probably assume that Lord Byron was the name of a contending fighter. (When asked what he thought of Shakespeare, Two-Ton Tony Galento replied, "I'll murder the bum.") Bill Bradley, the Princetonian banker's son from the Midwest, was a source of curiosity to his fellow basketball players, most of whom were products of the urban black slums.

In virtually every sport, there have been several out-standing personalities, men who seemed unlikely can-didates as professional athletes. But no man in the history of any sport was as unusual a phenomenon as Moe Berg, a major league catcher in the years before and after the se-cond world war. In a sport where men with any kind of ad-vanced education were relatively rare, Berg was an intellec-tual giant by any standards. His education included degrees from Princeton, Columbia and the Sorbonne. He was a successful lawyer and businessman. As a radio per-sonality, he became famous for his ability to answer ob-scure questions on any subject. A master of some dozen languages, including Latin and Sanskrit, he was a brilliant linguist of international renown who made phonetic and scholarly contributions to Japanese and other languages. And in recent years, the fact has emerged that before and after the war, he was America's top atomic spy, playing a major role in the counterintelligence that helped the allies win the war.

Born in New York at the turn of the century to Russian immigrant parents, Moe startled his family by being in-terested in baseball from the very beginning. "Moe was simply a genetic deviant," says his brother Sam, himself a doctor. "The Berg family tree shows it produced about twenty-five doctors in North and South America during the first half of this century, but Moe didn't like the sight of blood. Ever since he was two years old it was 'Hey, Sam, let's catch.' It could be a ball, an orange, anything."

After graduating from Barrington High School of Newark at the top of his class (his family had moved to Newark, where his father was a pharmacist), Moe was accepted at Princeton University, an extraordinary achievement at that time for a poor Jewish boy. He rapidly became a famous figure on that campus: both as a marvelous linguistic scholar who spoke numerous languages fluently, and as the star shortstop for the baseball team. The Princeton nine was so good that in Moe's junior year, they played an exhibition game at the Polo Grounds against the world champion New York Giants, and the Giants were lucky to win, 3-2, coming from behind in the last of the ninth.

In his senior year, Moe hit .337 and led the team to a record eighteen straight wins. The *Princeton Alumni Weekly* characterizes his play this way: "He was slow and lacked hitting power but had a slingshot arm and an ability to hit in the clutch."

A Princeton classmate named Crossan Cooper, who played second base on the team, also studied Latin in Moe's class. The two often bewildered their opponents by communicating with each other on the ballfield in that ancient tongue. "Moe and I would shout 'your turn' or 'my turn' in Latin so that the other side would not know which of us was going to cover second base on a given play. Of course, we assumed the first base coach for the other side didn't understand Latin," Cooper recalls to Kaufman,

Fitzgerald and Sewell, the co-authors of *Moe Berg: Athlete, Scholar, Spy,* a study of Moe's life.

Moe graduated *magna cum laude,* and received votes in his class poll for the "Most Brilliant" member of the class. Although Princeton offered him a teaching post in the Romance Languages, Moe wanted to go to Paris to study experimental phonetics at the Sorbonne, but he did not have the necessary funds. Baseball also beckoned: he was offered a contract by the Brooklyn Dodgers. Uncertain what to do, he sought advice from his Princeton coach, Bill Clarke, who pointed out to him that the money he got for playing ball would pay for his courses at the Sorbonne when he took them in the off-season. Still unsure that he could last long in the major leagues, Berg spoke to Dutch Carter, a successful lawyer who had been a legendary hurler at Yale.

"Take the baseball career," advised Dutch, according to Arthur Daley's account in the *New York Times.* "The rest can wait. When I was your age I had a chance to pitch in the National League. But my family looked down on professional sports and vehemently opposed my accepting. I've always been sorry I listened to them, because it made me a frustrated man. Don't you become frustrated. At least give it a try."

So Moe decided to give baseball a whirl, and joined the Dodgers immediately. In his first major league at-bat, he singled to drive in a run against Philadelphia. He played with Brooklyn for the rest of the season, fielding beautifully at shortstop but hitting rarely. Actually, Moe's shortcomings at bat were responsible for one of the classic remarks in baseball history. A scout named Mike Gonzales, told to wire a report on the young infielder, had sent the deathless four-word message: "Good field, no hit." It was a reputation that Moe carried with him for the rest of his career.

In the off-season he went to Paris; when he returned he spent the next two seasons in the minors, having a great year in the International League in 1926, when he hit .311 and drove in one hundred and twenty-four runs. He was called up to the Chicago White Sox, and arranged his schedule so that he could attend Columbia Law School when he wasn't playing ball. Despite his hectic schedule in pursuing both vocations as well as linguistics, Moe went on to place second at Columbia in a class of more than a thousand students.

For most of the 1927 season, Moe rode the bench with the White Sox, seeing limited action at short. But then came a day in August that was to alter his entire career. In a series against Philadelphia, the first and second string Chicago catchers had been injured in successive games. Now, playing in Boston, the White Sox faced disaster when their last backstop, Harry McCurdy, was hurt in the fifth inning. Player-manager Ray Schalk, himself one of the injured catchers, roared on the bench in confusion and disbelief, and ordered his road secretary to "get us a catcher, quick!"

Berg turned calmly to his distraught skipper and said, "What do you mean, get a catcher, we have a catcher on this bench."

Schalk whirled on the youngster. "Okay," he snarled, "get in and catch, wise guy."

"The funny thing is," Berg mused later in recalling the incident, "that when I said we had a catcher, I didn't mean myself. Earl Sheely, a first baseman, was a pretty good backstop and I had him in mind."

But as it was, Moe, eager for a chance to play, hustled out to the field and donned "the tools of ignorance," as catcher's equipment is sardonically known. He did astonishingly well for the rest of the game, although his first throw to second base got wedged between the bag and the ground. When he returned to the dugout, his mates needled him, explaining that the ball is meant to be thrown above the base. "Now you tell me," Moe deadpanned.

Chicago's next game was in New York against the mighty Yankees, and White Sox ace Ted Lyons asked for Berg behind the plate. When Babe Ruth, who became a good friend of Moe's, came to bat for the first time, he glanced down at the neophyte catcher and assured him that he'd be the fourth wounded White Sox catcher by the fifth inning. "That's all right," Moe responded, "I'll only call for inside pitches, and we'll keep each other company at the hospital." They both laughed, and Moe proceeded to catch an excellent game. He had found his natural position, and he never again returned to the infield, becoming one of the best defensive catchers in baseball.

"I'm elated over becoming a catcher," Berg confessed. "Being allowed to catch is the best break I've ever had. I'm not fast on my feet and my arm has saved me lots of times as an infielder. I've never been able to stay in the lineup long enough to develop as a hitter."

Casey Stengel offers this evaluation: "Now, I'll tell ya. I mean Moe Berg was as smart a ballplayer as ever come along. Knew his legs wouldn't cooperate in the infield and when the catching job opened up he grabs a mask and there he was. Guy never caught in his life and then goes behind the plate like Mickey Cochrane. Now that's something."

Ted Lyons, Moe's lifelong friend, accounts for some of Moe's success in his new position: "He had good reactions and a strong arm and great hands. His signal calling was flawless and in the years he was to catch me I never waved off a sign; few pitchers did. He became clinical in studying batters, knew their weaknesses and strengths. He took full advantage of this and pitchers simply felt confident with Moe doing the catching. And his shortstop experience showed behind the plate. No catcher could pick up short hops like Moe could."

While he became a shrewd and accomplished backstop, Moe still struggled at the plate. One day, after Berg trudged back to the dugout after another strikeout, a teammate and fellow catcher Buck Crouse drawled, "Moe, I don't care how many of them college degrees you got, they ain't learned you to hit that curve ball no better than the rest of us."

Still, Moe hung in and worked hard at improving. In the 1929 season, he reached the peak of his career. He led all catchers defensively, making only seven errors all season. His improved hitting earned him a thoroughly respectable .287 batting average. He even received votes for Most Valuable Player and was considered to be the best at his position except for the great Bill Dickey himself.

But in spring training the next season, a serious injury crippled all the bright promise of his career. Hustling into a base, Moe's spikes caught and the ligaments in his right knee were ruptured badly. He realized that he would never again be able to approach the standards he had set in 1929. But with intelligence and application, he continued to be one of the truly valued catchers in the league. Over the next years, he was traded to Cleveland, then went to Washington and Boston; and he was welcome wherever he went. He always played the game with enthusiasm, no matter how rarely he was put in. He became a legend in the bullpens around the league: he would not only help develop young pitchers and catchers, but keep them spellbound with tales of travel, history and women from all over the world.

He contributed on the ballfield in every way he could. As a part-time catcher, he went four seasons (1930-33) without making an error. When he joined Washington in 1932, manager Joe Cronin put him into seventy-five games, and Moe came through with several clutch hits as well as a steadying influence on the young pitchers. One of the key hits he had, which won an extra-innings game against the White Sox, was against his old buddy, Ted Lyons. Ted chased Moe into the Washington locker rooms. "He was doubled up with laughter," Lyons remembers fondly. "I gave him a couple of friendly punches. I said, 'Why'd you have to pick on me? You haven't had a hit in twenty years.' I told him he would have to pay for dinner that night."

In 1933, Berg realized the dream of every ballplayer when he played on a pennant-winning team. The Senators upset the powerful Yankees and won the championship of the American League, though they lost the series to the Giants.

Moe's fame as a person and as a ballplayer already extended well past the shores of his native America. In 1932, he went on a tour of baseball-mad Japan with Lyons and slugger Lefty O'Doul. They gave baseball clinics to enthusiastic Japanese players, while Moe astonished the delighted Japanese with his knowledge of their language. Though he declined an invitation to lecture at the University of Osaka, he did teach a Japanese waitress to tell O'Doul, in English, "You're a lousy hitter and lucky to be a major leaguer."

During his long major league career, Moe Berg anecdotes abounded through the sport. Reporters loved him because he was always "good copy" for their stories; and his unlettered colleagues on the field were equally fond of the Princeton scholar. Berg himself appreciated being treated as an equal, and never looked down upon his uneducated companions. "In baseball," he said, "a player stands on his own feet, and the fact that he can talk in five or six languages avails him nothing when he is up there at the plate with the bases filled and two out."

Stengel, in his inimitable style, put it this way: "It was amazing how he got all that knowledge and used all them penetrating words, but he never put on too strong. They thought he was like me, you know, a bit eccentric. He was very well liked."

Always fascinated by the origins of names, Moe would sometimes tell a teammate things the man didn't know about his own history. "Costello, you're an Irishman now but you weren't always Irish," Moe would say. "You were Spanish until Drake beat the Spanish Armada in 1588." With his phenomenal ear for dialects, Moe could identify a speaker's home town just by listening to him talk. Kaufman, Fitzgerald and Sewell describe incidents where stunned onlookers saw Berg correctly identify strangers as being from Marseilles, France and Coffeyville, Kansas.

One day, one of Moe's Washington teammates, an uneducated but power-hitting outfielder named Sheriff Harris, showed up in the hotel lobby looking pained. According to columnist Larry Merchant in the *New York Post,* when Moe asked what the trouble was and told Harris to stick out his tongue, "Harris did, of course, because for all anyone knew Berg had a degree in medicine too."

"You have a touch of intestinal fortitude," Berg diagnosed. "Go upstairs to your room, take it easy, don't eat anything heavy and you'll be fine." The next day, Harris appeared again in front of Berg; this time, the outfielder looked much healthier. "It worked," he reported to the amused Moe. "I got rid of that intestinal fortitude."

Another time, Al Schacht, the Washington third-base coach who was a friend of Moe's, took over the team while Cronin was absent. Al put Moe in to catch the first game of a double-header, although Berg had been doing very little playing for a while. Then, according to Schacht:

"We win 6-5 and he's beat, and I have to start him in the second game because of injuries. We have a big argument over it but he goes out and plays. By the fifth inning he can hardly get off his haunches, he's so tired. It's really hot. Then the pitcher and the batter, Whitehill and Cramer, have a staring contest — on the mound, out of the batter's box, in the batter's box, off the mound. Four or five times. It's killing Berg. Finally he takes off his mask and his chest protector, puts them on home plate, walks back to the dugout and says, 'That's it. I'm going in for a shower.'

" 'Here's your shower,' I say, and I throw a bucket of water on him. Then I tell him about injuries and he says, '*Now* you tell me.' He goes back and Whitehill is laughing so hard he throws a wild pitch on the first pitch. Berg just sits there and says to him, '*You* get it.' "

Later on, when Berg, Schacht and Cronin were all with

the Red Sox, Cronin one day called for a pitcher named
Jack Wilson to be summoned from the bullpen to bail out
his faltering starter. Schacht informed Cronin that Wilson
was unavailable. When Cronin inquired what his coach
was talking about, Schacht explained that Berg, spinning
another of his famous tales, had Wilson somewhere in
Russia at the moment, and the pitcher couldn't leave the
place without a passport.

In another well-documented incident, the team bus once
got lost on side roads after exhibition games in the Deep
South. Night had fallen, and the driver was lost, the players
helpless. Moe got outside, studied the stars in their constel-
lations for a moment, and then informed the driver that he
was heading in the wrong direction. When Moe told the
driver precisely which way to head, the startled driver
asked how he knew. "So say the stars," was the catcher's
reply. Moe and the stars, naturally, turned out to be ac-
curate.

Moe's legendary intellectual accomplishments, well-
known to the baseball world, received national attention
when, in February of 1938, he was persuaded to make a
guest appearance on "Information Please," a popular
radio show on which panelists answered questions on any
number of esoteric subjects. Moe amazed all of America
with the depth and breadth of his knowledge, and shattered the image of the universally dumb ballplayer. He was
a sensational success. Tens of thousands of calls poured
into the show's offices, as people asked who this extraordinary fellow could be. Moe was urged to make a second
appearance in April, which he did; he was, if anything,
even more of a hit.

In a final effort to stump baseball's resident genius, a

group of reporters got together and prepared a list of questions. Berg agreed to this one last round of queries, and was asked to identify the Seven Sleepers, the Seven Wise Masters, the Seven Wise Men, the Seven Wonders of the World and the Seven Stars. Moe fully and correctly identified all of them, and added that it was really impossible to know the true number of stars in the Seven Stars, as the Pleiades, or Pleiads in the constellation of Taurus were bunched too closely together for anyone to tell how many there were.

In a final effort, the reporters asked Moe to identify the Black Napoleon, the modern Hannibal, Poppea Sabina and Calamity Jane. He did, flawlessly.

Moe was now a national celebrity, with admirers from one end of the country to another. The *New York Times* even took out an advertisement in which they pointed out that one day in Detroit, when the paper had been late to arrive, Berg's newsboy had brought him the *Times* in the Red Sox dugout. The incident gave rise to more anecdotes and cartoons.

Even while constantly furthering his intellectual pursuits, Berg was always doing his best as a ballplayer in the game he loved. When he joined the Red Sox in 1935, he played as a part-time catcher and hit .286. "Moe lived up to every expectation," said Joe Cronin, the manager. Tom Yawkey, owner of the Red Sox, insisted that Moe "had a tremendous impact on our players," and called his acquisition one of the best moves the Red Sox ever made.

In the 1939 season, Moe showed the sharpness of his baseball judgment by insisting to reporters that Boston rookie Ted Williams, who seemed like a brash busher to many, was destined to be a great player. "They call him

screwy," said Moe. "Well, he isn't any screwier than a college sophomore, or any kid of 20. And he asks more sensi-
ble questions than most kids coming up. He's always eager
to learn something.

"A little while ago, for instance, he came over to me and
said, what will Ruffing throw with two strikes and no balls
on a left-handed batter? How does his fastball break?
Questions like that."

Moe was, of course, right, as Ted Williams became the
greatest hitter of his time. But according to sports writer
John Lardner, the veteran catcher and the cocky rookie did
not hit it off at first sight. Lardner wrote in the *Newark
News:*

"Moe Berg, the scholarly catcher, picked a conversation
with Williams one day.

" 'So you come from San Diego, eh, young man?' said
Mr. Berg, who, if he pooled his information with Einstein's, would have all but about 2 per cent of the information there is.

" 'So what?' said Mr. Williams suspiciously.

" 'San Diego,' mused Mr. Berg. 'County seat of San
Diego County, about 15 miles north of the Mexican
border. An excellent harbor. Largest naval and marine
base west of Chicago."

"Mr. Williams made a dive for Mr. Berg. The strong
arms of his teammates caught him in time and held him
back as he yelled, "Lemme at him! I'll tear him apart!"

" 'What's the trouble?' the boys asked Theodore.

" 'He can't knock my home town,' "snarled Mr. Williams, and continued to gnash his teeth.

Later on, Williams grew to admire and like Moe. He
referred to Berg's "special uniqueness" and "real man's

guts," and tells of the time Moe slammed one of his rare hits and, returning to the bench, told the slugging Williams, "That's the way you're supposed to hit them, Ted. I hope you were watching."

1939 turned out to be Moe's last year in the major leagues as a player. On the rare occasions that he would be summoned to catch, he would hustle in from the bullpen and don the catcher's gear to the delighted applause of his teammates in the dugout. Sometimes he would amble over to his teammates and ask in a confidential tone, "Gentlemen, does everyone still get three strikes out there?"

Moe ended the season with a .273 average, giving him a lifetime mark of .243. In the last game he ever played, against Detroit, Moe slammed a home run; it was only the sixth of his whole major league total. Still, despite his struggles at the plate, Moe's defensive ability, hustle, intelligence and popularity had enabled him to be a major league ballplayer for sixteen years, an exceptionally long career.

Among the admirers of the intellectual catcher was a Red Sox bat boy who was destined to become better known in future years as the President of the United States. According to Ethel Berg, Moe's sister, in her book *My Brother Morris Berg: The Real Moe,* John Kennedy "spoke with Moe every time the team was at home, Fenway Park. They both met often even through the years in the White House."

Kennedy was hardly Moe's first acquaintance in government circles; but it wasn't for many years later that the public knew the extent of his work for the government. In 1934, he had visited Japan for the second time, this time as part of a barnstorming team of major league all-stars that included the likes of Babe Ruth, Lou Gehrig, Lefty Gomez and Charlie Gehringer. But Moe Berg was the only man on the team who carried with him a letter of introduction from Secretary of State Cordell Hull; and unknown to anyone in Japan, including his teammates, Moe was engaged in undercover work for the U.S. government. One of the most popular members of the enormously idolized American band, Moe was a guest speaker at Meiji University, where his eloquent speech was delivered in Japanese; but on another day, while his mates were playing ball, Berg skipped the game and took carefully selected pictures of Tokyo from the top of one of the city's tallest buildings, a hospital where he was ostensibly visiting an American mother who had just given birth. Berg never met the woman he had supposedly come to see, but his photographs were later among the chief ones used by Gen. Jimmy Doolittle's pilots in their attack on the Japanese mainland in 1942.

After his retirement in 1939, Moe spent two years as a coach with the Red Sox; but by 1941, the war that he had foreseen so clearly had arrived, and he felt an obligation to help his country in any way he could. "All over the continent men and women are dying," he told Arthur Daley of the *Times*. "Soon we, too, will be involved. And what am I doing? Sitting in the bullpen telling stories to the relief pitchers."

Not for long, though. When the season was over, Moe accepted a request from Nelson Rockefeller, the Coordinator of Inter-American Affairs, that Berg become a Goodwill Ambassador to Latin America. The papers, as might be expected, played up the story with enthusiasm.

"Berg without a doubt is the most remarkable man baseball has ever known," Frank Graham wrote. Tom Meany asserted that "Berg is destined to do a great job for his country. When the final victory of the United Nations is achieved, I venture that Moe's contribution will outweigh that of any other athlete." The *Washington Post* said that Moe's "diplomatic mission is almost without parallel in the annals of diplomacy."

Before he left for Latin America, though, Moe first made an extraordinary broadcast to the Japanese people over the radio. In fluent Japanese, he pleaded at length, "as a friend of the Japanese people," for the Japanese to avoid a war "you cannot win." He invoked examples of historical American-Japanese friendship over the years. Berg's address was so effective that several Japanese confirmed afterwards that they had wept while listening. President Roosevelt called Moe the next day, thanking Moe for the speech on both his own behalf and that of the American people. Within a year of Moe's speech, Japanese officials banned baseball, referring to it as a decadent American sport.

Relations between the United States and her neighbors to the south had been strained for decades, and the strain had lately been increased by Nazi Germany's skillful propaganda campaign aimed at discrediting the U.S. Moe's official task was to improve the welfare of U.S. servicemen stationed in Latin America, and the relationships between them and their hosts. His unofficial function was to assemble secret, high-priority assessments of leading political figures, as well as simply to win friends by the sheer charm and magnetism of his considerable personality, and his unusual background (baseball is highly popular in sections of Latin America, and some of today's finest major leaguers come from south of the border).

Moe's report on his mission reflected the skill and concern with which he had invested his efforts; he was particularly concerned about the fact that American soldiers were not taking adequate advantage of the opportunities available to mingle with and understand the native populations. Rockefeller was highly pleased with the results of Moe's trip, and wrote to him that his work "has contributed greatly to the inter-American programs. Only someone with your experience and knowledge of international as well as human problems could have handled this situation with such tact and effectiveness."

Moe's subsequent work for the Office of Strategic Services was considerably more vital, and far more secret. He was one of the very finest American undercover agents. Michael Burke, himself an OSS agent and later president of the Yankees and of Madison Square Garden, says of Berg:

"Moe was absolutely ideal for undercover work. Not by design; just by nature. One, because of his physical attributes. He could go anyplace without fear. He had stamina. Also he had that gift for languages. In addition, he had an alert, quick mind that could adapt itself into any new or strange subject and make him comfortable quickly. He was immensely involved intellectually and active in international affairs through reading and travel. He had the capacity to be at home in Italy or France or London or Bucharest. He was on familiar ground in all those places. He also possessed a great capacity for being able to live alone, and could do this for long periods of time. The life of an agent sometimes is a lonely one and some people aren't suited for that."

Berg's first mission was to assess the political and military situation in embattled Yugoslavia. He slipped into the country, probably by parachute, and spoke to the forces under Tito and to the Serbian camp of Mihajlovic. Moe's report that the Yugoslav people supported Tito turned out to be prophetic.

After Moe's successful work in Yugoslavia, his commander, General William Donovan, decided to send him on the crucial and sensitive mission that would determine the degree to which Germany had perfected the atomic bomb. When Moe was named to undertake secret work in Italy, a Donovan aide, seeing Berg's name, asked the general, "Do you know who they gave us for this mission? A ballplayer named Moe Berg. You ever hear of him?"

"Yes," Donovan answered. "He's the slowest runner in the American League."

Moe performed a secret mission in Norway, providing the U.S. with information that Germany had a crucial plant there producing heavy water, a component of their planned bomb development. The plant was subsequently bombed and shut down for good. In Italy, Moe learned that another German atomic center was based in Duisburg; that, too, was then devastated with bombing raids that hampered Germany's progress on the bomb. Berg located several important Italian scientists and engineers, and helped arrange eventual passage to the U.S. His work in Italy was so important that the University of Rome awarded him an honorary Doctor of Laws degree in September, 1944.

Another of Moe's vital assignments was to determine the

extent to which Germany was planning and developing radiological warfare. His investigations led to scientists in Switzerland and France, and his reports were important aids in Allied assessments. With his extraordinary mind and concentration, Moe was rapidly able to become an expert on the fine technical aspects of atomic energy and radioactive repercussions; expert enough to discuss them on even terms with the world's top specialists in those fields.

Moe's most sensitive, and probably most dangerous, mission involved locating and somehow making contact with Germany's top atomic scientist, Professor Werner Heisenberg. Only Heisenberg would know whether Germany was virtually ready to produce an atomic bomb, or was still lagging in its research. According to the account of the mission in *Moe Berg: Athlete, Scholar, Spy,* Berg was even prepared, if necessary, to "eliminate" Heisenberg, "if it meant world survival." With an elaborate scheme, Berg lured the German scientist to Switzerland to give a lecture on quantum theory; Moe carefully evaluated the lecture, and then managed to attend the dinner party afterwards. With his polished German, no one knew Moe was an American agent.

One of the remarks Berg overheard was Heisenberg saying that he did not believe that Germany would win the war. Such a comment from a man in his position was strong evidence that the German effort was not an immediate threat. British Prime Minister Winston Churchill, President Roosevelt and the scientists working on America's Manhattan project (to develop a U.S. bomb) were all briefed on Berg's invaluable report. Roosevelt got the report from a General and responded, "Fine, just fine.

Let us pray Heisenberg is right. And, General, my regards to the catcher."

Moe continued to work on numerous secret missions, all vital and dangerous, for the duration of the war. Time and again, his mission was successfully accomplished. On one assignment in Germany itself to trace development of aeronautical work, Moe's trip, according to U.S. reports, "produced the collections of approximately eighty percent of the information of the German development work on high speed aeronautical designs and tests."

In 1945, as the war drew to a close, America had a new concern: they were anxious that the U.S., and not Russia, capture Germany's top scientists. The Americans knew that the Soviet Union was anxious to utilize the best German brains for their own purposes. Moe Berg's detailed reports on the secret whereabouts of the top German scientists enabled American investigators to find and capture them.

But while Berg was one of America's most valuable and effective secret agents, he always remained a ballplayer at heart. One day, while visiting a front-line hospital in Germany, he saw a couple of American soldiers standing on a grassy bank, wearing baseball gloves and tossing a ball back and forth. According to Russell Forgan, OSS commander in the European Theater, this is what happened:

"Moe went down and said, 'Look, do you fellows mind if I catch with you?' The guy with the catcher's mitt said, 'Sure. Take this.' He handed Moe the mitt. So Moe put it on and started throwing the ball with that short, quick flip, like that, you know. And this kid, the one who had given him the catcher's mitt, kept looking at the way Moe threw the ball. The kid kept looking and looking and looking and said, 'Hell, I know who you are. The last time I saw you was in Sportsman's Park. You're Moe Berg.' And Moe came back and, boy, he was the happiest guy. Imagine, the middle of Germany with a war going on and this guy recognized him. It pleased him tremendously."

In coming back to the United States after the war, Berg escorted Paul Scherrer, a top Swiss physicist. The two men went to visit Albert Einstein at Princeton. During their visit, Berg told the great genius that he had read Einstein's article on atomic war, which had been published in the *Atlantic Monthly*. Much to his pleased amazement, Einstein answered, "I read your baseball story, Mr. Berg, in the *Atlantic,* also. You teach me to catch and I'll teach you mathematics." Indeed, Moe's article on the nuances of the national pastime had described in literate and fascinating terms the struggle between the pitcher and the batter in baseball and the duties of the catcher on the diamond. It had been highly praised by literary, as well as sports, figures.

The war over, Moe resigned from the OSS. Colonel William Quinn of the Strategic Service Unit wrote a ten-page letter of recommendation suggesting that Berg be given the Medal of Merit, the highest honor given to civilians during wartime. Quinn cited Berg for his "many accomplishments . . . and for several times risking his life." The medal was awarded to Moe, but, apparently disinterested in formal honors for all his services, he politely declined.

In his later years, Moe continued his beloved scholarship, always delighted to make new discoveries in the world of linguistics, or indeed in any field. John Kieran, the *New York Times* columnist who was also a regular on "Information, Please" relates a telling incident in *This Week* magazine:

"As a Princeton alumnus he was naturally interested in the annual Princeton and Yale football disputes. Moe and I made a date to ride down to Princeton on a train from New York. Being well acquainted with his taste for literature I brought a book along. It was an old, thick, dog-eared Latin dictionary. During the train ride we pored over the quotations from Caesar, Cicero, Virgil and Horace. We traced words through their gradual change in spelling and meaning from the original Latin and French into English. We grubbed among the roots of the Romance languages. Just as the football special arrived at Princeton Junction, Moe looked up and said, 'John, imagine wasting time and money in a nightclub when you can have fun like this.' "

But however deep his love of the academic world, on the baseball diamond he only wanted to be known as a ballplayer. I* remember a game years ago at Yankee Stadium. The Yanks were hooked up with the Red Sox and I watched the game from the deep bleachers. Moe was working in the bullpen early in the afternoon, about an hour before game time. I yelled down at him and asked him what he thought of Bob Grove, who was scheduled to pitch that afternoon. He answered in a language that resembled Polish.

"You're in New York," I called. "Why not speak something we can understand?" He answered in Yiddish, and the spectators roared. I said a few words in Hebrew and he replied without hesitation, giving the crowd a real thrill. That same afternoon he caught the slants of Lefty

*H.U.R.

Grove, one of the greatest pitchers in the game's history, and got two hits himself. Trapping him on the way to the showers, I asked him about this game which was so much more physical than mental.

"I don't want to be known as a ballplayer who read a book," he told me. "And I don't want to be known as a lawyer with a bat on my shoulder. I practice law in the winter and play ball in the summer and I am careful to keep the two apart in my life. And I love baseball."

And baseball certainly repaid the compliment. Berg was one of the most popular players to play the game, and in his entire sixteen-year career was never once thrown out of a ballgame. Always extremely elusive to find in his private life, he could always be found in the ballpark at World Series time, buying his way in to the fall classic like any other citizen. However highly educated he may have been, he was always deeply delighted and privileged to be a major league baseball player.

Dr. W. Hardy Hendren is a doctor who met Moe at a World Series game in Boston in 1967. Hendren didn't know who the dignified stranger was, but quickly realized that this was no ordinary former ballplayer. Berg seemingly knew about every subject that came up, not least what pitch was going to be thrown next. Hendren, fascinated, invited the elderly stranger to join him for dinner. The doctor remarks:

"When he entered my house, he immediately began translating the Latin on a brass rubbing on the wall.

"That evening, we had several guests, doctors, who were in Boston to work with me. As we were sitting in the dining room I said to Moe I was amazed to see him predict what sort of pitch was coming next. He said it was easy for a professional ballplayer to do that.

"Then he mentioned that it was easy for professionals to make mistakes, too. He said, 'Occasionally surgeons make mistakes. For example, when a surgeon is operating for appendicitis and discovers it was Meckels diverticulum.' Well, the doctors dropped their forks. They could not believe their ears."

On May 30, 1972, at the age of seventy, Moe Berg died after suffering injuries in a fall at his Newark home. Before he died, he turned to a nurse and spoke his last words.

"How did the Mets do today?" he asked.

Many people who knew him are convinced that Moe Berg's intellect was of genius caliber; that this extraordinary man could have accomplished anything he wanted in life. Some feel he wasted these tremendous gifts; others admire his determination to enjoy his life to the utmost. John Kieran believes that had he applied himself to law, Moe could have gone all the way to the Supreme Court, and "could have been a Brandeis." Berg's brother never did understand why Moe wasted his time in baseball, remarking that "all it ever did was make him happy."

Friend and batterymate Ted Lyons says that "a lot of people tried to tell him what to do with his life and brain and he retreated from this . . . He was different because he was different. He made up for all the bores of the world. And he did it softly, stepping on no one."

Moe Berg remains in memory as one of the most remarkable men who ever lived, and certainly the most fascinating personality in the history of American sports. That's quite a legacy for a Jewish kid from Newark who had trouble hitting the curve ball.

LARRY SHERRY, LOOKING OVER THE OPPOSITION

Larry Sherry

Hero for a Season

One of the Jewish sages, Judah HaNasi, is quoted in the Talmud as saying, "Some win eternity after years of toil, others in a moment."

So it was with Larry Sherry, a Jewish baseball player who had his moment of eternity in the exciting baseball year of 1959.

Few pitchers have performed as brilliantly as Sherry in any World Series as Larry did in 1959. He continued to play ball after that year, of course, but it was all anti-climactic. It was 1959 that placed Larry Sherry into the record books and made him one of the authentic stars of World Series history.

It was all started when Larry, in a relief assignment, beat the Chicago Cubs in an extra-inning game to keep alive the hopes of the Los Angeles Dodgers, who were tied in the standings with the Milwaukee Braves. It was the tenth inning when Sherry was called to the mound in a 4-4 game. Two men were on base and the next batter was Ernie Banks, who led the National League in home runs and runs batted in. He already had hit forty-five homers, the most recent in this very game. Now Sherry was facing him. Larry threw a slider on the outside corner to Banks. Ernie then fouled off the second pitch. The third delivery was a low slider, but not too low. It was a strikeout on three

173

straight pitches. In the next inning, Gil Hodges hit a home run and Sherry continued to retire the Cubs, fanning Dale Long on a 3-2 pitch. That was one big game, and Larry Sherry was the man called in to make these outs.

Sherry had become a significant player on this Dodger team. The pennant race was a hectic one and it ended with the Dodgers and the Braves tied for first place, with a play-off facing the two clubs, the best-two-out-of-three becoming the 1959 National League champions.

The young right-handed relief pitcher had done his share to get the Dodgers into the playoff. He completed the season with seven straight victories and in thirty-six innings of relief pitching had compiled an 0.74 earned run average. At this stage of his career, Sherry was twenty-four years of age and his baseball achievements had not been spectacular. His brother, Norm, a catcher with the Dodgers in 1959, told reporters that "My mother fell just before she gave birth to Larry, and he was born with two club feet. He had to undergo surgery for six weeks and after that he still had to wear special orthopedic shoes." Larry himself recalled it this way, "I remember all the trouble I had when I went out for my high school baseball team. I had to get special baseball shoes with a built-up arch." Larry attended Fairfax High School in the Jewish section of Los Angeles (Fairfax). He was small and thin and weighed about 130 pounds. He was not strong or good enough to make the first team, but he kept at it, playing second base when he was not pitching. He alternated positions with Barry Latman, another Jewish pitcher who performed in the big leagues, but never won Larry's headlines.

Sherry also played American Legion ball, and when he had grown and developed into a tall, 195-pounder, he was signed by Walter O'Malley of the Dodgers for a $2,500 bonus. And now Larry hit the minor league trails, pitching in Great Falls, in Newport News, in Spokane and other minor league towns. When Larry was recalled to the Dodgers from St. Paul in mid-1959, his record was not very impressive, only six victories against seven losses. For six years in succession, his minor league record was below the .500 mark, surely no indication that he was going to be anything special. But he caught fire almost immediately and become a factor of importance when talk got around to Dodger pitching strength in the World Series.

The reason one was able to talk about the Dodgers and the World Series in 1959 was that Sherry was the man largely responsible for getting them there. The first playoff game was played on September 28, 1959 at Milwaukee. The Dodgers scored in the first inning, but the Braves rallied and took a 2-1 lead before Sherry was called in to stop the activity. In the third inning the Dodgers tied the game and in the sixth catcher John Roseboro hit a home run to put his team ahead, 3-2. Sherry held onto that margin and did not allow a runner past first base during the last three innings. In all, he yielded four hits and struck out four batters in seven and two-thirds innings. The next day, the Dodgers won without Larry's aid, although it was a wild game and he was warming up in the bullpen throughout the contest.

Now the Dodgers, who had risen from seventh place to the championship in the National League in a single season, were to face the Chicago White Sox, who were heavily favored to beat the National League representatives. The Sox had broken a New York Yankee streak of four pennant victories in a row. They had a remarkable pitcher in Early Wynn and a dazzling keystone combination in Nelson Fox at second base and Luis Aparicio at shortstop. The Dodgers had struggled and stumbled to their pennant while the White Sox had rested, following the playoff games in the National League.

The first game of the Series was an overwhelming victory for Chicago, 11-0. And when the second game began, it appeared like another big day for the American Leaguers as the White Sox took a 2-0 lead in the first inning. But the Dodgers fought back when Charlie Neal homered in the fifth and again in the eighth, following a homer by Chuck Essegian. Now the score was 4-2, in favor of the Dodgers. Johnny Podres, the Los Angeles left-hander had given way to Essegian as a pinch-hitter and Sherry was called to action. In the eighth inning, he showed some brilliant pitching in a crisis.

Ted Kluszewski and Sherman Lollar singled and one run scored on a double by Al Smith. Lollar was out at the plate on a foolish running play, but Larry was still in trouble, for the Sox had the tying run in scoring position with only one man out.

Working carefully, Sherry struck out pinch-hitter Billy Goodman, a former American League batting king, and forced the dangerous Jim Rivera to pop out to the catcher. That ended the game's greatest threat. In the ninth inning, Sherry retired the side in order, getting Norm Cash, Luis Aparicio and Nellie Fox. Los Angeles had won its first 1959 Series game.

The third game was played at the Los Angeles Coliseum, before a record of 92,394 baseball fans. Dick Donovan of the Sox was outpitching Don Drysdale of Los Angeles, but the game was scoreless when the Dodgers scored two quick runs in the seventh on a hit, two walks and a grounder through the box. The Sox struck back in the eighth when Kluszewski and Lollar singled. By this time, Walter Alston, the Dodger manager, had got used to calling on Larry Sherry, so once again Sherry took over. He did not begin well. He hit Billy Goodman, filling the bases. But Sherry had the poise so necessary for a relief pitcher. He forced Al Smith to hit into a double play, one run scoring. That made it 2-1. Then Jim Rivera popped out and Sherry was nearly home safe. The Dodgers gave him an extra cushion with a run in their half of the eighth. He struck out Cash and Aparicio, gave up a single to Fox and then fanned Jim Landis for the third out — and another game for the Dodgers, this one an official victory for Sherry.

The next day, Roger Craig tried to beat the White Sox, but again Sherry was the winner. He shut out the Chicagoans over the last two innings assuring a 5-4 victory and now the Dodgers had won three games against one for the White Sox. It was not yet over, because the Sox shut out the Dodgers 1-0 in the fifth game.

The Series ended at Comiskey Park in Chicago, on October 8, 1959. Johnny Podres, the wily Dodger left-hander, carried an 8-0 lead into the fourth inning of the sixth game, and it seemed that it was all over except for toting up the World Series earnings. But Podres hit Jim Landis on the head and Landis fell quickly to the ground. The accident upset the southpaw who walked Lollar. Landis had recovered rapidly and had taken first base. Now there were two runners with the long-hitting Kluszewski at the plate. Ted connected with a powerful drive for a three-run homer and suddenly the game was no longer out of American League reach.

Sherry trotted out to the mound, for his fourth appearance in six games. He had won two and saved another. He had been almost an unknown, but within a week he was the most talked-about ball player in the country. He also had his fast ball and all the confidence he needed. He was tired, as he later admitted, but he pitched as though there were no tomorrow. For five and two-thirds innings, he simply threw his fastball, daring the batters to do something about it. The White Sox could not score and the game ended 9-3, with the Dodgers World Champions. Larry Sherry had given up only one run in twelve and two-thirds innings, and only eight hits.

"He's the guy who killed us. He was the guy we couldn't touch," Al Lopez, the White Sox manager, admitted.

Charlie Dressen, the White Sox coach and himself a manager of note, said of the last game and Sherry's reaction to the final challenge, "He snatched the ball from Alston's hand like he owned it. And why not? Baseball fans may never have heard of this kid before, but he's always had the moxie and skill of the greatest."

That was 1959, Sherry's year of immortality. Alston, recalling it, said, "I've never had a pitcher with so little experience who was thrown into so many tight situations as Sherry was. As a matter of fact, I can't think of a pitcher like him that anybody ever had."

But Sherry never again attained such heights. He insisted that he be given a chance as a starter in 1960 and had a fair-to-middlin' season, with fourteen wins and ten losses. In 1961, he had arm trouble and never again was as effective as he had been in that one incredible, almost impossible season when he was a superstar, an untouchable pitcher. Few obscure hurlers get into a World Series; fewer still

become the stars of the championship games which capture
the imagination not only of baseball fans but of sports followers everywhere.

Larry Sherry had his shining moment, his eternity.
Nothing he could accomplish on a baseball field would
ever equal his 1959 performance. Perhaps it was fate that
he should never have another such opportunity. Once is
enough.

SANDY KOUFAX, A GREAT PITCHER, RELAXES

Sandy Koufax

Hall of Fame Pitcher

In the long history of baseball there have been many great pitchers and so it is dangerous to call any one pitcher the most effective, brilliant, spectacular twirler in the annals of a game which has an army of statisticians. But an excellent case can be made for Sandy Koufax, the Jewish southpaw star of the Los Angeles Dodgers in the National League.

Let us begin with a night game between the Dodgers and the Chicago Cubs at Dodger Stadium, September 9, 1965. Koufax faced Bob Hendley, a tough opponent, and Sandy started off fast by striking out two of the first three batters in the opening inning. Byron Browne, a rookie playing in his initial major league game, solved one of Koufax' pitches and lined it hard to Willie Davis in center field for the final out in the second inning. This was the first time in the game that anyone had come close to hitting safely. But Sandy then "settled down" and his fast ball and curve had the Cub batters perplexed and puzzled. Throughout the proceeding innings, this game became one of the best-pitched any of the fans had ever seen. Bob Hendley kept pace with Koufax and it was a hitless, scoreless game up to the fifth inning. Lou Johnson, in the Dodger half of the fifth, drew a walk and was sacrificed to second by Ron Fairly. Johnson stole third and came home on a throwing error by rookie catcher Chris Krug and Koufax had a one-run lead over his brilliant foe.

It was a no-hit game for both pitchers going into the seventh inning and the 29,139 fans realized that they were in attendance at a remarkable game in baseball history: perhaps a double no-hitter. Who could tell, with a guy like Koufax being extended by a pitcher determined to match Sandy pitch for pitch?

In the seventh inning, Hendley yielded the first hit of the game, a double to Lou Johnson, but it proved to be harmless because it came with two out and Bob retired Fairly for the final putout of the inning. Koufax, meanwhile, had pitched like an absolute master. Going into the eighth inning, Koufax had struck out eight and only seven batters had managed to lift the ball to the out-field.

In that eighth inning, when the fans realized that Koufax had a no-hitter going, and a perfect game at that, the tension rose. The first batter was the dangerous Ron Santo, followed by Ernie Banks, the two toughest Cub batters. Sandy struck them both out and ended the inning with a flourish by fanning Browne.

In the ninth inning, Krug, unaccustomed to the big leagues and a pitcher like Koufax, followed the lead of his more illustrious teammates — and struck out. Joe Amalfitano, a pinch-hitter, was the next swinger, and he fanned on three straight pitches, swinging with futility at the last one. The score was 1-0 and Hendley had pitched a one-hitter. The Cubs were still in the game, or so they thought. Now they sent up another pinch-hitter, Harvey Kuenn, a former American League batting champion and a man who seldom struck out. Sandy had, at this moment, thirteen strikeouts for the game and five in succession. Kuenn proved to be no problem to Koufax, who struck him out, and recorded a perfect game, one of the extreme rarities of baseball. Hendley had been victimized by Koufax and this was the only game in professional baseball in which only one hit was given up by both sides combined.

This victory brought Koufax' record in 1965 at that phase of the season to twenty-two victories against seven defeats. It brought his strikeout mark to 332 and made him the only pitcher in the game to pitch *four no-hitters* in the major leagues.

It added another milestone to an incredible career, which included these highlights: struck out eighteen in two different games, to tie a major league strikeout record; pitched no-hitters in four successive years; struck out fifteen Yankees in the World Series and was a World Series star almost every time he was in the classic.

Even before his remarkable feats in the 1965 World Series, Koufax had gained the respect of his fellow players as the best pitcher they had faced. After his perfect game against the Cubs, Ron Santo said, "I've never seen Sandy throw as hard as he did when he struck me out in the eighth. He threw one fast ball right by me and I was waiting for it. He seemed to get a burst of energy in the late innings." Walt Alston, Sandy's manager, remarked that "I thought this was the best of all his no-hitters." Lefty Philips, a Dodger pitching coach, called Sandy "a better competitor than any pitcher in baseball. Most pitchers hate to be matched against a Juan Marichal, a Jim Maloney or a Bob Veale, but Sandy welcomes the challenge. And he pitches just as hard against the bottom clubs as he does against the pennant contenders." Ernie Banks chimed in with, "He was just great — it was beautiful," and Banks had struck out three times. "That guy will drive you to drink," another Cub said.

Koufax himself, tired after that history-making game, was calm about his feat. "I knew all along I was pitching a no-hitter, but it never crossed my mind that it might be a perfect game." As for Hendley, who was so good himself, he said sympathetically, "That's the best any guy has pitched against me in my career."

Leonard Koppett, writing in the *New York Times* a few days after the perfect game, wrote that "Koufax brings people into the park as no pitcher has since the heyday of Bob Feller." And he made this observation: "Thursday night's game was Koufax' thirty-fifth start this season, all advertised in advance. The attendance for those thirty-five games is 1,284,934. This represented more than ten per cent of the National League's total of 12,019,241 through Thursday's games — and the league total was on the threshold of a major league record. Another viewpoint on the same figures is more enlightening: in his appearances, Koufax has averaged 36,712 customers per game; for all other National League games, without Koufax, the average is 15, 247."

Obviously, baseball fans knew that in Sandy Koufax they were watching one of the immortals of the sport, a pitcher who was capable of throwing a no-hitter every time he went to the mound. It was no wonder that after eleven years as a major leaguer, Sandy Koufax had come to a point where baseball writers were speculating on whether there ever had been a better pitcher in baseball. He had won almost every award in the game that a pitcher could win. He had achieved miracles. He held strikeout records, earned run records and had won key victories for his team year after year, sometimes under physical handicaps. He had captured the imagination not only of the baseball world but of millions to whom baseball was of small importance. He had had books written about him, thousands of articles and hundreds of feature stories. He had his picture on the cover of the leading magazines in the United States and he had become one of the best-known names in the United States. Thus, he had also become one of the most famous Jews in America. If any athlete in this volume is "great," Sandy Koufax is that man.

There is no space in this volume to describe in full detail the entire career of Sandy Koufax, but a good place to start is not at the outset of that career but at the end of the 1965 season, for it was then that the sports historians had begun to analyze his accomplishments. There were two essays in particular that struck me,* in compiling a file on Sandy Koufax which I had begun just about when he came to the Dodgers. One is by Bill Libby in the 1966 edition of *True's Baseball Yearbook*, and the other is a feature by Dave Anderson in *Dell Sports* (March, 1966) entitled "Koufax: How He Compares With Six All-Time Greats." A summation of these two studies will offer some insight into the position that Koufax held after more than a decade of pitching in the major leagues.

Bill Libby asks, "How Great is Sandy Koufax?" and comes up with some conflicting answers. Libby quotes Atlanta manager Bobby Bragan as saying, "He is the greatest pitcher who ever lived," but Libby observes that Bragan was not yet born when some of the best pitchers had performed. Libby also quotes the retired baseball com-

*H.U.R.

missioner and former newspaperman Ford Frick: "The way he has pitched the last few years, his name belongs right up there with Cy Young as one of the great pitchers of all time."

But Libby then points out that at the end of 1965 Koufax had won only 138 games and had pitched only eleven years and had only two twenty-game seasons. Cy Young won 511 games and Walter Johnson 416. Warren Spahn, a contemporary of Koufax, had won 363, and, Libby remarked, of twenty-two pitchers in Baseball's Hall of Fame only one (Dizzy Dean) had won less than 190 games. Dean had won 150 and had his career cut because of injuries.

On the other hand, Libby writes, "Koufax is the only pitcher in history to ever pitch four no-hitters. Bob Feller and Cy Young had three each. Koufax has twice tied Feller's record of eighteen strikeouts in a single game. Last season, Sandy struck out 382 batters to surpass Feller's one-season mark of 347. And Sandy is the first ever to lead his league in lowest earned run average four seasons in a row. His recent accomplishments cannot be dismissed lightly. It does appear that at his best, he is as good as the best has ever been."

Libby goes on to examine the records of all the great pitchers and stresses that Koufax' early years were not impressive and that he came of age as a pitcher in 1961, when he began to live up to his promise. It was, therefore, only in his later years that Koufax began to bear comparison with the other outstanding pitchers. Libby makes clear that, to his way of thinking, Koufax had not been pitching brilliantly for enough years to be ranked with men like Cy Young, who won thirty-one, thirty-two, thirty-three, thirty-four and thirty-six games in single seasons, and Christy Mathewson, who won thirty, thirty-two, thirty-three and thirty-seven games. Walter Johnson won twenty or more games twelve times, ten years in a row. And Libby records the lifetime records of Spahn, Early Wynn, Robin Roberts, Whitey Ford and Lefty Grove to show that they won far more games than Koufax over many years of service to their clubs.

Yet Koufax' earned run average was 2.93, lower than Carl Hubbell, Grove, Spahn, Feller or Dean. And Sandy had thirty-five shutouts, eight more than Dean, only one less than Hubbell. But Grove had 135, Johnson 113 and Grover Cleveland Alexander 90. Thus the statistics are quoted and they do not, of course, stand alone, for baseball has changed. There are night games and more difficult schedules today than in the past. One cannot necessarily offer statistics as the only measurement of greatness, but Libby concludes that Koufax "is just about as good right now as any pitcher has ever been," which is a fair statement, for if a man is to be judged at his best, how can anyone improve on Koufax' accomplishments since he became a first-rank pitcher?

Dave Anderson is more aware of the differences in generations than Libby. In his investigation, he remarks, "Sandy Koufax outclasses his contemporaries. He is too good. It is meaningless to compare him with today's other star pitchers: Don Drysdale, Juan Marichal, Jim Maloney, Whitey Ford, Mudcat Grant, Dean Chance. They are the first to admit Koufax is better. The Dodger lefthander must be judged against the great pitchers in baseball history."

Then Anderson writes that "it is not fair, perhaps, to

compare pitchers of different eras. The game has changed. The ball has changed. But the size of the plate and the distance from the mound have been the same for Koufax as they were for the six premier pitchers of the modern era: Christy Mathewson, Walter Johnson, Grover Cleveland Alexander, Lefty Grove, Bob Feller and Warren Spahn."

Here is how Stan Musial, one of the best hitters of the modern age, compares Koufax and Spahn, both lefthanders. "Koufax," according to Musial, "is the most overpowering pitcher I ever faced. He overpowers you with both his fastball and his curve. Spahn never really overpowered you. Spahn would work on you. Pitch you in and out, low and high. Spahn was a scientist." About Koufax, Musial adds, "Sandy throws as hard as any pitcher I ever saw. In my time in the National League, there were some hard-throwing pitchers — Johnny Vander Meer, Rex Barney, Bob Veale. But none of them threw harder than Sandy and none of them had his curve. Sandy has one of the best curves I ever saw . . . That's what makes Koufax great. He has the great fastball *and* the great curve. He just overpowers you with them."

Ted Williams compares Koufax with Feller, but he never batted against Koufax. Still, he recognizes Sandy's skill and says he has the same tricky motion that Feller had. "There's no doubt," he says, "about Koufax being the best of today's pitchers. His curve is a big pitch with him. Feller used his curve as his strikeout pitch and I've noticed that Koufax does the same thing."

In comparing Koufax with Grove, Luke Appling, who is in the Hall of Fame together with Williams, reports, "I've never batted against him so I can't really say if he's faster than Grove or not as fast. I just don't know. But it seems that Koufax works on a hitter more than Grove did. Grove had good control. But he never tried to set you up. He didn't have the curve ball to do that."

Edd Roush, also in the Hall of Fame, remembers Alexander well and says that Sandy is faster, but that the eras in which they worked differed greatly and so he couldn't be sure just how Koufax would rate against Alexander. Roush does concede, for example, that Walter Johnson, considered the king of the speed pitchers, did not have a curve ball nearly as good as Sandy's.

George Sisler, another Hall of Famer, played against Johnson and, as a modern-day batting coach, also has seen much of Koufax. His opinion, therefore, is of particular interest. "It's hard to compare pitchers of different eras," he admits, "but Koufax is a great pitcher and would be a great pitcher in any era. He has a great fastball, a great curve, and he has poise and control. He has a better curve than Johnson. In fact, I don't think anyone has ever had a better curve than Koufax. It breaks down and it breaks sharply, but it breaks big, too. It's a great curve. I've always said that I thought Walter Johnson was the best pitcher I ever saw. And at his best he was tops. But if Koufax' arm stays sound, he has a chance to equal Johnson."

Max Carey, on the other hand, insists that Mathewson is the best he ever saw. Christy worked with his brains, according to Carey, a Hall of Famer. Mathewson could have been faster, if he wanted to be, but he did not operate along those lines. Carey does say, however, that "Koufax is terrific. He's got the stuff. Both the curve and the fastball. He's a natural."

Anderson concludes that, so far, Sandy's problem is

durability, for he has had trouble with his health. "But it is also the *only* flaw. He has everything else. He has something on all the premier pitchers except Feller. He is faster than Spahn, Alexander and Mathewson, and he has a better curve than Grove and Johnson. He has something on Feller, too. Koufax already has four no-hitters. Bob Feller had three."

At the height of Sandy's career, awed admiration was expressed by hosts of his contemporaries. "Hitting against Koufax is like mining hard coal with a toothpick," said Joe Garagiola, catcher and TV broadcaster. "The size of the ballpark means nothing to Koufax. He could pitch shutouts in a telephone booth," added Hank Bauer, the one-time Baltimore manager.

The immortal Casey Stengel made this dry observation: "Umpires often can't see where Koufax' pitches go so they have to judge from the sound of them hitting the catcher's glove. He's very tough for umpires who are hard of hearing." Sam Mele, former Twins manager, said of Sandy that "He's the only pitcher I'd pay my way into the park just to watch him warm up."

Two pitching colleagues offered these perspectives: teammate Don Drysdale said that "I expect him to pitch a no-hit, no-run game every time he starts. I'm only surprised when somebody gets a hit off him." And Twins hurler Jim Grant said flatly that "Koufax is the greatest pitcher alive. And maybe dead. The only thing I can do better than Sandy is sing and dance."

Paul Richards, longtime baseball executive who has seen so many of the sport's great players, feels that "Koufax is so good he could beat a team made up of the nine best players in the history of baseball." After Jack Mann of the

New York Herald Tribune watched Koufax massacre the mighty Yankees, he wrote, "the archaeologists ... will review the films of the 1963 World Series and conclude that it was a tough league in which Sandy Koufax could lose five games." Comedian and baseball fan Milton Berle summed it all up when he announced that "Koufax is the greatest Jewish athlete since Samson."

It is obvious that Sandy Koufax had to be considered every time a list of great pitchers was compiled. He truly had won the admiration of the baseball world, of his own contemporaries, of former stars, of Hall of Fame players, of managers, coaches, fans and sports writers. In the course of this chapter, some of the great moments of his baseball career will be spelled out in greater detail. But meanwhile, one cannot conclude that Koufax attained baseball heights suddenly, that he came to the major leagues and immediately conquered them. In spite of his later success and his constant potential, he struggled hard to attain the eminence he later won. Pitchers are not born; they are developed. And Sandy surely did not start his career as though he was going to have any easy time of it in professional baseball.

He was born Sanford Koufax on December 30, 1935, in Brooklyn. He lived in various sections of the borough and spent his time with a group of boys to whom basketball was more interesting than baseball. Neither of Sandy's parents were baseball fans. His father was a lawyer and his mother worked and they did what they could to raise their children, but certainly did not stress professional sports. Sandy played ball at the Jewish Community House in Brooklyn, in schoolyards and at Lafayette High School. He played on Lafayette's basketball team but did not even think of trying out for baseball until he was a senior at Lafayette, and then he played first base! It was while he played sandlot ball that he attempted to pitch. His coach, Milt Laurie, admired Sandy's fastball and a Brooklyn sportswriter, Jimmy Murphy, told the Brooklyn Dodgers that he had just seen a fifteen-year-old sandlotter with a tremendous amount of speed. The Dodgers put a scout on the boy's trail. And it was a long trail, for Sandy won a basketball, not a baseball, scholarship at the University of Cincinnati. He made that team, too. He pitched some six games and he was so startlingly effective that he soon had a herd of baseball scouts watching him. In thirty-two innings, he struck out fifty-one batters. In two games in succession, Sandy fanned thirty-four, eighteen in one game and another sixteen in the next one.

After his first year at college, Sandy was invited by the New York Giants to work out at the Polo Grounds. Sandy was wild, as lefthanders often are, and the Giants lost any interest they may have had in him. But other scouts could not forget Koufax' blinding speed, and they kept after him. The Dodgers, following the Giant lead, invited Sandy to try out with them. Manager Walt Alston was among those who watched Sandy, but there was no serious talk after that. Sandy then tried out with Milwaukee and Pittsburgh, but no offers were forthcoming and Sandy returned to Cincinnati for his sophomore year.

Al Campanis, the Dodger scout, made Sandy a firm offer on December 22, 1954 — a $14,000 bonus and a $6,000 salary. The Koufax family, unacquainted with baseball values, did not know quite what to do. They waited for other bids for a while, but none came and Campanis was persistent. Campanis also said it would be nice if a

Brooklyn boy signed to play for a Brooklyn team. Finally, Sandy signed and he now was a professional player, although he had not pitched in more than fifteen or sixteen games and a total of 100 innings. What is more, being a bonus player, he could not be farmed out to the minors. He had to learn his craft the hard way, in the majors, with veteran players looking askance at bonus rookies.

Sandy joined the Dodgers in 1955 and was wild and un-impressive. "I was so nervous and tense," he remembered, "I couldn't throw the ball for ten days. When I finally started pitching, I felt I should throw as hard as I could. I wound up with an arm so sore that I had to rest it another week." The Dodgers were fighting for the pennant in 1955 and could not gamble with a bonus player without ex-perience or control. He started his first game in July and lasted less than five innings against Pittsburgh. In August, the Dodgers were leading the National League by a com-fortable margin and they gave Sandy another chance as a starter. On August 27, 1955, Sandy Koufax gave baseball fans a glimpse of the pitcher he could eventually become. He beat the Cincinnati Reds, shutting them out with two hits. He fanned fourteen and showed that when he had his speed under control, he was extremely difficult to solve. Somewhat encouraged, he started again, and Milwaukee knocked him out of the box in the first inning. The next time around, he pitched another shutout, against the Pirates, yielding five hits and fanning six. He was, as one can see, uncertain and undependable, and although the Dodgers won the pennant, Sandy did not feel he had con-tributed anything to the victory.

For the next few years, Koufax was learning how to pitch. In 1957, he won five games and lost four and split twenty-two decisions in 1958. Koufax, at this time, was merely another lefthander with occasional good days. It was in 1959, another indifferent year, that Sandy had one of his first great days, or nights. It happened on August 31, 1959. In June of that year he had struck out sixteen Phillies. Now, he was facing the Giants. There were 82,794 fans in the stands in Los Angeles and Sandy won, 5-2, but that was the least of it. Sandy felt loose and he struck out the first batter, Jackie Brandt, on three pitches. Willie McCovey was the next hitter and he did not do much hitting, for Sandy fanned him on a swinging third strike. That was the beginning. Sandy had control and speed and had the Giants popping out and fanning. In the sixth inning, he struck out the side and by this time had eleven strikeouts. In the seventh, Brandt and McCovey fanned again, for No. 12 and No. 13. In the eighth inning, with the score 2-1 in favor of the Giants, Koufax had to bear down harder than ever. He got Willie Mays when Roseboro, his catcher, held Mays' tipped third strike. And then Orlando Cepeda became Sandy's fifteenth victim. In the ninth, Koufax realized that if he fanned the side he would shatter the National League record of seventeen, held by Dizzy Dean, and the major league mark of eighteen by Bob Feller would be equaled.

Eddie Bressoud was the first batter in the ninth. Sandy struck him out on four pitches. Danny O'Connell was the next batter. The second baseman carried the count to 2-2 and then watched a curve break over the plate for strike three. This was No. 17 and Koufax had tied Dean's record, set in 1933. The batter was now Jack Sanford, the pitcher. There was no point in lifting him for a pinch-hitter because Sanford was all tied up with Koufax in a 2-2 game.

Sandy wound up and threw three bullets and history had been made. Sanford was the eighteenth strikeout and Koufax had tied Feller's mark. But the game was not yet over. And, as though this were a game out of fiction, the Dodgers won it in the last half of the ninth inning. With one out, Koufax, a weak hitter, shocked everyone by singling to left. Jim Gilliam also singled to the same area and now the Dodgers had their pitcher on second and Gilliam on first. Wally Moon then hit a home run and the Dodgers won the game, thanks to Koufax' brilliant pitching and timely hitting. With these eighteen strikeouts and the thirteen in his previous game against the Phillies, Sandy now had a two-game record of thirty-one, breaking another Feller record of twenty-eight in two games and a National League mark of twenty-seven, set by Karl Spooner, another Dodger pitcher, in 1954.

This game, a highlight in Koufax' career, was only one game. Sandy was not as effective in others. And in 1960, he was angry that he had not done better and that Buzzy Bavasi, the general manager of the Dodgers, had not given him more opportunities to pitch. He had lost a game in the 1959 World Series, but he was not, in his view, getting the chances he felt he deserved.

One night, in 1960, Sandy got into a fight with Bavasi, which was overheard by many reporters. "I want to pitch," Sandy yelled at Buzzy, "and you guys aren't giving me a chance!"

"How can you pitch," Bavasi responded to the challenge, "when you can't get the side out?"

"How can I get anyone out sitting in the dugout?" Sandy replied.

It was no wonder that Sandy was dissatisfied. By the end of 1960, he had won thirty-six games and had lost forty. One of his teammates had said of Koufax that "He has a bad competitive spirit. He never had to ride the bush leagues. He doesn't realize what it means to pitch and win in the majors."

During that winter, Koufax gave serious thought to quitting the game. He had been playing for six years and had little to show for it. He was not even a pitcher who could win as many as he lost. He was erratic and apparently did not have the stuff to become a star.

Joe Becker, the Dodger coach, said of Koufax that he was "overanxious," and Bavasi said that he tried to overpower the hitters and you cannot do that indefinitely against major league batters unless you mixed up your pitches.

Sandy Koufax began to develop into a real pitcher in 1961. He had the benefit of the advice of a Jewish teammate, Norm Sherry, one of the team's catchers and the brother of Larry Sherry, the Dodger pitching star in the 1959 World Series.

Riding in a bus together during training, Sherry said, "Sandy, I think your troubles would be solved if you would just try to throw easier, throw more changeups, just get the ball over."

Koufax was a man willing to listen, even if the advice came from a "secondary" player. He thought about it and decided not to attempt to overwhelm every batter with every pitch. "I used to throw each pitch harder than the previous one," Sandy later told a reporter. "There was no need for it. I found out that if I take it easy and throw naturally, the ball goes just as fast. I found that my control improved and the strikeouts would take care of themselves."

He got off to a fine start in 1961. He had won only eight games in 1960. In 1961 he already had won eight games in June. He had become a regular, steady pitcher. He was used in forty-two games and pitched more than 200 innings. He won eighteen games and lost thirteen. He struck out 269 batters, thus breaking a National League record of 267 held by Christy Mathewson for fifty-eight years. The batters said that Sandy now had control of his fastball and that his curve was more effective than ever before because his control gave him an opportunity to mix up his deliveries.

The baseball fan will recall that 1961 was famous for another reason as well. That was the year Roger Maris of the New York Yankees strained to beat the most famous record in the books: Babe Ruth's sixty home runs in a single season. The pressure on Maris was tremendous. Reporters followed him everywhere. Television cameras were fixed on him on the ball field, almost to the exclusion of the other Yankee stars. Maris got his sixty-one home runs, but he never came close again to being a superstar.

It was during this turmoil that Sandy Koufax was trying to break an older record than Ruth's, which had been set in 1927. The National League record for strikeouts for one season was Mathewson's 267, set in 1903 by one of baseball's greatest pitchers. Koufax, working hard to establish himself with the Dodgers, was having a good year, an especially fine one for him. On August 29th, he beat the Chicago Cubs for his fifteenth win. In the process, he fanned twelve batters, giving him, as of that date, 212 strikeouts and bringing his goal somewhat closer. It also was the eighth time in 1961 that Sandy had struck out ten or more men in one game. On September 15th, Sandy won from the Milwaukee Braves, chalking up his sixteenth victory. He now had 243 strikeouts, beating the record set for lefthanders by Rube Marquard of the New York Giants in 1911. In whipping the Braves, Sandy beat the great lefthander Warren Spahn, then seeking his twentieth win of the year. It was also the ninth time in the year that Koufax had struck out ten or more in a game. A few days later, on September 20th, Sandy won his eighteenth victory, licking the Cubs, fanning fifteen of them and bringing his strikeout output to 259. In another appearance he got three batters on strikes. He now was up to 262. On September 27th, Sandy pitched brilliantly against the Philadelphia Phillies. He received no batting support and lost 2-1. But he struck out seven, smashing Mathewson's record. Another point: Christy worked 367 innings to attain his mark; Sandy pitched in only 255 innings.

How did the wild, ineffectual, sometimes brilliant pitcher become so steady and so good? Sandy had an answer of sorts for Leonard Koppet, then writing for the *New York Post.* "In a strange sort of way," Sandy said, "I think the terrible season I had last year had a lot to do with it. I learned to lose. I used to want to win so badly that I couldn't get myself to stop thinking about the last thing that went wrong. If I lost a game, I'd be thinking about making it up in the next one. If a batter got a hit in the first inning, I'd still be mad and worrying about it with the next hitter, or the next inning. But last year I lost so often that something finally got through to me: that even when you lose, you start out the next game even. There's a certain number of times you're going to get beaten, and there's no sense worrying about it if you can just concentrate on the next thing coming up."

This kind of talk indicated that Koufax was maturing as a player and as a man. He now was twenty-five, finally a winning pitcher, a record-holder and a regular on a good team. The year of 1962 was one to which he and his fans were looking forward with confidence.

And 1962 was one of the most remarkable seasons ever experienced by a major league pitcher. Koufax proved forever that at his best, no one was better. But he also demonstrated that his luck was not always of the best. He won fourteen games and lost seven, which does not seem to be too impressive. The reason for the 14-7 record was due to an injury that nearly ended Sandy's career. But until he was stricken, he was brilliant. He struck out 216, walking only fifty-seven, and he won the earned run average title for pitchers with a low of 2.52. Notwithstanding his injury, he pitched a no-hit, no-run game and also became the first pitcher to have *two* eighteen-strikeout games in a career.

On April 24, 1962, Sandy Koufax again went into the record books as a strikeout pitcher when he beat the Chicago Cubs in Chicago by a score of 10-2.

While the victory itself was an easy one, Koufax had to work hard for his record. He fanned eighteen Cubs, to repeat his 1959 feat and to become the only pitcher to do this job more than once. It happened early in the 1962 season and the achievement proclaimed to all that Sandy's 1961 successes were by no means an accident. Sandy allowed the Cubs six hits, including a lead-off homer to Billy Williams in the ninth inning, when the score already was a lopsided 10-1. Sandy struck out nine of the first ten batters to face him. He also fanned the entire side in the first, third and ninth innings.

This performance led to an even greater one two months later, against the New York Mets, who had become the clowns of major league baseball, but who also had won a fanatical following in New York City, after the loss of the Brooklyn Dodgers and the New York Giants. Koufax, living as he was on the West Coast, remained at heart a New Yorker and he pressed more than usual when he played in New York. For example, he pitched against the Mets in the Memorial Day double-header at the Polo Grounds in 1962 and won by a score of 13-6. Surely this was not one of Koufax' finest victories. Yet he told Arthur Daley of the *New York Times* that "It was the most exciting game I ever pitched in my life." Daley was shocked to hear this statement from a man who already had pitched record-making games, for Sandy had had a ten-run lead and had pitched sloppily after that, yielding thirteen hits. The reason for Sandy's satisfaction went beyond statistics.

He told Daley, "Maybe it was just being back in the big town again. I was higher than a kite. It was an emotional jag and I couldn't relax. That crowd was unbelievable and it added to the excitement. It was such an enthusiastic crowd and it never stopped cheering for the Mets, no matter how hopelessly they were out of it."

Then Koufax reminisced. "The Mets, in a way, reminded me of the first Dodger team I ever saw. When I was a small boy, my father took me to Ebbets Field to see my hero, Pete Reiser. The other team had a ten-run lead, just as we did yesterday. But the Dodgers refused to quit. They kept pecking away and finally Reiser won the game in the ninth with an inside-the-park home run."

With this sentimental attitude about the Mets, Sandy Koufax must have had a special thrill on the night of June 30, 1962 at Los Angeles, when he pitched the first no-hit, no-run game of his career. He beat the Mets, striking out thirteen and winning 5-0. In retrospect, even this no-hitter was not the best performance of Koufax' career, but it was enough to make him an immortal of the mound.The Dodgers gave Sandy a four-run lead in the first inning, so there was no pressure on the pitcher almost from the outset. In the first inning he needed only nine pitches, all strikes, to eliminate Richie Ashburn, Rod Kanehl and Felix Mantilla. Two Mets fanned in the second; two more in the third; Kanehl again in the fourth; one in the fifth and two in the sixth. Sandy missed a strikeout in the seventh because with a man on base with one out, he forced Frank Thomas to hit into a double play. In the eighth Sandy got two more strikeouts for a total of thirteen. Meanwhile, not a single Met got a hit and no runner reached third base, although Sandy walked five.

After the game, many ballplayers were interviewed and, of course, Koufax was the man they talked about. Solly Hemus, who was a Dodger coach, needled Sandy throughout the game and perhaps kept him loose as pressure mounted. Once, in 1960, Sandy had pitched a one-hit game, against Pittsburgh, and so he knew what the feeling was like. After the three strikeouts in the first inning, Hemus said to Sandy, "It isn't really that easy, is it?" Halfway through the game, Hemus reminded Sandy that he had not yet given up a hit. "I've had one a lot later than this," Koufax replied, and went back to work.

In the second inning, the Mets almost hit safely, when Thomas drove a ball sharply to the right of Maury Wills, the fine shortstop of the Dodgers. Wills made a backhand stab and quick throw to first. Fortunately for Koufax, Thomas was a slow runner and so a threat did not materialize. That was the only time the Mets came close to a hit.

It is no wonder that after the game the players raved about Koufax. Gene Woodling, a former Yankee who pinch-hit in the ninth inning, said, "Koufax is the kind of guy who sends you back to the farm, and happy to go." Rod Kanehl observed of Sandy, "He throws the ball hard until he's got two strikes on you. Then he throws it harder." Richie Ashburn chimed in, "The way he was throwing, he had you completely at his mercy."

Sandy himself had a great deal to say. First, he denied that the no-hitter was "tainted" because he had thown it against the weak Mets. He also said he had trouble getting his curve ball over the plate in the middle innings and that his arm stiffened on him in the fourth inning. Still, the no-hitter was an exciting experience for him, as it must be for any pitcher. "It doesn't happen very often," he said, not knowing what the future held in store for him. "A lot of great pitchers never got one. Sal Maglie had to wait almost to the end of his career to get his. And he said it was the biggest thrill of his life. I remember thinking after the game, 'Now you've got it. Nobody can take it away from you anymore.' It's a hard feeling to describe."

At this point in 1962, Sandy had won eleven games and lost four. In his last five starts, he had given up only three earned runs, for a 0.63 earned run average. Over the season, his earned-run average was 2.33. Sandy was on his way to his best season. He was named to the All-Star game, and by that time had won thirteen and lost four. He had more than 200 strikeouts and his earned run average was the lowest in the National League. With Sandy to lead them, it appeared that the Dodgers were on their way to the pennant.

Why not? Koufax had been burning up the league with his pitching form. He had struck out eighteen in a game; he had pitched a no-hitter; he hit his first major league home run in a game to win from Warren Spahn, 2-1. In eight starts, from June 13th to July 12th, he had been as overwhelming as a pitcher can be. He gave up only four earned runs, and his strikeouts had mounted to 209.

Then tragedy struck. Sandy did not start another game that year, and made a few hapless appearances on the mound in September. The Dodgers, minus his talents, slowly fell back among the other teams in the league. The Giants caught up with the Dodgers and won the pennant in a playoff.

What had happened to Sandy Koufax? The entire baseball world was wondering. At first it appeared to be a blood blister on Sandy's index finger. The finger had been numb for a while, but it had not affected Sandy's pitching. Then it grew so numb that he could not throw a curve ball effectively. He could not spin the ball off his fingertips, and he noticed this after the All-Star game break. He saw his curve fail him in a game against the Giants; then he left a game against the Mets in the seventh inning. He started one more time but could not pitch and quit after the first inning. In August of that year, Sandy told Milton Gross, a *New York Post* columnist and a good friend, that his finger was "sort of useless right now. It doesn't hurt or anything, but there's a half inch of finger that's raw, virtually no skin on it. The skin had just died."

It was a blood clot, a dangerous one, and throughout the hot August month, when the pennant race was getting closer and closer, Koufax was visiting doctors. He learned later that he had been in danger of losing the finger. After the blood clot, infection had set in. Drugs and medication to repair the blood vessels had been successful. "All I care about," Sandy said, "is the future. I can't help being a little worried. Will it come back?"

No one knew. He hardly did any more pitching in 1962, although he made a final appearance on September 27th in a game against Houston. In that effort, Sandy pitched four scoreless innings and struck out four. Then he weakened and gave up a two-run homer. He left the game ahead, 4-2. His catcher, John Roseboro, reported that Koufax had his "usual good stuff." Sandy himself was relieved. "That game," he said at the time, "meant more to me than any other I had ever won, and that includes the no-hitter I pitched against the Mets. Although I wasn't as sharp as I would like to have been, I was satisfied. More than that, I was relieved. I had looked awful in two previous turns on the mound after the long layoff and I didn't want to spend the winter wondering whether I'd ever be able to pitch again. My finger wasn't completely healed — although there was no more pain — but I had to pitch and find out. I did."

The Dodgers lost the pennant and Koufax thought his finger would be all right. Could anyone tell about Koufax? The sports magazines and columns were full of stories about the Jewish lefthander. Bob Hunter, writing in the *Sporting News* in February, 1963, put the story in proper focus when he wrote: "Sandy Koufax, the man with the golden arm and the tinplate finger, without a doubt will be the most spotlighted Dodger when the club opens spring training in Vero Beach. He'll be the center, the key, the crux of the double comeback as both the Dodgers and Sandy strive to reach the goals that each barely missed last season." Hunter added that "Koufax was headed for twenty wins, easily, and his strikeouts would have just about rewritten the record books for keeps . . ." Now, Koufax is the man being looked upon to perform the double comeback — for himself personally, and for the team as a National League entry."

Robert Creamer, writing in *Sports Illustrated* (March 4, 1963), on the subject of "An Urgent Matter of One Index Finger," reported that "The Finger cost the Dodgers the National League pennant, it will have a great deal to say on whether the Dodgers win or lose in 1963 and it had brought Koufax more publicity than his extraordinary pitching achievements ever did."

Koufax was constantly being asked — and the magazines and newspapers were dutifully recording his replies — whether his finger was still bothering him. "It feels all right. I don't think it's going to give me trouble," was his answer to all reporters. Would the pressure of the finger against the ball cause a recurrence of his difficulty? "No, it shouldn't," Koufax said, again and again.

The baseball fans of America waited for Sandy's first 1963 mound performance. It was a fine one. On April 10, 1963, he beat the Chicago Cubs in Chicago, by a score of 2-1. Sandy gave up only five hits and struck out ten. It was his first complete game since the previous July and he was in excellent form, for he walked only two batters. "The finger didn't bother me a bit," the southpaw stated to reporters. "The one thing that pleased me was that I had no trouble with the cold weather and I was making good pitches in the last few innings. There was a little numbness in the finger, but that was due to the cold."

Two starts later, Sandy gave the Cubs two hits and shut them out 2-0, fanning fourteen. All seemed to be well with him and the Dodgers. But on April 23rd, Sandy was working against the Milwaukee Braves and yielded only two hits in six and two-thirds innings. He suffered a muscle spasm and left the game, with a 1-0 lead. The Dodgers won the game, but Koufax' condition was far more important to the club than a victory in April. Dr. Robert Kerlan, who had worked on Sandy's finger the previous year, analyzed his new trouble as an injury to the "posterior capsule of the left shoulder joint." Sandy had stretched or torn the membrane which covers the muscles there. "I'll try not to let it get me down," Sandy said. And he did not. After a two-week absence, he pitched an 11-1 win over the St. Louis Cardinals. Alston, Bavasi and Sandy relaxed and made jokes. Koufax was back in the shape that assured the Dodgers of a serious run at the pennant.

At Los Angeles, on the night of May 11, 1963, Sandy Koufax pitched his second no-hit, no-run game, and it was a better performance than his no-hitter against the Mets. He retired the first twenty-two men he faced and then walked Ed Bailey, the Giant catcher. Jim Davenport then hit into a double play. Sandy walked one other man and faced twenty-eight batters in all, only one more than the minimum of twenty-seven. He had walked Willie McCovey with two out in the ninth, as the pressure grew. The final batter was Harvey Kuenn, who hit the ball back to Koufax on the mound. Sandy tossed the ball to first for the putout. More than 55,000 fans screamed in admiration and

Koufax had had another night to be remembered.

As though repeating a recording made again and again, Koufax told the reporters hovering over him, "This was my greatest thrill. To pitch a perfect game would really have been something great. I'm sorry I had to walk those two guys. But it's still my biggest thrill."

That game was, of course, Koufax' best of the 1963 season, but it was by no means his only excellent performance. Throughout the year he demonstrated the kind of skill that propels a player into the Hall of Fame. On June 17th, Koufax won his tenth game of the year against three defeats, by shutting out the Giants 2-0, for his sixth shutout of the year. On July 6th he had his eighth shutout of the season and his seventh straight victory. Already, his shutouts were the most marked up by any National League pitcher in any season since 1942. Sandy kept rolling along. By July 15th, he was the leading winner in the major leagues, with sixteen victories. By mid-year, *Time* magazine reported that Koufax was the best pitcher of the year. He had pitched a no-hitter, two two-hitters and four three-hitters and he had nine shutouts. "His fastball," *Time* said, "comes in like a 20-mm. cannon shell; his curve breaks so sharply that it acts, says Dodger catcher John Roseboro, 'like a chair whose legs suddenly collapse.' Control? 'When an umpire calls my pitch a ball,' says Koufax casually, 'that means it is either high or low. It's never outside or inside.' All in all, agrees St. Louis Cardinals' slugger Ken Boyer, 'Koufax is just too damned much.' "

Through July 23rd, Koufax was the major league's standout pitcher, the *Sporting News* concluded. On the basis of a point system for low-run games, in which a shutout is worth five points, Koufax had a twenty-point bulge over his nearest competitor and his great pitching was bringing his club closer and closer to the National League flag. But he had difficulty in winning some of his best-pitched games. For example, he pitched one-run ball twice in succession and failed to win either decision. He did not lose, but neither did he gain victories. He gave up one run in twelve innings against St. Louis and left before the game went one way or the other. A few days later, he tried for his twentieth victory of the year and limited the Milwaukee Braves to three hits in eight innings. His eleventh shutout was also in the offing. But Sandy weakened in the ninth. With one out, he allowed Eddie Mathews a double and with two out Gene Oliver tied the score with another double. The Dodgers eventually won but the decision went to Bob Miller.

In spite of his brilliance, Koufax never had a twenty-game victory season until 1963. On August 28th, he finally made it, with an 11-1 win over the Giants. He thus became the second Jewish twirler in major league history to win twenty games in a season. Erskine Mayer had been the first. Mayer won twenty-one games with the 1914 Phillies and repeated in 1915.

Koufax did not cease to win after achieving this goal. He set a major league record of eleven shutouts in a season for lefthanders, when he blanked the Cardinals for his twenty-fourth victory. Again, it was one of Sandy's most masterful efforts. He made a 1-0 lead hold up until the seventh inning. He did not give up a hit until Stan Musial singled in that frame. He allowed three more hits only after the Dodgers stretched their lead to four runs.

What made this game especially significant from a

Jewish point of view was that Sandy had altered his pitching schedule to avoid working on the Jewish High Holidays. He had pitched in Philadelphia with two days rest and in St. Louis with three days off so that he could miss working during the holidays. In winning, Koufax added to his National League strikeout record, bringing his total to 288. His twenty-four victories was the most any lefthander in the league had won since Carl Hubbell had twenty-six in 1936.

Koufax ended the year with twenty-five wins against five losses. He started forty games and completed half of them. His twenty-five wins and eleven shutouts were tops in the majors for the year. His earned run average of 1.88 was the lowest in the league since 1943, when Howie Pollet finished with 1.75. Sandy yielded only sixty-five earned runs in 311 innings. He also averaged nearly a strikeout an inning, with 306 in the 311 innings he pitched.

It was Koufax' performance in 1963, against his shortened 1962 season, that made the difference for the Dodgers, who won the pennant in 1963. As Larry Sherry, his Jewish teammate, said of him in the midst of the 1963 season, "He has incredible confidence. He should have, of course, he's that good, but it's more than that. He just doesn't seem to have any doubts at all. He knows, he just plain *knows,* he's going to get them out. It's made a tremendous difference in him."

As exceptional as Koufax was during the year, he attained new heights during the 1963 World Series against the New York Yankees. No matter how a player performs in the course of the long baseball season, he is best remembered for his World Series feats. And even Sandy Koufax, who entered the Series as the pitcher who could make all the difference in the world in a short series, was not expected to be as overpowering as he proved to be. After all, the Dodgers were facing the Yankees, the most feared team in the game, with sluggers like Mickey Mantle and Roger Maris and a pitcher like Whitey Ford. Moreover, the Yankees had the reputation of seldom losing to the National League in the World Series; when they did, it was considered to be an accident.

Some experts favored the Dodgers because of Koufax, Don Drysdale and Ron Perranoski, the relief pitcher. Others continued to believe that Ford, Jim Bouton, a promising new righthander who had won twenty games, and Ralph Terry, with the support of Mantle, Maris, Tresh, Elston Howard and other Yankee regulars, deserved backing as ultimate winners.

Dan Daniel, a veteran baseball expert, always had been a Yankee man and if ever he had an opportunity to favor anyone, it would be the Yankees. Prior to the World Series, Daniel, comparing Koufax with Ford, implied that Ford would prove to be the better pitcher, but that the Series had "the makings of one of the greatest southpaw battles of classic history between Whitey Ford and Sandy Koufax." While Koufax had won twenty-five games, Ford was a twenty-three game winner. Ford, according to Daniel, had a wider variety of pitches, with Koufax being primarily a fastballer. "Sandy is muscle bound," Daniel told his readers. "He has the back of a blacksmith. This makes for strength but not for fluidity. The bachelor from Brooklyn never worked in a mine. He never had a construction or road job. . . . Some critics fault Koufax for what they allege to be a lack of color . . ." and so on, and on.

Milton Gross, a competing columnist, had a different attitude. In analyzing the Dodger chances for the World
Series, he wrote a column entitled "It All Depends on
Koufax." In it, Gross said, "If Koufax loses the opening
game, forget it. The Yankees will do what they customarily
do in the Series." John Podres had beaten the Yankees
before, but now he was older and less impressive. Drysdale
was a righthander and the Yankees "ate them up." Or so it
was said. "The Dodgers," Gross insisted, "have come to
regard Sandy as a super pitcher. He is the one responsible
for this NL pennant, just as he was the one who could have
won it last season if not knocked out of action by the cir-
culatory ailment in the index finger of his pitching hand.
When Sandy works the Dodgers feel that they must win."
Gross quotes Don Drysdale as saying about Sandy, "He's
the only pitcher I've ever seen who wouldn't surprise me a
bit if he pitched a no-hitter every time he went out there. I
am surprised if he doesn't strike out everybody or if
someone hits the ball off him." Podres, who had made
World Series history himself, said of Sandy, "I think he is
the greatest." And Casey Stengel, who had seen them all,
said, "The fella is positively amazing and it almost takes a
miracle to beat him." Stengel made this observation immediately after Koufax won his twenty-fifth game of the
year, beating the Mets, 1-0.

The first game of the World Series, on a pleasant day on
October 2nd at Yankee Stadium, saw Ford and Koufax
locked in what at first seemed to be a pitching duel. Who
was the better lefthander?

On this day, Koufax bested Ford as, before and later, he
proved to be better than other great pitchers in the game.
More than 69,000 fans settled down to watch these two

stars. In the first inning, Whitey retired the Dodgers in order: two strikeouts and a bouncer to third. Well, then, here was good old dependable Whitey, at his best in the World Series, when it counted. Koufax showed the Yankees that his strikeout record was no freakish thing, that the Yankees were merely batters and not supermen. He merely struck out the first five Yankees, as though he were eliminating gnats! Tony Kubek was the first Yankee batter and he struck out, swinging. Bobby Richardson, a cute batter who was known for his good eye, was no more effective. Sandy also got him swinging, fooling him badly. Tom Tresh took a called third strike and Koufax had demonstrated to the Yankees they were in for a rough afternoon.

Ford, however, was not in good enough form to keep pace with the National League lefthander. Frank Howard, with one out in the second inning, hit a long drive down the middle lane of Yankee Stadium. It went 460 feet in the air in front of the center-field bleachers. Mickey Mantle chased it and chased it but had no chance to make the catch on the fly. Howard, a 255-pounder, was slow around the bases and so had to settle for the longest double in Yankee Stadium history. Moose Skowron, who earlier had been a Yankee star and now was playing for the Dodgers, singled over second and Howard scored the first Dodger run. Dick Tracewski, a rookie, also hit safely and then John Roseboro hit a drifting fly to right field which came down just inside the foul pole. It was a home run and Koufax had a four-run lead over Ford, who had won ten previous World Series games.

Mickey Mantle was the opening Yankee batter in the second inning. Like Tresh in the first inning, Mantle took a called third strike. The next batter — and victim — was Roger Maris. He went down swinging on the final strike and Koufax had now fanned five Yankees in a row! Sandy's curves, fastball and floaters had confused the great Yankee hitters. He had imposed his will on them and, one could guess, this series of outs made its impression on the Yankees. They now knew that they were facing a pitcher the like of which they had not met on their path to the American League pennant.

Joe Pepitone struck out in the third inning, and by this time Koufax had a five-run lead. In the fourth frame, Koufax repeated his exploits of the first inning: he retired the side on strikeouts, with Kubek and Richardson swinging vainly and Tresh again being fooled on a call. In the fifth, Mantle struck out and Maris was retired. Sandy had a perfect game and the fans began to buzz. But Elston Howard singled, Joe Pepitone did the same and Clete Boyer beat out an infield hit to fill the bases. Now the Yankee fans woke up and called for their team to knock Koufax out of the box. It may be that the Yankees were not listening, for Hector Lopez, batting for Ford, went down swinging and the side was retired, with Koufax marking up his eleventh strikeout.

With one out in the sixth, Richardson drew a base on balls and Koufax was a bit disturbed by this temporary loss of control. He walked Tresh and the Yankees again had cause to hope, with Mantle and Maris the next batters. Koufax, however, regained his form and forced both muscle boys to pop out to infielders. Sandy was on his way to a shutout and had a chance to better Carl Erskine's record of fourteen strikeouts in a World Series game, set ten years earlier.

In the eighth inning, the Yankees finally scored. Kubek singled. Richardson fanned for the third time and then Tresh hit a home run into the lower left-field stands. The shutout was gone, but the game was still in hand.

In the final inning, Koufax already had his fourteen strikeouts and three outs to go for victory. Howard lined out. Pepitone singled, Clete Boyer flied out and Koufax had one more out to nail down and he needed a strikeout to set a new World Series record. He faced a pinch-hitter, Harry Bright. A dangerous long ball hitter, Bright swung desperately at a third strike, missed, and Koufax had his record and the Dodgers had won the first game.

"Everything they were writing about him is true," Mantle said after the game. Richardson, who had fanned only twenty-two times in 630 times at bat during the regular season, had been victimized three times. He asked, "How come he only won twenty-five? If Koufax is this consistent, I've never seen anyone like him." Bright had a semi-joke. "I wait seventeen years to get into a World Series and I strike out. That isn't bad enough, 69,000 people were rooting against me." Howard was calm, saying, "He can't pitch every day." Koufax said he got a little tired around the sixth inning, but then regained his strength. Like a gentleman, he said that he was a little sorry he had broken Erskine's record for Carl had been a Dodger pitcher himself, but Sandy admitted that "I wanted that last strikeout so badly, I could taste it."

Apparently, Dan Daniel was not correct when he thought Koufax did not have the "fluidity" a great pitcher needed, and Sandy did not have to work in the mines to overpower the Yankees.

The Dodgers had shown the Yankees their best pitcher.

Johnny Podres, who pitched the second game, was only a
trifle less effective. He beat Al Downing 4-1 in the second
game at the Stadium. He tired in the ninth, yielding one
run and being saved by Perranoski. The Dodgers had won
both games in New York and returned home as the
favorites to win the Series. Everyone knew that Koufax
would pitch again in the fourth game and that was enough
for most fans to know. Meanwhile Don Drysdale, who had
been the big Dodger winner before Koufax came along,
pitched an even better game than Koufax and Podres. He
faced Jim Bouton, the Yankee twenty-game winner, and
the Dodgers scored one run in the first inning. It was a
cheap run. Bouton walked Jim Gilliam, who advanced to
second on a wild pitch, and Gilliam scored on a single by
Tommy Davis. The Davis hit bounced off the pitching
mound toward Richardson, who partially lost sight of the
ball against the shirts of the crowd, the ball then bouncing
off Richardson's left shin. It was enough for Drysdale, who
pitched a shutout and won 1-0. The Yankees, already
proud, were now faced with the humiliation of losing a
World Series in four straight games, and it was a distinct
possibility with Koufax on the mound.

This time, Whitey Ford was much better than he had
been in the opening game. There are those who believed he
was better than Koufax on this afternoon in Los Angeles,
but you pay off on the score.

Koufax got the first nine Yankees, four on strikes, and it
began to appear that the Yankees never would solve his
serves. Ford kept pace with Sandy, facing only twelve batters in the first four innings. It was 0-0 and this one was a
grim pitchers' duel. Frank Howard had singled in the second inning and Skowron had hit into a double play.

Whitey then got the next seven batters. He did not have the same luck with Howard, who had hit that long double off him in the first game. In the fifth inning, Howard lashed another one of his powerful drives, this time 450 feet into the left field stands, for the first run of the game.

In the fifth inning, Richardson hit a pop fly that fell for a double when two infielders and an outfielder messed up the play. It was a lucky hit, but Koufax was not invincible. In the seventh, Mantle finally got a hit off Koufax. He hit the first pitch into the left-field bleachers and the score was tied 1-1. The tie did not last long. Gilliam, in the bottom of the seventh, hit the ball to Boyer who stretched, caught it and threw perfectly to Pepitone. Joe lost the ball in the crowd and it bounced off his chest. When the scrambling was over, Gilliam was on third. Willie Davis hit a long fly to Mantle, who caught it but could not throw Gilliam out at home. Now the score was 2-1 in favor of the Dodgers. Koufax held that lead to the end. Richardson began the ninth with a single, and Koufax, who had fanned only six batters, now struck out Tresh and Mantle for a total of eight. It seemed to be all over when Howard grounded to Maury Wills, but Tracewski dropped the ball on a force play on Richardson and the Yankees had two runners instead of the last out. Koufax, however, was not fazed. He got Hector Lopez to hit a dribbler to Wills, who made the final out by tossing the ball to first.

Koufax had won two of the four games; the Yankees had dropped four in a row and the Dodgers were the world champions, thanks to Koufax' season and World Series performance. Now the praise rolled in like waves. Koufax won a Corvette from *Sport* magazine for being the outstanding player in the World Series. The City Council of

Los Angeles passed a resolution commending the Dodgers for their showing and the County Supervisor, in a moment of excitement, proposed that Fairfax Avenue be renamed Koufax Avenue, at least for a while. Sandy was the only United Press International 1963 Major League All-Star player chosen overwhelmingly. He received sixty-eight of seventy-one votes. The *Sporting News* named Sandy the No. 1 National League pitcher. And he became the winner of the Cy Young Award as the outstanding hurler in the major leagues. He won this honor unanimously, getting all twenty votes cast by a committee of the Baseball Writers Association of America. It is interesting to note that this vote was conducted before the World Series.

Late in October, Sandy won the National League's Most Valuable Player Award. Twenty members of the Baseball Writers Association did the picking and fourteen of them chose Sandy as their first choice. In the total vote, Koufax received 237 points to Dick Groat's 190. This was only the seventh time in thirty-three years that a pitcher had been named for this honor. Koufax, when informed of the vote, said, "I'm awfully surprised to win this. I honestly never thought they'd name a pitcher most valuable. I'm especially proud of this honor. I feel it is the most important one in baseball." Sandy's manager, Walt Alston, said that Koufax "had a great year and he deserved every honor he got. I haven't done much else than pat Sandy on the back all year long, so I think he knows how I feel about him."

In its February, 1964 issue, *Sport* magazine named Koufax its "Man of the Year." In an editorial, Al Silverman, editor of the magazine, wrote, "In a pitchers' year, one pitcher stood above them all. In a year of heroic performances in all sports, one man stood above them all.

Not since 1934, when Dizzy Dean blazed to thirty victories plus two more in the World Series, had a pitcher enjoyed such a year as Sandy Koufax." Then Silverman gave the details of Sandy's 1963 season and concluded, "*Sport's* Man of the Year for 1963 — the Dodgers' Sandy Koufax — without argument."

Life magazine, in a close-up on Koufax, called Sandy "the best pitcher in the past decade," and called attention to his "remarkable year, following his finger injury."

What could Koufax do in 1964 after having conquered all possible worlds in 1963? Milton Gross asked this question in a magazine article between seasons: "What do you do after you've won twenty-five games, set a National League strikeout record of 306, pitched eleven shutouts, had a 1.88 ERA, won the Cy Young Award by unanimous selection and the National League's Most Valuable Player Award?"

It should be borne in mind that no matter how successful Koufax was, ill health dogged him throughout most of his career and 1964 was no exception. It was a year of some brilliance, but it ended on a question mark, for before the season was over, Koufax had another injury and baseball fans were asking if this great pitcher was not brittle, if his sports life was going to be a long one.

He won his first start of the year by shutting out the St. Louis Cardinals, 4-0. It was his tenth consecutive victory, counting the two World Series wins of 1963, and his twentieth in his last twenty-two decisions. It appeared that he was going to be as good as ever — if not better. He hurt his arm on April 22nd and then recovered, winning from the Chicago Cubs 2-1 in ten innings, and striking out thirteen batters. But he also was losing games and had five victories against four defeats when he faced the Philadelphia Phillies on the night of June 4th. He had been worried about a soreness in his elbow, but on this night he pitched the third no-hit game of his major league career, facing the minimum number of twenty-seven batters. Richie Allen drew a walk in the fourth inning and then was thrown out trying to steal second. He fanned twelve batters and by striking out ten or more men for the fifty-fourth time in his career, he tied a record held by Bob Feller and Rube Waddell. Only Feller had three no-hitters before Sandy tied him. Koufax won the game when Frank Howard hit a three-run homer in the seventh. The fantastic lefthander was so invincible that only four balls were hit to the outfield by the Phillies. Sandy was as strong in the ninth as he was in the early innings. He struck out the initial batter, made the second one pop to the first baseman and then only a pinch-hitter, Bobby Wine, stood between him and his third no-hit game. The count went to two strikes and one ball. Then Wine struck out.

By June 13th, Sandy was on his 1963 schedule of victories and there was no doubt in the minds of the fans that he was going to reinforce his reputation as the premier pitcher in the game. On the last day of June, he won his seventh straight game and his eleventh of the year, and for the fifty-sixth time he fanned ten more hitters. In his next start, he ran his streak to eight in a row, getting his fifth shutout and his twelfth victory, by defeating the Mets. He had yielded only eleven earned runs in his last ninety-five innings. And so he rolled on and on and by mid-August he had nineteen victories. How much better could anyone be? Was he meeting the challenge of 1963? Of course!

But he remained injury-prone. In a game in Milwaukee

on August 8th, he hurt his elbow sliding into a base. He continued to pitch, but the pain persisted and it became clear at the end of the month that he was through for the year. It was a terrible blow to the Dodgers who were unable to repeat their pennant victory of the year before. And so the 1964 season ended on a sour note for Koufax. He had won nineteen games and lost five. He led the National League with seven shutouts and had 223 strikeouts in 223 innings. Don Drysdale finally overcame this mark by pitching steadily all year long. Sandy's earned run average was 1.74. Brilliant, of course. But what could one do? Jimmy Cannon, the sports writer for the *New York Journal-American,* in a sensitive series on Koufax, said of his injuries, "It came at him again, like a tiger who lulls the trainer into temporary serenity by acting like a house cat . . . He awakened one morning and the elbow was swollen and stiff, like a snake in death. The doctors examined him and could not recognize the symptoms of any injury or disease. He had won nineteen by then and requested they allow him to try to get twenty but they persuaded him that leisure would repair it."

Koufax remembered that August morning when he discovered the bad elbow. "My arm was as big around as my knee. I didn't know what it was. But we got the swelling down. I started to throw and it started to swell again. I possibly could have pitched at least one game. But the season had ten days to go. I had won nineteen, and would have liked to have won twenty. But the club wasn't going anywhere. The doctor said forget about pitching. The rest would be beneficial and I wanted to be right."

It was not surprising that Koufax started the 1965 season with the feeling that he would go as far as he could, pitching from day to day, hoping against hope that his arm would not collapse. True, he had been wonderfully good. He had gained national acclaim for his feats. He had proved his ability under pressure of a tight pennant race and he had shown his staying qualities in the World Series. He had demonstrated that he was more than a strikeout pitcher, that he was a winning pitcher. But had he pitched himself out? Did he have the stamina required of the truly immortal hurlers of the game? Or was he going to break down every once in a while, during critical moments, and become an uncertain player, one who might — or might not — break down? How would he rank when compared with those steady pitchers who lasted for ten or fifteen or more years? After all, his early years were indifferent. Now, when he finally had learned the art of pitching, when he had shown the skill of the best pitchers in the game, was he going to be like Herb Score, who had started well and then, following an injury, faded away? Of course, he had done more than Score and even Dizzy Dean, but he still was young enough to accomplish even more. What was to happen in 1965?

Sandy proved, if ever further proof were needed, that in spite of his uncertain arm, he was a great and dazzling pitcher. In spring training, the baseball world was watching him closely. He pitched two complete games and seemed as good as ever. But he knew that at any moment, his career could end. Yet he hoped to be a regular starter, regardless of the arm flare-ups.

On April 18, 1965, Sandy had his first start of the season, against the Phillies in Philadelphia. He had pain earlier in the spring and his ailment had been diagnosed as "traumatic arthritis." According to the Associated Press,

"A struggling Sandy Koufax, showing definite signs of his pitching ailment," beat the Phillies 6-2. The AP reporter said that Sandy appeared to be far from the invincible lefthander of the previous season. But Leonard Koppett of the *New York Times* had a different view. He wrote, "Accounts of the game in Philadelphia say Sandy 'struggled' — but only by the superhuman standards people have been imposing on Koufax since his record-breaking performances of 1963. Actually, Sandy pitched a five-hitter against the team that almost won the pennant last year; he struck out seven, which is about normal, and walked five, which is high for him but not surprising in view of his interrupted training schedule."

The important thing was that Sandy had no after-effects following his opening victory. And he retained his form throughout the year. On June 12th, he shut out the New York Mets for his ninth win of the season against only three losses, and a week later Sandy again won from the Mets, 2-1. He had twelve strikeouts and marked the seventh time in 1965 that he fanned ten or more, and the sixty-eighth time in his career that he had accomplished this feat. By mid-July he still had only three losses, against sixteen victories, with three shutouts. He had completed fifteen games in twenty-two starts and, for the fifth consecutive year, had marked up a minimum of 200 strikeouts, which was a National League record. This was rather impressive for a pitcher who did not know, from one start to the next, whether his arm would blow up on him — and on his team, which was fighting for another National League pennant.

By the end of July, the Dodgers — and Koufax — were flying high. But at the end of the month, the pitcher and his team had another scare. Sandy had won eleven in a row and had not missed a turn all year, when he lost a night game to the Cincinnati Reds, 4-1. Sandy pitched eight innings, striking out eight and allowing five hits. In the early innings, he experienced a stiffness in his left arm and his doctor, Robert Kerlan, admitted that "I would say the arthritic condition in his elbow, which is chronic, was perhaps a bit worse last night."

Sandy had a response. "I haven't missed a turn this year and I don't intend to." He was scheduled to pitch against the Cardinals in his next start and he did not let his team down. He went all nine innings for a 3-2 win. He yielded only five hits and fanned eleven batters. He won his twentieth game when he beat the Mets 4-3 on August 10th and a few days later chalked up his twenty-first victory, in a ten-inning, 1-0 game over the Pittsburgh Pirates. Again, Sandy was in strikeout form, getting twelve Pirates.

Already, the 1965 season was a successful one for Sandy Koufax. His arm, while not always strong, was good enough to serve him through a difficult season. He was winning and striking out batters as in the past. It was all quite satisfactory. But on the night of September 9th, he achieved a pitching performance better than any in his life and equaled by very few pitchers in the history of the game. He pitched a perfect game against the Chicago Cubs and thus became the first twirler in baseball history to pitch four no-hitters in a career. What made the game even more remarkable was that Sandy's opponent, Bob Hendley, gave up only one hit. But the reader will remember that this chapter began with a description of that game, Sandy's "finest hour." Up until the moment Koufax pitched this history-making game, he was one of only four hurlers to have three no-hitters: Larry Corcoran beginning in 1880 and then Cy Young and Bob Feller. Now Sandy stood alone, the only man who put together four no-hitters — and four years in succession!

Meanwhile, quite apart from Sandy's exploits, the Dodgers were engaged in one of the hottest, closest pennant races in many years. This was an unusual Dodger team. It had the pitching of Koufax and Don Drysdale, but Tommy Davis, one of the team's best players and finest hitters, was injured in May and never came back in 1965. Jim Gilliam, who had started as a coach, was reactivated as a player and minor leaguers were brought up to fill various holes in the lineup. The Dodgers fought their way to first place in early July, then faltered and recovered enough to keep the lead into mid-August. On September 6th, the Dodgers led the Giants by a single game, and then the Giants ran off a fourteen-game winning streak and appeared to be "in" as the next National League champions. On September 16th, the Giants held a four-and-a-half-game lead over the Dodgers and hardly anyone held any hopes for the Los Angeles club, which had Maury Wills stealing bases, Koufax and Drysdale winning, but the rest of the team lagging behind them.

At this moment in the race, the Dodgers took hold of themselves and started to play brilliantly. They won five in succession, including three shutouts. In thirteen games, Dodger pitchers held the opposition so tightly, that seven of those games were shutouts. Claude Osteen and Ron Perranoski joined Koufax and Drysdale and the race became so tight that on September 30th, with only four games left to both the Dodgers and the Giants, the Dodgers held a two-game lead. Sandy won his twenty-fifth game of the year the night before, shutting out the Cincinnati Reds and fanning thirteen and bringing the Dodger winning streak to twelve. On October 1st, the Dodgers lost to the Milwaukee Braves and the Giants also were defeated, so with the race that close, no champion would be declared until almost the very last day of the season.

Sandy had pitched steadily all year and now he was called on by Walt Alston to nail down the pennant. Sandy was pitching with only two days of rest. He was bone-tired, but now, if ever, he had to win. The Braves were a tough team, and eager to play the role of spoilers. But Koufax was not going to allow *this* season to end sourly. He rose to the challenge and won, 3-1, striking out thirteen and giving up only four hits. The pennant was won, Koufax had won twenty-six games and the Dodgers were now in the World Series. Koufax had an earned run average of 2.06 and set a major league record with 369 strikeouts for a single season. He surely had made a major contribution to the 1965 pennant chase. And his personal records kept coming. Not only did he have his perfect game and his strikeout record. He also fanned ten or more men in a game eighty-one times (a new mark), twenty times in 1965 alone. His last four victories of the year, coming at moments of extreme pressure in the race, were shutout wins.

The 1965 World Series opened in Bloomington, Minnesota, October 6th, with the Dodgers trying to win the world championship from the Minnesota Twins, a new power in baseball, a team that had easily beaten back the challenge of the once-great New York Yankees, and every other American League team as well. Normally, Koufax, the Dodger ace, would have been the first Dodger pitcher to take the mound. But it was on Yom Kippur and Sandy already had told Alston — and the sports world — that he would not play ball on the Jewish holiday. This act of faith made for a good deal of discussion throughout the nation, but Koufax won the admiration of almost everyone by making clear he did not think that even a baseball game, a World Series game at that, was as important to him as observing Yom Kippur. After this game, Alston permanently kept a Jewish calendar on his desk so that he would always be aware of any upcoming holiday.

Don Drysdale opened the Series and, to the surprise of many, lost 8-2 to Jim Grant. The Twins showed both power and speed to lick Drysdale, but the Dodger fans remained confident, for Koufax was scheduled to pitch the next game, and who could beat Drysdale and Koufax back-to-back? Hardly anybody, was the usual reply to that question. But the Twins did it and consternation took over among the Dodgers.

Koufax lost to another southpaw, Jim Kaat, in what started out as a close game but became a rout when Sandy left the mound. For the first five innings, Sandy pitched shutout ball, although he later said that he had control trouble. Kaat was quoted after the game, saying, "Nobody expected me to beat Koufax. When I saw him throw after an inning, I thought I'd better not give up a run." And he did very well, keeping pace with Sandy for those five scoreless innings. In the sixth, Zoilo Versalles, the aggressive Minnesota shortstop, hit a ball to Gilliam, which took an unexpected bounce, hit Gilliam's right shoulder and caromed into left field. It was called a two-base error and Koufax was in trouble. Struggling for control, he allowed Tony Oliva to hit safely and then Harmon Killebrew singled Oliva home and the Dodgers were two runs behind.

In the Dodger seventh, there were two singles and then a sacrifice, advancing both runners, and Alston lifted Sandy for a pinch-hitter, after John Roseboro singled to drive in one Dodger run. The Twins stopped the rally and Koufax was out of the game. Dodger pitchers gave up another three runs to allow the Twins 5-2. When Sandy had left the game, the score was 2-1 in favor of the Twins.

Now it seemed that the Dodgers were in deep trouble. Their two top pitchers had been beaten. But Claude Osteen pitched a 4-0 shutout in Los Angeles and then Drysdale won an easy game 7-2, with his teammates running wildly and effectively on the bases and showing the old Dodger style of run, run, run. The World Series was all tied up with two victories apiece.

In the fifth game, the last one at Los Angeles, Koufax faced Jim Kaat and Sandy was back in his "normal" form, which meant that the Twins could not score a single run off him. Sandy won a 7-0 shutout and gave the Dodgers a one-game lead in the World Series, three victories to two. Sandy was again almost perfect. He faced only twenty-nine batters, two above the minimum, and pitched perfect ball until the fifth inning, when Killebrew looped a hit into center field. He yielded only three other hits, walked one and struck out ten — a standard performance by the southpaw. It also was Sandy's twenty-eighth complete game of the year and the twenty-second game in which he struck out ten or more batters. Jim Grant said after the game, "There should be one Cy Young Award for him and another for the rest of us to shoot at." But Koufax amazed not only the opposition players; he also astonished the medical profession. The team physician of the Twins, Dr, William E. Proffitt, Jr., said, "You would never have thought that Koufax could pitch consistently with that arthritis condition in his elbow. At least he might've had to rest every three or four pitching starts. But the way he's performed this year is amazing."

Jim Grant, who had won the first game of the Series and lost the fourth, came back for a third start — and won the sixth game, by a score of 5-1, hitting a three-run homer to clinch the victory. This brought the Series down to a fateful seventh game, and again it was Koufax who carried the hopes of the Dodgers and the National Leaguers. He had only two days rest and he was tired, as he had repeatedly said during the week. He had not missed a turn in the regular season and already had pitched twice in the Series. But he was the man who had to do it.

He showed, in the first inning, that he was not as sharp as usual. With the first two batters retired, Sandy walked Oliva and Killebrew. He met this opening challenge by striking out Earl Battey. In the third inning, Versalles got the first hit for the Twins. The following inning gave Sandy a two-run margin on which to work. Jim Kaat yielded a home run to Lou Johnson. Ron Fairly doubled and scored on a single by Wes Parker. It was a thin lead, but Koufax nursed it along. He had his troubles in the fifth. Frank Quilici doubled and Rich Rollins walked. Sandy was upset by the umpire's calls and showed some temper — which was rare for him. Versalles then hit a sharp grounder toward third base. Gilliam, old as players go but a veteran who did not panic, made a good catch and barely made a force play at the bag. That was the last time the Twins had a real chance to score.

It was still 2-0 when the Twins came up for their last chance against an exhausted pitcher fighting to keep a shutout, to win a game, clinch a World Series. Oliva was the first batter and Koufax got him on a grounder to third. Sandy was pitching a two-hit game and had eight strikeouts. The game was one of his patented ones, but the fans realized that here was a pitcher fighting fatigue as well as the Twins. Killebrew singled and the crowd, rooting hard for Minnesota, screamed with anticipation.

Now Battey was the hitter. The first pitch was fast and over the plate. Battey looked at it. On the second strike, Battey swung and missed. Sandy had him puzzled. The next pitch was a curve, and as it hooked the plate, Battey stood there, bat on shoulder. He was the ninth strikeout victim of the day for Koufax.

Killebrew remained frozen to first base as Bob Allison strode to the batter's box. It was Allison who had homered in the sixth game to tie the Series and bring it down to this seventh contest. He fouled back the first pitch for the initial strike. Then Sandy was low and then high for two balls. Again, Allison swung and missed for a second strike. Koufax reached down for another fastball, threw it — and Allison missed it one more time, a final time, and the World Series was at an end. Koufax had his second shutout, another game with ten strikeouts, and a world championship for his mates and himself.

Walt Alston, the Dodger manager, had to make a major decision for this seventh game. He had Drysdale ready and a well-worn Koufax. Whom was he to pitch? The fans buzzed over it, but Alston made the winning choice. It was no wonder that after that last game, he said that Koufax was the best in the world. "If there ever was a better pitcher, it was before my time," Alston told reporters. Sam Mele, the losing manager, agreed. "He's in a class by himself."

Newsweek magazine called it "Sandy's series." *Sports Il-lustrated* said that "the best pitcher in baseball proved to be the difference between two very different ball clubs." Tommy Holmes, writing for the *New York Herald Tribune,* reported that "there was only one story as the long baseball season came to its end. That was Mr. Koufax." He also pointed out that in this World Series, Sandy had pitched twenty-four innings, allowing one earned run and striking out twenty-nine.

The honors came frequently for Koufax after the season ended. He won a Corvette from *Sport* magazine for being the outstanding player in the Series. *Sports Illustrated* named him "Sportsman of the Year." On the same day, January 8, 1966, he was named to receive the Sid Mercer Memorial Award (for player of the year) and the Babe Ruth Award (for being the top World Series star) by the New York Chapter of the Baseball Writers' Association. He was the first player to win the Ruth Award more than once and only Joe DiMaggio, Ted Williams and Mickey Mantle had repeated as Mercer winners. The *Sporting News* selected Sandy as "Player of the Year," and the pitcher was chosen "Male Athlete of the Year" for 1965 in an Associated Press Poll. He also had won this honor in 1963. Sandy also won the Van Heusen Award "for grand performance in baseball," outpolling Willie Mays and other fine players. And, to make it just about unanimous, he won the Cy Young Award for best pitcher in baseball by unanimous vote of a committee of the Baseball Writers' Association and was the first player to win the award twice. The committee stressed that Sandy had led the major leagues in total wins, with twenty-six; most innings pitched, 336; most strikeouts, 382; and lowest earned run average, 2.04.

After the remarkable 1965 season, Koufax entered into financial negotiations with the Dodgers, and once again he won national headlines. He and Don Drysdale attempted to deal with the management not as individual players but as a team — a tactic never before used by baseball players. They asked for a $1,000,000 three-year package. It shook the baseball world, not only because of the huge sum of money but also because the two outstanding pitchers were negotiating in tandem. The two men held out for more than a month and finally settled for record-breaking sums, Koufax for a reported $125,000 for 1966 and Drysdale for a reported $110,000.

"Our fight," Koufax said later, "was to establish ourselves at a certain plateau salarywise. That's the battle of every ball player." He added that "We accomplished what we set out to accomplish, and that is the right of a baseball player to bargain."

Fans wondered whether Koufax would be effective in 1966, without the benefit of spring training. "Don't let anyone tell you spring training isn't necessary," he told reporters. But one week-end before the season opened, he pitched six innings of no-hit ball against the Cleveland Indians. He began the year a bit uncertainly. Soon, however, he hit his normal stride. On May 19th, he pitched a shutout over the Giants, for his sixth win of the season. Almost as usual, he struck out ten in this victory. On June 1, he pitched another shutout, this time a 1-0 win over the St. Louis Cardinals, for his ninth triumph. He ran off an eight-game winning streak and by mid-June, he led the National League with a pitching record of 11-2 and in earned run averages and strikeouts. Obviously, the long holdout had no effect on his ability.

Yet shadows did not pass over the great pitcher. As the 1966 season continued, Koufax kept winning, but, for a while, he was no longer overpowering. He did not overwhelm the batters. He struggled for control, even though he added to his victory list and strikeout victims piled up. At the end of July his arthritic elbow acted up again and he required, for the first time in the season, heavy shots from his doctor. On July 23, he won from the Mets, 6-2, but he was wild and unhappy with his performance. It was victory No. 17, but Sandy, a perfectionist, knew that something was wrong. As Maury Allen of the *New York Post* phrased it, "Sandy is 17-5 on the season with a 1.70 ERA but has not been the same, smooth overpowering pitcher in the last few weeks."

It was thought that Sandy would have to miss his next mound turn. He didn't. Instead, he was his brilliant self again. On July 27, he went eleven innings against the Phillies. He yielded one run, four hits and scored sixteen strikeouts! He left after the eleventh inning and his team won 2-1 in the twelfth. His fourth strikeout of the game was his 2,267th of his career, moving him ahead of Lefty Grove and into tenth place among the lifetime leaders. His fifteenth strikeout, which came in the ninth inning, was his 200th of the season. This was the sixth year in a row he reached that high figure. Clearly, Koufax, when healthy, was extraordinary. Equally clearly, his arm had its uncertainties.

Before the season had ended, Sandy had decided to make this his last year in the game; but the team was in the thick of a pennant race, and the decision remained private.

The pain in his arm grew worse all the time. The doctors had warned him that on any given pitch in any game, the elbow might stop working, and Sandy would lose the use of his arm not only for pitching, but for doing anything at all. He risked becoming a cripple, but he felt obliged to finish the season as best he could. He wanted to honor his commitment to his team and his teammates.

Writing in *Sport* magazine, Milton Gross observes: "It wasn't generally known that as the season progressed into the tight stages of the pennant race, Sandy had begun to receive injections directly into the elbow two days before every pitching assignment. In the days immediately following each game, the pain was intense. In the day following each shot, the pain was even worse, but Koufax continued the pretense that he was going about his daily routine normally."

On the final day of the season, the Dodgers played a doubleheader against the Phillies. Los Angeles needed to win one of the two games to win the pennant. They were losing in the first game, and Sandy went to Alston in the eighth inning and volunteered to go to the bullpen and pitch relief if he was needed, and then pitch the second game as well if they couldn't win the opener. Alston had no intention of relieving with Sandy, and the Dodgers did drop the first game. The second game simply had to be won or it was goodbye pennant. Despite the aching pain in his arm, Sandy went out to the mound for the nightcap.

The Dodgers gave him an early six-run lead, and normally, with Sandy on the mound, that would have been the ballgame right there. But in the fifth frame, with one out, Sandy threw a pitch and heard a crack as he felt a sharp pain rocket into his back. Despite his agony, he got the

third out of the inning, then went into the clubhouse while
the Dodgers came to bat.

Sandy had slipped a disc. The trainer snapped it back
into place while Sandy literally fell off the table. Then
Koufax returned to the field and grittily hung on to finish
the game and save a 6-3 win that won the pennant for
his team. Afterwards, Sandy confessed that he really didn't
even know how much he was hurting during the game
"because I was full of codeine. It was the only way I could
pitch." The pain-killer was added to the dosages of cortisone and butazolidine with which he had already been in-
jected.

Koufax retired after the 1966 season because he felt he
simply could not pitch without pain or up to his established standards. But it is a telling tribute to his brilliance that in this last season, during which he toiled in un-
remitting pain, he compiled statistics that would be
awesome in any day or age. In leading his team to another
pennant, he won twenty-seven while losing only nine, compiled an E.R.A. of 1.73, and struck out over 300 batters for
a record-breaking third season. All this while gravely han-
dicapped by a serious injury.

In the fall classic that year, the Dodgers were swept in
four games by the Baltimore Orioles, a result that shocked
the baseball world. Sandy lost his last game in professional
baseball when centerfielder Willie Davis lost two consecutive fly balls in the sun, adding a wild throw on the second misplay for an unforgettable three errors on two plays.
The two ruinous plays gave the Orioles three unearned
runs and, ultimately, the ballgame.

"When Davis returned to the bench," Gross relates,
"the rest of his teammates avoided Willie as though he

were unclean. The centerfielder fled to the corner of the dugout as if he were trying to hide. He was hurt by the hoots and the boos. Koufax was hurting just as much, physically as well as mentally, but he went directly to Willie.

" 'Don't let them get you down,' Sandy said.

" 'Sandy,' said Willie, near to weeping. 'I'm sorry.'

" 'There's nothing to be sorry about,' Sandy said, trying to console his teammate. 'These things happen.' "

When Koufax retired after the season, accolades for the great southpaw poured in from everywhere. Leonard Koppett, in an article bluntly titled "Why Koufax belongs in the Hall of Fame," wrote these observations:

"In January, 1972, Sandy Koufax will be voted into the Baseball Hall of Fame. He'll have to wait that long because of the rule that forbids a vote until five years after the player's retirement. But it will be a formality; everyone recognizes that . . .

"He led the National League in earned run average for five consecutive years. No one else ever did that in either league. Only three men who won more than 150 games in modern times have better won-lost percentages: Christy Mathewson, Lefty Grove and Whitey Ford. In strikeouts, Koufax was in a class by himself. Only Sandy was able to strike out 300 or more men in three different seasons. Only Koufax, in the whole history of baseball, struck out more than one batter per inning pitched throughout his career. Only Sandy pitched four no-hitters, in four consecutive years.

"So Sandy will go into the Hall of Fame at the earliest possible moment for the simplest possible reason: he belongs."

Baseball fans everywhere, even the most sophisticated, marveled at the Dodger ace's feats; and their appreciation increased when they considered the physical difficulties that plagued his pitching arm. Mel Durslag, in the L. A. *Herald-Examiner*, called Sandy "the pin-up boy of the Arthritis and Rheumatism Foundation." But that arthritic arm struck out ten or more batters in a record ninety-seven games.

In *The Great No-Hitters*, Glenn Dickey notes that in the start prior to his fourth no-hitter, Sandy had been removed for a pinch-hitter in the eighth while trailing Houston, 2-1; Koufax had been so frustrated that he had picked up a rubbing table and tossed it against the wall. The next day, his elbow improved, and when he pitched the no-hitter the elbow felt as good as it had all year. "Maybe it was the exercise he got throwing the table," Dickey says dryly.

Arthur Daley of the *Times* makes the point that "the Dodgers begged Sandy not to announce his retirement when he did. They didn't want to be hung over a barrel at trading time, nor did they want to risk impeding the flow of their advance ticket sale. He could have taken a $150,000 salary for the next season for doing nothing. But Sandy had too much character for that. His high ethical standards could not permit him to be a party to such deceit. So he quit with his head held high."

Without question, Sandy went out a winner. His dazzling record in the last pennant-winning season capped his marvelous career. Just as impressive as his regular-season feats were his marks in interleague competition. Along with his four World Series wins, his cumulative E.R.A. in Series play was 0.95, the fourth-best in history (Babe Ruth, better known as a hitter, was second-best). Despite being in

only three Series, his sixty-one strikeouts is the fourth best
mark ever. He is second only to Bob Gibson in compiling
the most Series strikeouts per nine innings (9.63), and his
paltry allowance of only 5.68 hits per nine inning game
puts him seventh in that category. He was also the winning
pitcher in the 1965 All-Star game, and started the 1966
classic which his team won, 2-1. One can only imagine the
dizzying heights to which his career might have led had his
arm remained healthy.

In January, 1972, Sanford Koufax was elected to
Baseball's Hall of Fame in Cooperstown, New York. At
thirty-six years old, he was the youngest man ever so
honored. He joined an elite group of only nine men who
had ever been elected in their first year of eligibility. He led
everybody on the ballot with three hundred forty-four of a
possible three hundred ninety-six votes; his total of votes
was the highest ever received by any player in baseball
history. His judges had awarded him the highest possible
accolade, and had confirmed what everyone always
suspected: that there had never in the history of the game
been any pitcher any better than Sandy Koufax at his peak.

Observing Koufax hurling against the Twins in the
World Series, Roger Angell, in his splendid book *The Summer Game,* offers these reflections:

"I concentrated on watching Koufax at work. This is not
as easy as it sounds, for there is the temptation simply to
discredit what one sees. His fast ball, for example, flares
upward at the last instant, so that batters swinging at it
often look as if they had lashed out at a bad high pitch.
Koufax's best curve, by contrast, shoots down, often barely pinching a corner of the plate, inside or out, just above
the knees. A typical Koufax victim — even if he is an excel-

lent hitter — having looked bad by swinging on the first pitch and worse in letting the second go by, will often simply stand there, his bat nailed to his shoulder, for the next two or three pitches, until the umpire's right hand goes up and he is out. Or if he swings again it is with an awkward last-minute dip of the bat that is a caricature of his normal riffle. It is almost painful to watch, for Koufax, instead of merely overpowering hitters, as some fast-ball throwers do, appears to dismantle them, taking away first one and then another of their carefully developed offensive weapons and judgments, and leaving them only with the conviction that they are the victims of a total mismatch. Maybe they are right, at that; the records of this, Koufax's greatest year, suggest as much. In the regular season, he won twenty-six games, struck out three hundred and eighty-two batters (an all-time record), and pitched his fourth no-hit game — a perfect game, by the way — in as many years, which is also a new record. In the Series, he won two shutouts pitched within three days of each other, and gave up exactly one earned run in twenty-four innings. He was the difference between the two clubs; he won the Series."

Other great hurlers and strikeout specialists always have been and always will be part of baseball's lore, and sooner or later most all of Sandy's many records will fall, as records are made to do; but Koufax has left his mark indelibly upon this sport. The Jewish boy from Brooklyn had become much more than a baseball star, more even than a Hall of Famer. He had become, as Angell puts it, "maybe the best pitcher in the whole history of baseball."

KEN HOLTZMAN, ACE SOUTHPAW

Ken Holtzman

Ace Southpaw

On July 20, 1974, the Oakland Athletics played a baseball game in Cleveland, and the Indian pitcher, a young right-hander named Dick Bosman, blanked the A's with a no-hit, no-run game. When the reporters invaded the post-game Oakland clubhouse to solicit comments about Bosman's feat, one of the first players they sought out was Oakland's Ken Holtzman.

"The man pitched a no-hitter and he didn't pitch it scared," said the A's ace left-hander. "He didn't pitch around anyone. He came right at you." Ken's remarks drew particular attention because he himself knew all about no-hitters. The masterful southpaw had pitched two himself while establishing himself as one of the top professional hurlers in the game.

Ken's twin no-hitters were thrown while he was with the Chicago Cubs in the National League; when he was traded to Oakland in the American League, he became a member of the most celebrated three-man rotation in baseball, a twenty-game winner, a three-time world champion and a World Series hero. But when he was still a college student at the University of Illinois, he wasn't at all certain that he would even go into baseball professionally.

The talent, of course, was always clearly present. As a high school star in St. Louis, Ken was selected the Most

Valuable Player on the state championship team. But being an unusually thoughtful athlete, he considered carefully before accepting a baseball offer.

"I knew if I played baseball, I'd be behind when I entered business," he said in an interview with Glenn Dickey in *Sport* magazine. "Say I played until I was thirty-one; I'd be ten years behind the guys I graduated college with. So, I had to be assured that I would get enough money to make it financially worthwhile for me."

Ken signed for an estimated $70,000 bonus from the Cubs after his junior year of college; he left school and started his baseball career in the minors, but after only a couple of months, he was quickly promoted to the Cub team, becoming a full-fledged major leaguer in 1965. After the season, he returned to the campus and obtained his degree, majoring in French.

In his brief stay with Chicago in 1965, Ken had not been involved in any official pitching decisions; but he became a regular starter in 1966 at the tender age of twenty. His manager with the Cubs was the fiery and controversial Leo Durocher, whose relationship with Holtzman started well enough but gradually disintegrated until, after several seasons, Ken asked to be traded.

But "Leo and Kenny had a good relationship in 1966," says Ferguson Jenkins, the Cub's ace right-hander in those years, in his own autobiography. Jenkins points out that the press was calling Holtzman another Sandy Koufax, "which was unfair to him. Like Koufax, Kenny was left-handed and Jewish, but at the time he was only twenty and in his first year.

"Kenny had a good live arm, a good fast ball and curve, and a remarkable change-up with which he had great success. Kenny had a good attitude toward the game, liked to pitch and liked to win. Durocher made a great deal of him, always praising him, always kidding around with him."

In his rookie year Holtzman won eleven games, but lost sixteen. He was hampered not only by a losing team but by a bad habit of tipping off his pitches by opening and closing his glove. But he worked hard at correcting this flaw, and in 1967 he chalked up a sensational 9-0 undefeated mark in a season that was curtailed by his obligations to National Guard service.

He struggled a bit more in 1968 with an 11-14 record, but hit his stride the next year with a distinguished 17-13 campaign. The 1969 season was a watershed year for Kenny: that was the year that he hurled his first no-hit game, and it was the season in which the Cubs blew a big lead in September and lost the pennant to the New York Mets. It was during the strain of this pennant race that Durocher alienated a great number of his players, Holtzman among them.

William Furlong, in an article for *Look* magazine aptly entitled "How Durocher Blew the Pennant," describes the unpleasant situation:

"Leo was not much admired, even within his own ball club, for the way he handled his pitchers last year. One of them, Ken Holtzman, he had much earlier begun to call out to in the clubhouse: 'Hey, Jew!' or 'C'mon, kike!' There was nothing malicious in this. It was Durocher's way . . . no different from Durocher calling Ron Santo 'wop,' or college-grad Don Kessinger 'dumb hillbilly.'

"But in the case of Holtzman, though, Durocher really started to lose touch with his player when these labels were paired with a rumor sweeping the clubhouse that Ken

lacked guts, that he didn't hang in there when the pressure
was on.

"Holtzman suspected he knew the reason. Whenever he
was in a tight game, and Leo stomped out to ask him if he
was tired, he'd answer with the truth. Of course he was
tired. You can't pitch six or seven strenuous innings of
major-league ball without getting tired. But he wasn't tired
to death. He did not need to be relieved. He found out that
this is not the way the game is played. Managers are used
to being lied to. If a pitcher admits he's tired, then he's too
tired to pitch anymore. The result was that in his first few
years with the Cubs, Holtzman found himself being
yanked fast and early.

"The solution was simple. Holtzman learned to lie. He
stopped admitting he was tired. Last year, he completed six
of his first ten starts and had a 10-1 record by early June.

"When Leo learned of this ploy, he threatened to fine
anybody $500 who lied to him about being tired. At that
point, the only thing that counted was that Durocher was
no longer in contact with his young pitcher. A world had
come between them. In the September crunch, Holtzman
won one game, lost five."

Jenkins, confirming the 1969 conflict, adds that "Leo
started calling Kenny's pitches from the bench. Kenny
resented this, feeling that this was the reason he became a
seven-inning pitcher.

"Kenny would pitch well for six or seven innings and
then would lose control of the game. Leo would call for a
couple of pitches that Kenny did not want to throw. Leo
then would take him out for a relief pitcher. Often we
would be ahead when Leo took Kenny out of the game,
but the relief pitchers would be hit hard and we would lose.

This increased Kenny's resentment, and I, too, thought that if Leo had left him in he might have won a few more games and increased his confidence . . . from 1969 on Leo was always picking on Kenny, who was on the defensive all the time."

But even though his manager made life difficult for him, Kenny was too professional a pitcher not to do his very best whenever he was on the mound; and on August 19, with a 13-7 record, Kenny fired a no-hitter against the Atlanta Braves at Chicago.

Holtzman had come close to the feat before, but had never quite made it all the way. As a rookie in 1966, he had faced the great Sandy Koufax at Chicago in what would be the Dodger immortal's last game against the Cubs; he retired after the 1966 season. In the match between the two best Jewish left-handers in history, the rookie sparkled even more brightly than the Hall of Famer; Kenny had a no-hitter through eight innings, and settled for a 2-1 victory over the Dodgers and Sandy. And earlier in the 1969 season, he had pitched seven perfect innings against St. Louis before yielding the first Cardinal hit in the eighth frame.

But on this August afternoon at Chicago, he set down the hard-hitting Braves without a single safety. Warming up before the game, Kenny had realized that he had little control of his curve and change-up, and decided to stick with his fastball. That turned out to be enough, as his teammates supported him with exemplary defense. Left-fielder Billy Williams leapt to pluck a drive just at the wall off the bat of the great Henry Aaron in the seventh, second sacker Glenn Beckert twice robbed Felipe Alou of potential hits, and shortstop Don Kessinger made a nifty play on a grounder by opposing pitcher Phil Niekro. Niekro himself pitched eight shutout innings and gave up only five hits — but one of them was a three-run home run to Ron Santo, and that was the ball game.

Interestingly, in the course of his 3-0 masterpiece Holtzman did not strike out a single batter, although he was averaging about six whiffs a game. At the time of the game, the Cubs were still in first place, fighting to stay ahead of New York; and although the Mets eventually passed them, Kenny's no-hitter provided an opportune boost to team morale. In the errorless contest, Holtzman allowed Atlanta only three walks.

In the 1970 season, Kenny again won seventeen games, and this time he only lost eleven. In one of his victories against the Giants, he had a 9-0 lead after two innings, and the final score was 15-0; but instead of letting up, as another pitcher might have, Kenny hurled with his customary professional concentration and had a no-hitter going until one man was out in the eighth inning.

Despite his successive seventeen-win seasons, Holtzman's disenchantment with his situation in Chicago increased, and in 1971 he won only nine games, disagreed openly with the carping Durocher and many of the local sportswriters, and expressed a desire to be traded somewhere else. But despite his unhappiness and the uncomfortable pressure to which he was subjected in this disappointing season, he was still able to spin out another no-hit masterpiece on June 3 against Cincinnati. At the time, Kenny entered the game with a poor 2-6 record and a miserable E.R.A. of 5.40.

As in his 1969 gem, Kenny noticed while warming up that his curve seemed unreliable. Again, he relied exclusively on his extremely effective fastball. He fanned six Reds, walked four and allowed no one a base hit, winning 1-0. The game's only run, in fact, was scored by Holtzman himself in the third. He reached first on an error by Tony Perez, moved to second on an infield out and was driven home when Beckert singled.

There were only two serious Cincinnati threats to break up the no-hitter, and both came in the seventh inning. Perez, never fast afoot, was barely thrown out on a slow roller to Beckert, and Johnny Bench almost managed to bunt for a hit; but at the last second, the ball spun foul. The Cincinnati fans, heckling Kenny about the no-hitter for much of the game in an effort to break his concentration, were cheering the southpaw by the ninth inning, when he put the finishing touches on his masterpiece by fanning Tommy Helms and Lee May to end the game.

After the season, Kenny's request to be traded was granted. "I had asked to be traded," he says, "but I didn't make any demands. I never asked to be traded to a contender. When John Holland (a Cub executive) called me and told me I'd been traded to Oakland, it didn't really dawn on me for a minute because I wasn't that familiar with teams in the other league. I just said, 'Fine, thank you,' and hung up. But then I got to thinking: the A's had to be a good club because they'd won their division the year before, and I'd have a chance to get into the World Series with them."

"That was the break of his career," says Glenn Dickey in his book, *The Great No-Hitters*. "Taking a cue from his no-hit games, Holtzman relied more and more on his fastball as he won nineteen, twenty-one and nineteen games in his first three seasons with the A's — and the A's won three straight World Series. Better the Cubs should have traded Durocher. After all, he couldn't throw a no-hitter."

Grateful as Kenny was to be coming to Oakland, he was no more pleased than were the A's in getting one of the game's best left-handed hurlers. "I've never seen a pitcher who throws as fast as he does who has his control," marveled Wes Stock, the Oakland pitching coach. "He's amazing. He gets the ball exactly where he wants it time after time. You keep waiting for him to miss, but he almost never does. He's like a machine."

"Holtzman's pitching seems almost effortless," says Dickey in *Sport*. "He has a definite rhythm and he believes pitching quickly keeps that rhythm intact. It is not uncommon for his games to finish in two hours."

"His control is what makes him effective," observed Kenny's new catcher, Oakland's Ray Fosse. "He's got good stuff, too, of course, but the main thing is he can get the ball where he wants it. Sometimes he doesn't have his control at the start of the game, but he'll keep working on it until he gets it. Some pitchers, when they're off at the start of the game, start fighting themselves, but he never does."

"Like Jim Hunter, Holtzman is a thinking man's pitcher, not a flame thrower," analyzes Tom Clark in *Champagne and Baloney,* a history of the champion Athletics. "His forte is not the velocity of his fastball but his ability to control it. Pitchers like these don't look for strikeouts; they *want* the hitter to put the bat on the ball, and hit it harmlessly on the ground or up in the air."

Holtzman himself explains that the change in ballparks helped his pitching enormously. He had averaged three walks a game with Chicago, but reduced that number to less than two with Oakland. "Wrigley Field is a hitter's park," he says of Chicago. "You always have the feeling that if you make a mistake, it's a home run. And even when the wind is blowing in, it's still a good park for hitters because it has a good hitting background and it's almost impossible to foul out because the stands are so close to the field. I'm a fastball pitcher, but I felt I had to use my curve a lot there and I couldn't control it as well.

"My fastball is my best pitch. I have much better control with it than with the curve. If I get in a tight spot, ninety-nine percent of the time I'm going to throw my fastball, my best pitch. I don't want to leave here knowing I got beat because I threw the batter my second best pitch.

"There's a lot to pitching," adds the studious southpaw. "I'll give you an example: concentration is the biggest part of pitching, but sometimes when I've had trouble, it's because I've been concentrating too hard on each pitch and not thinking in sequence. You have to think in terms of two or three pitches at a time. You put one pitch in one spot to set up the next two pitches. One time I might start a hitter out with an inside pitch to let him know I've got it. Another time I might throw a couple of pitches outside to set him up for an inside pitch. Different situations affect you."

The two Oakland pitching stars Kenny joined were Jim Hunter and Vida Blue; but Blue was involved in a grueling contract dispute with mercurial A's owner Charlie Finley in 1972, and Ken's strong left arm was sorely needed. Holtzman was the A's most effective pitcher all spring, compiling an impressive 19-11 record while leading his team to a match with the powerful Detroit Tigers in the American League playoffs. Although Kenny lost a playoff game to Detroit when Tiger hurler Joe Coleman set a playoff record by whiffing fourteen batters while pitching a 3-0 shutout, the A's won the series from the Tigers and advanced to the World Series against the National League champion Cincinnati Reds.

Kenny was excited to have achieved his boyhood dream of being in a World Series at last. "That whole week, I walked around like a little kid," said Holtzman, normally a detached, cerebral athlete. "I was just so happy to be there. Ernie Banks used to tell me you had to have a lot of kid in you to play this game, and I know now what he meant."

Kenny received another thrill when A's manager Dick Williams named him as his starting pitcher in the opening game of the series. "He and Hunter were our stoppers," Williams said. "They kept us from ever going into a long losing streak."

So Holtzman took the mound against the Reds and stymied Cincinnati's powerful batting order in registering a 3-2 victory. In the fourth game of the series, Kenny was again the starter, and again the Redleg batsmen were helpless when swinging at his canny serves; they spent the afternoon "struggling against the experienced and capable Oakland left-hander," Roger Angell remarks in his book *Five Seasons*. But although the Reds had still not scored on Ken and trailed 1-0 in the eighth, Williams relieved Holtzman with Blue, who gave up two quick runs. But Oakland rallied in the bottom of the ninth to come from behind to win, 3-2. The A's went on to take the series in seven games, and Kenny Holtzman was the ace southpaw of the new world champions.

In 1973, happy and established in Oakland, Ken enjoyed his finest season. For the first time in his career, he joined the magic circle of 20-game winners, registering a remarkable record of 21-13. In April, he was the team's most solid hurler. In May, he spun a four-hitter against the White Sox, then stopped an Oakland losing streak with a masterful one-hitter against the Yankees. In June and July, Holtzman and Hunter led the A's as the team racked up 29 wins in 43 games. By mid-July, both pitchers had 15 wins to their credit. On August 17, Kenny beat Milwaukee and put the A's into first place for good. The next week, he shut out the Yankees again, and put Oakland ahead by five games. In September, he whipped the Angels for his 20th victory.

Oakland met arch-rival Baltimore in the three-of-five playoff series. With the series tied at one game apiece, Williams sent Holtzman to the mound for the crucial third game, and Kenny responded with what Tom Clark characterizes as an "almost perfect" effort. Holtzman locked horns with Baltimore star Mike Cuellar in a billiant pitching duel that went eleven innings before the A's triumphed, 2-1. When Bert Campaneris homered to finally win the game, A's skipper Williams, with joyful gratitude, grabbed Holtzman and kissed him in the dugout!

Having disposed of Baltimore, the A's moved into the World Series for a second time, this time against the immensely popular New York Mets. Once more, Kenny was selected to start the opening game, and he again emerged as a winner. In the third, Holtzman came to bat and stunned Met pitcher Jon Matlack by slapping a 3-2 pitch into left field for a clean double. The distracted Mets then committed two straight errors that allowed first Holtzman and then Campaneris to score in the two-out rally. Those two unearned runs were the only ones the A's could get off

Matlack, but Holtzman made them stand up for a 2-1 A's win.

The Mets gallantly fought back, and the series was tied 3-3 as the two teams prepared for the final game that would determine the world champion. For this decisive effort, Oakland again called on their southpaw ace, and Kenny again came through. Once again, Holtzman faced Matlack in the third inning and cracked a double; Campaneris homered on the very next pitch, and the A's went on to win the game and the series on Holtzman's 5-2 victory. Oakland thus became the first team to win consecutive world championships since the mighty Yankees of 1961-62. What made Kenny's slugging feats even more astonishing was that, because of the American League's designated hitter rule, he had come to bat only once during the entire 1973 season (he drew a walk in that appearance).

In the 1974 season, Holtzman once more helped lead Oakland to a pennant as he compiled a 19-17 record. In what had become an annual event, the A's again faced Baltimore in the playoffs, and again Oakland emerged trimphant, thanks in no small measure to Holtzman's contribution. After the Orioles had whipped Hunter in the opening game, Kenny stepped in and beat Baltimore in the second game, yielding only five harmless hits in the course of a 5-0 shutout. For the second consecutive year, the A's fought past the Orioles to enter the World Series.

This time, their opponents were the young, impressive Los Angeles Dodgers. The A's had a new manager, Alvin Dark, but an old strategy — start Holtzman in the opening game. For the third consecutive year, each time facing a different team, Kenny justified this confidence, pitching his team to a 3-2 win. As in the previous fall classic, Kenny starred at the plate as well as on the mound. He had never gone to the plate at all during the American League season, but when he batted for the first time this year he smashed another two-bagger to left, his third double in his last four series games. The Dodger pitcher, Messersmith, was as unnerved as Matlack had been, and in short order threw a wild pitch that advanced Ken to third, from where he scored on a lovely suicide squeeze bunt by Campaneris.

In the fourth game of the series, the A's took a commanding 3-1 lead in games when Holtzman hurled them to a decisive 5-2 whipping of the dazed Dodgers. Once again, Kenny contributed not only sparkling clutch pitching, but also what Angell characterized as "another personal editorial on the subject of the designated hitter — this time, a home run." The round-tripper was the third of Ken's entire career. The demolished Dodgers were dismantled in the fifth and final game, and the Oakland Athletics had established themselves as one of the greatest teams in baseball history with their amazing accomplishment of three consecutive world championships.

But while no other team could seem to crack the skills of the colorful, brawling A's, with their mustaches, long locks and marvelous play on the field, their owner could. Charlie Finley was so universally unpopular among his employees that dislike of their outspoken boss was one of the ties that bound the players together in common cause. Williams had already left in a dispute with Finley, and after the 1974 campaign Hunter had left Oakland and joined the Yankees. Many, if not most, of the world champions were threatening to quit, play out their options, or demand trades. Along with all his fellows, Holtzman had his share of hostilities with Finley, but he continued to pitch with exemplary professionalism.

During the troubled 1975 season, Kenny was used at irregular intervals and received little support; but he still managed to pitch excellently and stay a winning pitcher. On June 8 in Oakland, he faced the Tigers on a pretty California afternoon, and pitched one of the finest games of his career. For eight innings, he mowed down the overmatched Detroit hitters. No one got a hit, and only one Tiger had even reached base on a walk — and he had been instantly eliminated on a double play. As the Oakland spectators watched anxiously in their seats, Kenny took a 4-0 lead into the ninth and final inning, needing only three more outs for a no-hitter. Only eighteen men in major league history, including Holtzman himself, have ever pitched two no-hitters, and only Sandy Koufax and Nolan Ryan (with four and five) have claimed more than two. The fans rooted fervently for the Oakland lefty to retire the next three Tiger batters.

Holtzman set down the first batter, and then retired the second as well. Needing only one final out to achieve his place in the record book, Kenny faced light-hitting Tom Veryzer, a shortstop batting only .230. With concentrated cunning, Kenny induced Veryzer to lift a fly ball to center field. A sense of triumph swept over the stands for a moment as they sensed a routine out that would end the glorious pitching show. But to the horror of the onlookers, Oakland center fielder Bill North misjudged the ball, then, realizing his mistake, tried desperately to recover and lost his footing. Finally, he made a futile dive for the ball as it bounced over his head onto the warning track. North finally caught up with it and threw it to second base. He never

touched the ball until after it had fallen, so it was scored as
a base hit. In despair, North flung his glove into the air,
walked to the centerfield fence and slammed it angrily with
his clenched fist. Holtzman stared at the next Tiger batter
for a moment, then struck him out on three pitches to end
the game.

"Kenny's near classic doesn't exactly bring about a
clubhouse party," remarks Clark dryly in his account of
that day. "In fact, an extra-inning World Series loss
couldn't leave a team more dejected-looking than the A's
appear after this victory. Holtzman, author of two earlier
no-hitters, contains his disappointment admirably and tells
reporters with typical grace and class that it was only
'justice' that Veryzer's ball had dropped in, calling attention to several fine plays made behind him earlier. But
among his teammates there's some grumbling about the
one that got away. Gene Tenace says bluntly that Veryzer's
hit 'looked catchable.' Around the room the other players
dress quietly, in tacit agreement. Told that broadcaster
Monte Moore had said he'd 'drifted in on the ball' before it
went over his head, Billy North snaps, 'Let *him* play center
if he thinks he's so good.' The ball sailed away from him at
the last minute, the speedy little center fielder explains in
his diffident basso. 'I thought I had it, but the wind just
carried it away. I was the most disappointed person in the
park.' "

It's doubtful if North could have been any more disappointed than the man on the mound, but Kenny continued
to pitch as professionally and expertly as ever. In June, he
sparked an eight game winning streak by whipping the
Twins; on July 4, a full house in Oakland watched him
blank the Angels. Even with the weakened Oakland team

clawing their way to another division title, Kenny still managed to turn in a formidable 18-14 record.

Facing the talented and exciting Boston Red Sox in the playoffs, Dark announced that, with the absence of Hunter, Holtzman would be his starting pitcher in the opening game. "Kenny has a history of getting up for the big ballgames," Dark explained. "The bigger it is, the better he pitches."

But the unhappy A's no longer played like three-time champions, and their horrendous play behind Holtzman's brave pitching made it clear that these were not the Oakland A's who would always find a way to win. Angell describes the first game vividly:

"In the bottom of the very first inning, Yastrzemski singled off Ken Holtzman, and then Carlton Fisk hit a hopper down the third-base line that was butchered by Sal Bando and further mutilated by Claudell Washington, in left. Lynn then hit an undemanding ground ball to second baseman Phil Garner, who muffed it. Two runs were in, and in the seventh the Sox added five more, with help from Oakland center fielder Bill North, who dropped a fly, and Washington, who somehow played Lynn's fly to the base of the wall into a double."

Boston whipped the A's in the second game as well, and Oakland was down to the last gasp. With no Hunter around to complement Holtzman — Kenny called Catfish "our invincibility shield," but Hunter was a Yankee now — the A's turned desperately to Holtzman. Finley and Dark apparently felt that even a tired Holtzman pitching on only two days' rest was a better gamble than any of their well-rested hurlers who lacked Kenny's proven skill and pitching savvy.

"Holtzman himself doesn't find out about it until he strolls into the clubhouse at the Coliseum for Monday's non-workout, which is washed out by a rainstorm that restricts the athletes to card games and interviews," Clark writes in his account. "Told that he'll be the finger-in-the-dike starter, Kenny acts about as excited as the 2000-year-old-Man. He shrugs, says he's 'tired of the season' ('It's been going a long time'), promises offhand to do his best despite the lack of rest ('I don't care, I pitch when they tell me to'), then jumps into the nearest bridge game. Around the room his down-at-the-mouth teammates mumble half-hearted attestations of confidence, sounding as rote and hollow as a crew of cheerleaders practicing their act in an undertaker's parlor. Could *this* really be the end of the line, a T.S. Eliot ending in Oakland, without so much as a minor beef, a single squawk out of the clubhouse of the once-angry A's?"

In any case, it was the end of the Oakland dynasty. Once again, a fine, courageous effort by Kenny was undone by incompetent play by his fielders. The A's barely survived a bad relay throw and a fly ball lost in the sun, both in the very first inning; but the reprieve was brief. Kenny pitched valiantly for three innings, taming the potent Boston bats; but in the fourth, the Oakland defense collapsed completely. After Holtzman had retired two of the Red Sox, Lynn lined a ball at Washington which dropped right out of the left-fielder's glove. When Claudell had difficulty picking up the ball, Lynn hustled to second base. The next batter singled to right field, where Reggie Jackson, intending to make the play at home, slipped instead and ended up sitting on the grass while Lynn raced home with the game's first run.

The next inning "is Holtzman's sad finale," Clark
writes. "Rick Burleson starts it off by doubling past the immobile form of Bando, who's playing third in this series
with all the range of the Rock of Gibraltar; two more hits
and a run later, Kenny comes out, deserving the respectful
ovation he gets. He sits on the bench for a minute or so,
hanging his head, then gets up and walks back toward the
clubhouse runway. No one talks to him as he goes."

The bickering A's were thoroughly broken up over the
next season. Hunter and Dick Green had already left; in
short order Reggie Jackson, Bando, Tenace, Rollie
Fingers, Campaneris, Rudi and Ken himself had escaped
Finley's clutches. Holtzman was glad to get away from the
abrasive Oakland owner. "You can't imagine how that
man can demean you in negotiations," he told Maury Allen of the *New York Post*. Finley traded Kenny and
Jackson to the Orioles before the 1976 season; both were
playing out their options, refusing to sign a contract.
Neither signed with Baltimore that year, either. On June
14, Baltimore traded Ken to Kansas City, but the trade
was called off when the Royals were unable to agree with
Ken about a contract; they were unwilling to concede him
the courtesies of a no-trade clause and some deferred pay-
ments. So Ken returned to Baltimore, but not for long. The
ambitious Yankees, anxious for some quality left-handed
pitching, were willing to offer Kenny a five-year contract
worth somewhere around a million dollars. An involved
ten-player deal was arranged, and Holtzman became a
Yankee, ironically joining Hunter and Jackson as new
teammates.

Despite the enormous difficulties of concentrating on
pitching while he was shuffled back and forth between four

ball clubs, Kenny's consummate professionalism was evident in his ability to fashion a winning record in 1976, even with all the pressures and distractions. He ended the season with a 14-11 won-lost ledger.

But for reasons known only to himself, Yankee manager Billy Martin chose to overlook Holtzman's tremendous record and used him sparingly, and not at all in postseason play. Kenny was a proven winner of big games, a top performer of enormous experience, but the temperamental Martin — as mercurial as the other bosses whom Kenny kept encountering, Durocher or Finley or Yankee owner George Steinbrenner — did not call upon him for an appearance in either the playoffs or the World Series. The Yanks barely squeaked by Kansas City in the fifth playoff game, and then were unceremoniously swept by Cincinnati in four games in the series.

Holtzman, with characteristic tact and class, defended the manager who seemed to be slighting him. "I don't think I'm owed any explanation," he told the *New York Times.* "We have very competent pitchers. Just because I've pitched well in postseason games before doesn't have anything to do with what's happening now. I'm not disappointed . . . if he wants me in the bull pen, I'll do it. I told Billy when I came here in June from the Orioles that if he wants me in the bull pen, I'll do it. If he says you'll never pitch or if he says you'll pitch every day, I'll do either.

"As long as we win, that's the most important thing. That's the professional attitude and I take no other attitude. Never do I forget that I'm a professional only. I respect Billy's baseball knowledge. He put a competent pitcher out there. Don't try to make anything more out of it than that."

Although Cincinnati's massacre of the Yankees in the 1976 World Series seemed to highlight the Yanks' need for a pitcher of Holtzman's caliber, Martin continued not to use him in the 1977 season, even after three of his top pitchers — Hunter, Don Gullet and Ed Figueroa — incurred injuries. In fact, in early August Holtzman heard the news that Martin planned to pitch him against a Syracuse farm club in an exhibition game; instead of raging or sulking, Kenny laughed uproariously at the absurdity of the situation.

"He has not lost his sense of humor — of the absurd," wrote Murray Chass admiringly in the *Times.* "Ken Holtzman does not cry. He does not complain. He has learned, he explains, to control his emotions." This self-discipline led some to assume that Holtzman was indifferent to events as long as the checks kept coming — that he was a kind of baseball mercenary who doesn't care what he does so long as he is paid well. But as Chass discovered, "the image becomes distorted, shattered, when one hears what Holtzman really is saying."

"I feel I should be trying to earn the money," confided the frustrated left-hander. "I don't think any professional athlete who has played at this level would say he'd rather sit down and get paid. Certainly I want to play. How discouraging is it to come to the ball park and not play? I've reconciled myself to it. I don't run around looking for someone to complain to."

Chass added that "if anyone has reason to complain in this Yankee season of complaints, it is Holtzman. But he has uttered not one complaint publicly." Allen, discussing the same problem in the *Post,* characterized Kenny as "a young man, thirty years old, healthy, a professional athlete of enormous skills, a bright man, witty, in total control of his life, his emotions and a great part of the future."

When he finally did confide his feelings to Chass in August, Kenny observed that both the Baltimore and New York front offices had been less than honest with him, as both had assured him they wanted him on their teams so that he would pitch regularly for many seasons to come. The southpaw observed that Steinbrenner was "a fool" to give him so much money and not give him a chance to earn it. After all, it had been Steinbrenner who suggested the long-term contract so that his investment would be secure.

"I was excited about playing for the Yankees," Kenny reflected sadly. "New York was a good place to play, I had heard that Billy was a good manager to play for, a winning manager, and it was a chance to get back to the World Series. I didn't come to the Yankees as a stepping stone to going somewhere else. I came with the intention of finishing my career with the Yankees."

With infallible logic, Kenny suggested to the Yankees that they trade him to Milwaukee, an area he likes, so that they would at least be able to get a player in return who would help them more than he would sitting on the bench. When no trade was made during the 1977 season, despite wide expectations that one would be arranged, Kenny pointed out a glaring contradiction in the position of Yankee management.

"They're saying that my trade value is high enough that they could turn down trades for me," he noted, "but I don't have any value to the Yankees. People ask me why I'm not pitching. I have to come up with an answer and I can't."

Martin continued to use Holtzman very rarely, and Ken

asked, more than once, to be traded to another team. Finally, on June 10 of the 1978 season, Ken was sent to the Chicago Cubs, the very team with which he had started his career. The Cubs were in the midst of a pennant race, and desperately needed some capable, experienced left-handed pitching.

Ken himself was ecstatic. "I'm going to the park early tomorrow," he announced upon learning of the trade.

"I'm not bitter at anybody," he said later, "I'm not pretending I wasn't unhappy in New York. Of course, I was unhappy. Now, I'm happy to be back home." He noted that he hadn't pitched regularly in a year and a half, and expected that it would take a little while to work back into the groove. But he looked forward enthusiastically to making a contribution, and a chance once again to hone and display the skills which had given him such a marvelous career.

He was particularly pleased to be able to live near his family in Illinois. "Family, home and religion are very important to Holtzman," pointed out George Vass in *The Jewish Post.*

"I believe in Jewish values and my religion," Kenny observed. "We do keep kosher at home, and I try to as much as I can on the road during the baseball season, though sometimes it's difficult. When it's feasible, I order kosher food in advance on the airline trips. Of course, that has its advantages, because the kosher menu is much better food than the usual airline fare."

So Kenny came back home to his original club. At the age of thirty-two, he was starting a new phase of a career which had already established him as one of the premier southpaws of his era: three-time world champion, great clutch hurler, and two no-hitters to his credit. His career ended in less than two years. Yet it should be remembered that Kenny Holtzman was an intelligent, articulate athlete and a master of the pitcher's craft as well as a consummate professional.

STEVE STONE ON THE MOUND

Steve Stone
To Stardom from Obscurity

When the 1980 baseball season began, Steve Stone was just another journeyman right-handed pitcher who, in a decade of playing, had managed to hang on in the major leagues.

He was now thirty-three and had come back from an arm injury. He had played for the San Francisco Giants, the Chicago White Sox, the Chicago Cubs, then back again with the White Sox, and then finally he had signed with the Baltimore Orioles as a free agent.

His nine-year major league record was unexceptional. In fact, he had lost more games than he had won (seventy-eight wins to seventy-nine losses), and he did not possess that good live fast ball which made a pitcher a glamorous figure in the national game. Yes, Stone did have a major league curve ball. That, and pretty good control, had kept him in the sport. But he was nothing to write home about. He seemed to be just another major league pitcher lucky to have a contract.

So what happened? In 1980, he became the biggest winner in the game, with twenty-five victories. He kept the Orioles in the American League pennant race, the steadiest pitcher of an excellent staff. From May 9 onwards, he was virtually unbeatable; he put together a fourteen-game winning streak that lasted until the final day of July. He finished the season with a twenty-five and seven record and a 3.23 earned-run average. Early in November, he was named the pitcher of the year in the American League by the *Sporting News* (Steve Carlton was the winner in the National League). A few days later, he was awarded the highest accolade given a big league pitcher: The Cy Young Award as the season's best hurler (in the American League. Again, Carlton won National League honors).

How did it happen?

In 1979, Stone was a struggling pitcher. The Orioles won the American League pennant but his contribution was minor. He won eleven and lost seven, but he gave some evidence of improvement when he won his last five decisions.

In talking to Ken Nigro of the *Sporting News* about the 1979 season, Stone confessed, "I was our only weakness. Everybody else was having a renaissance year. Every time I picked up a newspaper, I read that I should be banished to the bullpen. There were some unpleasant noises whenever my name was announced. The fans booed the hell out of me and that was not a pleasant experience. I wasn't pleased with what was going on." He added, "I realized I had to realign my thinking." He did. Through August 10, 1980, he had won twenty-three of twenty-seven decisions since the 1979 All-Star break, and people began to think his season was something of an accident.

Stone didn't think so, and in many interviews to reporters in newspapers and magazines, he spelled out his own ideas. He told Nigro, "Remember, this is the first time I haven't been with a fifth-place club. Before now, every club I've been on has been poor defensively or couldn't hit or couldn't run the bases. I'll bet the collective record of the clubs I was on was under .500, possibly .400. It's difficult to have a .600 winning percentage on a team like that. Coming over to Baltimore was an important change for me."

A pitcher needs confidence to win. This statement cannot be overemphasized. And Steve Stone, like any pitcher, had to make a believer of himself before he could convince major league hitters. "I used to try not to lose before," he told Henry Hecht of the *New York Post* before taking the mound and starring in the 1980 All-Star game in Los Angeles. "Now, when I go out, I go out to win every time, and I'm certain I am. I try to envision myself literally walking off the mound a winner. I allow no negatives in my thinking. When certain ones start creeping in, I erase them and make it like a blank blackboard waiting to be filled in with things like, 'The team is going to play well, is going to score some runs, I'm going to throw strikes, I'm going to win.' "

At the age of thirty-three, Steve Stone had finally achieved superstar status, gaining recognition as the league's best pitcher; but the journey to that lofty plateau had not been easy. Like so many other young ballplayers who try to make it in the major leagues, Steve had starred in sports when he was growing up. In his native Cleveland, he won several tennis championships and was a proficient golfer. Attending Kent State University, he starred on the bowling and volleyball teams, and was no mean hand with a pool cue. His prize "victim" was the late Thurman Munson, his catcher at Kent State, later to be the All-Star receiver for the New York Yankees. "Thurman fancied himself a pool shark," Stone confided to Ray Kennedy of *Sports Illustrated,* "and I was careful never to disillusion him — especially when I was in the process of beating him twenty-five matches in a row."

As a college pitcher, Steve was outstanding. He was selected to the All Mid-American conference team, and was named team captain as a junior. By the time he graduated in 1970 — with a teaching degree in history and government — he had been signed to a contract by the San Francisco Giants, who assigned him to their Fresno farm club. At Fresno, when he wasn't pitching, Steve took advantage of his environment with the lively curiosity about the non-baseball world that has always distinguished him from many of his peers. He quite literally labored in the vineyards.

"All the wineries in the area had tasting rooms," he explained to Ray Kennedy, "and on the days we weren't pitching, another pitcher, Bill Frost, and I would sip our way across the Napa Valley, taking notes and learning all we could about where wine came from." Stone became a recognized expert on wine, and part-owner of no fewer than nine restaurants.

After two minor-league campaigns, Stone joined the Giants for spring training in 1971 — and as an eager rookie, he wasted no time trying to be noticed. His first assignment was to pitch batting practice. The first man to step into the batter's box was the legendary Hall-of-Famer Willie Mays. A young, hard-throwing fireballer in those days — his fastball had been timed at an overpowering ninety-five miles per hour, and he had averaged better than a strikeout per inning in the minors; he struck out one hundred eighty-four batters in one hundred sixty-seven innings in Fresno in 1969 — Stone figured "that with twenty-two other pitchers around, I had to impress the organiza-

tion right away. So I started blowing the ball in. Mays missed a few, fouled some off and then said to the catcher, 'Who *is* this guy? Tell him to just throw the ball in.' "
Stone ignored the advice. "Willie stayed in for one more pitch — thrown right under his chin — then threw down his bat and never took batting practice against me again that spring."

Steve succeeded in being noticed, and he made the club. But from the very beginning of his big-league career, the articulate, witty Jewish hurler had to contend with outmoded but prevalent baseball stereotypes. Speaking of his struggle against some of the doggedly unimaginative minds that are not uncommon in professional baseball, Stone told Steve Jacobson of *Inside Sports:* "Charlie Fox [manager of the Giants in 1971] felt the only way a ballplayer could perform was to chew tobacco, wear a sloppy uniform and, as he put it, not be afraid to get a bloody nose, and eat, drink and sleep baseball. I never thought a bloody nose was all that comfortable, and tobacco upsets my stomach. I like to eat — but not baseball — and I never thought sleeping with the game would be all that enjoyable. I think he thought reading hurt your eyes.

"But the best was Johnny Sain [White Sox pitching coach when Stone was with Chicago]. He told me he never met a ballplayer who smoked a pipe who was aggressive enough to be successful. He also thought the fact that I was close to my parents was a liability."

Stone was also unfairly, and stupidly, penalized for not being more physically imposing than he was. "I'm a shade under five-foot ten, and I weigh one hundred seventy-five pounds. Every manager who ever looked at me said, 'Well, maybe he could start ten or twelve times, but he's not durable enough to pitch a whole season for me,' " Steve told Murray Chass of the *New York Times*. "Charlie Fox started that in San Francisco. He said, 'I don't think he can start a whole year for me,' and I didn't. There are a whole lot of people out there telling you you can't do things. They put restrictions on you. I was starting to believe I couldn't be a starting pitcher for a whole year. The worst thing that can happen is for you to start believing the tags they put on you."

To compound his problems, Steve developed a sore arm, and was traded to the Chicago White Sox in 1972. The following season, he was sent uptown to the Chicago Cubs, where he struggled to win games for a poor team. Although he had lost some of the smoke from his youthful fastball, Steve nonetheless had learned the craft of pitching well enough to go 12-8 for the hapless Cubs in 1975, when he was one of only two pitchers on the staff with an earned run average of less than four runs per game. The Cubs suggested that he accept a cut in his salary. Steve understandably refused, and decided to play out his option and become a free agent. But during the 1976 season, he suffered a torn rotator cuff in his pitching shoulder — a dreaded injury that has almost invariably ended the careers of even the most brilliant pitchers.

Now Stone faced a crucial dilemma. Despite heavy pressure from the team's management, Steve resolutely refused to undergo an operation, or even to take pain-killing drugs that might permanently damage his arm. He bluntly refused to let the team doctor stick cortisone shots into his arm.

"I think I was the first person ever to reject any course of treatment suggested by a team doctor," the independent-minded pitcher said to Jacobson of *Inside Sports.* "I told him I wanted to rehabilitate my career on my own. He said, 'If you don't start pitching, you don't have any career.' " But Stone stuck to his guns. "I had no idea what was right, how to solve the problem," he admitted to Chass. "I just had an idea of what was wrong — and that was cortisone shots and surgery."

Determined to do it his way, Steve found a kinesiologist at the University of Illinois who put him on a special program that involved cryotherapy — where the arm is frozen — and then subsequent exercises which ultimately involved lifting weights. The theory was that the body's effort to get the frozen area back to normal temperature would double the blood flow — which would, in turn, help heal the tear; the exercises would then strengthen the area. The treatment worked, and by the end of the season, Steve was pitching effectively enough to have his rights in the free-agent draft selected by five teams. He signed with his former team, the White Sox, now run by maverick owner Bill Veeck. "Bill Veeck wagered sixty thousand dollars that my arm would hold on," remarked Stone. "I owe that man a tremendous debt." Roland Hemond, Chicago's Vice-President of player personnel, recalls finalizing the deal with Stone over lunch in Chicago's elegant Pump Room Restaurant where Steve, a part-owner, was filling in that day as manager. Hemond observed that it was the first time he had ever signed a player in a tuxedo, and he picked up the check as "a sort of bonus to Steve."

Steve richly rewarded Veeck's faith in him by becoming a bulwark of Chicago's pitching staff, winning fifteen games — the most he had ever tallied in a season — and then signing another one-year contract, this time for one hundred twenty-five thousand dollars. "I owed Bill that year," said Steve loyally. "But then, we were even." Stone added another twelve wins in 1978. Then, with a number of young, promising pitchers looming on the White Sox scene for 1979, Veeck was reluctant to give Steve more than another one-year contract; so, by mutual agreement, Steve became the first player in baseball history to enter baseball's re-entry draft for free agents twice. Again, five teams bid for negotiating rights to the right-hander. Still cherishing every big-leaguer's dream of playing in a World Series, Steve chose Baltimore, a perennial pennant contender. The Orioles signed him to a four-year contract for a then-handsome sum of seven hundred sixty thousand dollars — not bad for a journeyman hurler with a losing lifetime record who had only won as many as fifteen games once.

"I also felt," Steve later said to a reporter, "naively, as it turned out, that I could come here and secure a spot in the four-man rotation. Once again I was proven wrong. Earl [Weaver, the manager] sat me down at the beginning and said there would be no competition. He had a four-man rotation, and I would be the fifth."

Used only as a spot starter, Steve struggled in the first half of 1979. By the All-Star break, his statistics were unimpressive: six victories, seven defeats, and an earned run average of 4.40.

"His performance wasn't what we expected it to be," conceded Earl Weaver, the Baltimore manager. "We got him as a veteran pitcher who could serve as insurance and who could be spotted. I was disappointed that he thought he couldn't do it."

"I was pitching irregularly, and he'd take me out in the

third inning losing two to nothing," Stone pointed out. "A breaking ball pitcher needs regular work. I felt that wasn't helping my rhythm."

So Steve took a long, hard look at himself and the situation, and sought support wherever he could find it. He studied and listened to some of the brilliant pitchers on Baltimore's pitching staff: Cy Young winners Jim Palmer and Mike Flanagan, and clever southpaw Scott McGregor. He adopted specific routines when he won: playing the same tape on the way to the ballpark, eating the same meals at the same restaurants. He kept a lucky toy elephant inside his locker. He consulted a psychic. He meditated, and concentrated on positive thinking.

"No one who has played this game has ever said it was anything less than eighty percent mental," he observed; and in an effort to improve his approach to the game, he read the autobiography of his boyhood idol, Sandy Koufax, the Jewish left-hander who had pitched his way into the Hall of Fame. Steve read the book five times — and he changed his uniform number from twenty-one to Koufax' old number, thirty-two. "I admire Sandy Koufax for the way he conducted himself," said Stone of his idol. "Everything I have ever read or heard about him has shown me that the man has class. He always has conducted himself with dignity and I want to emulate him. I've said it before — and I know this will come back to haunt me, too — but I would have liked Sandy Koufax if he had been an Arab."

There were physical adjustments that helped, too. After the Oriole infielders had grumbled to pitching coach Ray Miller about their difficulty in maintaining concentration behind Steve because he took so long between pitches, Miller urged Stone to speed up his delivery.

"After one game in California, we decided that something had to be said," Stone's teammate, third baseman Doug DeCinces recalled. "I think it was the fourth inning, and it was two hours into the game. It's tough to play behind pitchers when they take five minutes between pitches... Since he picked up his pace," DeCinces added, "it's great to play behind him."

In adjusting his pace, Stone reflected thoughtfully to Chass, "Perhaps when you take a long time between pitches, psychologically you're not confident about your pitches."

Miller also made another major suggestion. Stone's best pitch, his "money" pitch, was his curveball. But he also threw a fastball, a slider and a forkball. The trouble, as Miller saw it, was that Steve tried to throw them all early in the game. The coach advised Steve to concentrate on only two pitches early, then go to the others later in the game if he needed them to further confuse the hitters. So Steve relied primarily on what he calls a "very good major league curveball." When the curve's not working, he says, pitching "is like the Allied forces going out to face the Germans and finding they left their ammunition at home." He also utilized "a fastball I'd call just a touch above average major league. An above-average major league slider. And a well-above-average major league head."

Oddly, in contrast to the usual result, his fastball actually *gained* velocity after his recovery from his injury. What apparently happened is that after building up the shoulder muscles by lifting weights, he discovered that his muscles had added more bulk than he needed to pitch most effectively. So he stopped lifting the weights, with the result that the newly strengthened shoulder muscles became more limber — and his fastball picked up about five miles an hour, a substantial difference on the major-league level.*

Perhaps as important as any other factor was Steve's maturity as a person. He now had confidence in his ability and only awaited an opportunity to prove himself, but he kept everything in proportion. He is a man, as reporter Murray Chass put it, "who understands himself, who has placed his life in perspective. He can laugh at himself, can poke fun at where he has come from in his baseball career — even at where he could conceivably go. He has endured too many setbacks in that career to allow himself to lose sight of who he is."

"I've always been a person to whom the game was not a life-or-death situation, even when it was the sole means of my support. I always felt that if I lost, I lost, and I'd get them next time. I didn't throw things around the locker room. When I was eight and eight, I was happy, and I'm happy now," explained Steve after emerging as the league's premier pitcher.

With a revamped delivery, a faster fastball, a mature perspective, and a strong new confidence in himself and his ability, Steve waited for a chance to pitch regularly. After the 1979 All-Star break, he got that opportunity. Injuries struck the Baltimore staff. McGregor hurt his elbow, Palmer his back, Dennis Martinez his shoulder, and Flanagan suffered through a slump. With very little choice, Weaver made his six and seven right-hander a regular

---

*"He was the only pitcher I have ever seen," remarked Oriole skipper Weaver, "whose fastball gained a foot over the winter."

starter. Steve responded to the challenge by going undefeated for the rest of the season. He won five and lost
none, with an E.R.A. of 2.94. He was particularly dazzling
in Baltimore: his record at home, for the season, was eight
wins to only one loss, with an unbelievable E.R.A. of 1.97.
What's more, in three additional home games, Steve went
nine or more innings, for no decision, in games which the
Orioles eventually won.

Still, despite his late-season flourish, skepticism persisted. After all, his season record for 1979 was only eleven
victories and seven losses, and he was not yet regarded as a
leading pitcher on the club, let alone in the league at large.
The Orioles reached the World Series that year, but though
Steve had carried the club the second half of the season, he
was the forgotten man when the Series got under way, ap-
pearing for only two innings in just one game. "Sixty million people watched the World Series — and I was one of
them," was his dry observation.

When word got out that the contract Steve had signed
with Baltimore included a bonus provision of ten thousand
dollars should he win the Cy Young Award in any given
season, the reaction around major league clubhouses was
predictable amusement. Steve Stone? The Cy Young
Award? You must be kidding. The guy's seventy-eight-
seventy-nine lifetime, and he's never won more than fifteen
games in a season.

Stone himself chuckled when he recalled the clause. "I
think it was something my agent just threw in there," he
has said. "I don't think he thought it was a serious
proposal. I didn't. A bonus for a winning season would
have made more sense. It was like an insurance salesman
telling you, 'We'll give you fifty thousand dollars if an

elephant falls on you,' because he knows darn well an elephant isn't going to fall on you."

It wasn't long before the laughter stopped. On June 16 of the 1980 season, Steve had a three and three won-lost record, with an E.R.A. hovering around four runs a game. That night, he beat Cleveland 4-1, yielding only six hits, and shutting the Indians out until the ninth inning. His record rose to four and three. Between then and the All-Star game on July 8, he won eight more games without a loss.

When the All-Star game was about to commence in Los Angeles on July 9, Steve was the possessor of a gaudy twelve and three record. The manager of the American League squad — none other than Earl Weaver — named as his team's starting pitcher the man who had established himself as the league's best hurler that year — Steve Stone.

Musing over this meteoric rise, Henry Hecht of *The New York Post* reflected before the game: "Consider this: Stone started the year seventy-eight-seventy-nine lifetime with a 4.06 E.R.A. He was just another pitcher . . . He was known for being Jewish, for writing poetry, for being a delightful guy and a fun interview, for being involved in the restaurant business and for having an excellent curveball. He was not known for his won-lost record."

But he was now — and in the clash between the best players in professional baseball, Steve more than justified his manager's confidence. He did what no pitcher had managed to accomplish for fourteen years: he pitched three perfect innings, retiring every batting star he faced, as he turned in what *The New York Times* emphatically characterized as "the most outstanding performance of the game."

Taking the mound for the American Leaguers in the bottom of the first inning, Steve retired the Dodgers' Davey Lopes on a grounder to third baseman Graig Nettles of the Yankees. He then got the Dodgers' dangerous outfielder Reggie Smith to fly out to Red Sox centerfielder Fred Lynn, after which Steve faced powerful slugger Dave Parker of the Pittsburgh Pirates — and struck him out.

In the second inning, Steve pitched to perennial All-Star Steve Garvey of the Dodgers, and induced Garvey to foul out. The legendary Cincinnati star, Johnny Bench, was Stone's next victim, as the slugging catcher grounded out harmlessly. Dave Kingman, a prolific home-run hitter, was Stone's next challenge — and strike three sent Kingman back to the dugout.

When Stone took the mound in the third inning, his American League teammates had not managed to scratch out a single run in his support; but then, their National League counterparts had not even managed a baserunner against the Orioles' ace right-hander. Steve kept the amazing streak intact. The Cardinals' Ken Reitz grounded out, the Dodgers' Bill Russell flied out, and — ending with a flourish for the third consecutive inning — Stone fanned his final National League batter, hometown hurler Bob Welch.

Though the Nationals eventually won the game, 4-2, Steve's flawless pitching was the glowing highlight of the game. Not since 1966, when Denny McLain managed the feat, had any pitcher worked three perfect innings in an All-Star contest. Even more amazing, Steve had required only twenty-eight pitches to retire all nine batsmen.

He reacted to his bravura performance with characteristically deadpan humor. "I was always very

tough in All-Star games," he remarked after his initial appearance in the major league classic. "In 1965 I pitched in
the Ohio high school All-Star game, and I won that."

A bit more analytically, he then observed: "Being
primarily a breaking-ball pitcher, the National League
guys were looking for the curveball. But when I went out to
the mound, I didn't have a good curveball so I threw a lot
of fastballs." In other words, Stone had set down nine in a
row of the best the National League had to offer — and he
had done it all without effective use of his best pitch. It was
a stunning achievement, as he himself conceded. "I'll sit
back and perhaps tomorrow or the next day, it will hit me
as to what I've done."

"I couldn't look at this lineup as a group," he remarked
of his accomplishment. "I had to face each one as a single
entity. As a group, it would have seemed too big a task but
one by one, I was able to handle nine guys." Stone, before
the game, had acknowledged that "My ultimate fantasy
was to start an All-Star game, but I knew it was all a pipe-
dream — now that I'm here, it's a great, great thrill." He
not only started such a game, but starred in it as well!

The rest of the season continued as a series of triumphs
for the now-masterful right-hander. On July 16, Stone
retired the first eight batters he faced as he beat Milwaukee
for his twelfth straight win and improved his record to
fourteen and three. By the time he faced the archrival
Yankees on August 9, he was the major leagues' win-
ningest pitcher with an astonishing seventeen and four
record. After that night's contest, it was eighteen and four,
and Baltimore had chopped to three and a half games a
Yankee lead in the standings that had once swollen as high
as eleven games. In the game, Stone was touched for a two-

run homer by Oscar Gamble in the very first inning; and that was all the Yankees scored for the rest of the night. Stone, as the New York reporters glumly reported the next day, was "masterful."

Five days later, Stone faced the Yankees again — and yielded only two hits as he whipped the New Yorkers six to one. Reggie Jackson, the Yankees' slugger, led off the second inning with his thirty-second home run of the season — and the only other hit the Yanks managed all evening was a fifth-inning single by shortstop Bucky Dent. Stone, nineteen and four now, had beaten the Yankees in a route-going performance for the second time in five days. In eighteen innings he had allowed just three runs and nine hits — and no runs at all, in either game, after the second inning. Baltimore had cut the Yanks' lead to two and a half games behind what *The New York Times* referred to as Stone's "dazzling pitching that has made him the standout in the American League this season."

Bob Watson, the Yankees' good-hitting first baseman, offered an interesting opinion as to what made Stone so formidable. "He doesn't give you a good ball to hit," he noted with admiration. "He throws at corners, spots his fastball and changes speeds. What happens is it looks so good to hit, guys are too anxious and they wind up swinging at his pitches."

Steve himself offered an insight into his approach. "Willie Mays," he recalled after mowing down the Yankees again, "told me that if he hits a home run off a guy on a curve ball, the next time he faces the guy, he's looking to hit a home run off a fastball." So, after Reggie Jackson had socked Steve's second-inning curveball into the right-field seats, he came to the plate again in the third and was fed, not a fastball, but a steady diet of slow, tantalizing curves. The result was an easy fly ball to the center-fielder.

"Jackson is a wonderful hitter," Stone explained to Thom Greer of the *New York Daily News*. "But I was thinking about what Mays said and I wasn't gonna throw him any fastballs. I wanted to show Reggie I was going to get him out with the curve. If he's going to hit a ball to beat me, he's going to do it on my pitch."

All of which was an example of Stone's newfound confidence, an element which Baltimore coach and the former star, Frank Robinson, insisted was crucial to Steve's phenomenal success. Steve agreed. He felt he had the Yankees under control. The Yankees could not help but agree. When asked whether he really thought that Stone was all that good a pitcher, Charlie Lau, the Yankees' highly-respected batting coach, answered, "He hasn't proved to us that he is not. And he's getting somebody else out, too," he added in a wry reference to the rest of the league's lineups.

Earl Weaver cheerfully agreed that Stone had earned his status as the league's ace hurler. "I always thought Stone could be a winner," he insisted. "There was never any doubt in my mind that this guy could be a winning pitcher with the Baltimore Orioles, not because of the Baltimore Orioles but because of his ability. It's the pitchers who make the club good. If it wasn't for him now, we'd be a losing team," Weaver admitted.

"But it's for damn sure we didn't go out and get him last season because I knew he would be nineteen and four today," Weaver acknowledged. "I got him for insurance. I told my general manager I thought he could win in the American League. But he was only my fifth starter. But

Steve pitched his way into the rotation. Some guy missed a turn and Steve got in." Weaver grinned. "And it looks like he's gonna be there awhile, doesn't it?"

In his next start, five days later on August 19, Steve faced the California Angels in search of his twentieth win — a plateau he had never achieved in his career, nor had any other pitcher won so many at this stage of the season. Steve not only got his coveted twentieth win, he actually came within five outs of pitching a no-hitter. Keeping the Angels hitless through the first seven innings — combined with his last outing against the Yankees, this gave Steve an incredible streak of twelve consecutive hitless innings pitched — Steve entered the eighth inning fully aware that he was within reach of a no-hitter. But after retiring the leadoff man in the eighth, Steve finally yielded a single to shortstop Bert Campaneris, who grounded one up the middle past the grasp of the Oriole infielders. Steve gave up one more hit that inning — a bloop single to Dan Ford — and then, with relief help from teammate Tippy Martinez, ultimately won the game, five to two, having allowed only those two hits sandwiched around a couple of walks. Was he disappointed at losing his chance at the pitching masterpiece? Hardly.

"I feel terrific," said Steve afterwards. "I've never ever been close to twenty wins before. I never thought much about winning twenty games before. I didn't know if I'd ever get the chance. I was only with fourth, fifth and sixth-place clubs.

"You don't go twenty and four pitching overpowering games every time out. I've only got one shutout, so I get just enough runs to win. It's the ballclub," he said modestly. "I would have liked the no-hitter," he admitted, "but I just didn't get it."

Steve thus became the twenty-second Oriole pitcher to win twenty games — but he was the earliest twenty-game winner in the club's history. Having had his remarkable fourteen-game winning streak finally stopped July 31, he had now reeled off another four victories in succession, almost singlehandedly keeping the Orioles in the race with the Yankees. "Without Steve," Weaver again admitted, "we would not even be in contention."

Pursued by reporters who kept searching for the key to his spectacular success, Steve again explained his pre-game rituals. Always think about the game ahead of time. Take the phone off the hook. Lie down on the bed, close your eyes. Then pitch the entire game-to-be in your head, getting every batter out at least four times, plus a couple of pinch hitters. Don't stop until you envision pitching coach Miller congratulating you on a complete game. "I'm a good pitcher," Stone told Diane Shah of *Newsweek*, "but not a great one. So I have to outsmart the opposition. If I go on instinct, I go to the shower."

Shah saw a parallel between Steve's careful preparation for the game and the thoroughness with which he had prepared for the possibility of celebrating his twentieth win. He had shipped two cases of white wine to Anaheim before the game, in case he should register his twentieth victory in the Angel game. "I hope the guys don't mind, but I don't like champagne," he explained. After the near no-hitter, though, he got a dose of champagne anyway — poured over his head by his celebrating teammates.

Stone now faced new individual challenges. Could he continue to lead the entire major leagues in wins? Could he match the Oriole club record, held by Dave McNally and Mike Cueller, for most wins in a season (at twenty-four)?

On September 4, he whipped Seattle five to one, for his twenty-second win. It was the one hundredth win of his major-league career, and reaching that milestone was sweet indeed. "I had great control," Stone said afterwards, "the best of the season. My curveball was working very well and I was getting them to hit my pitch. It's nice to win my hundredth career victory. It was a long time coming. I hope to have a hundred four or five wins before the season is over."

In the game itself, Steve had demonstrated real mastery. In defeating the Mariners for the third time that season, he had required a total of only one hundred nineteen pitches, of which seventy-nine were strikes. He walked only two, and struck out three. But as the numbers suggest, he was consistently able to get the batters to swing at his pitch, and hit either harmless popups or routine grounders.

"Stone mixes up his pitches so well it is almost impossible for a righthander to hit him," moaned Mariner Tom Paciorek, a right-handed hitter whom Steve had fanned twice in his four hitless trips to the plate. "His slider moves so well over the plate, and he just keeps you off balance all the time." Such is the art of pitching.

"Steve just throws the pitches he wants to throw," explained Weaver succinctly. "He throws the ball over the plate and tells the batter to try and hit it. He gives them what they aren't expecting, and he gets them out."

On September eleventh, Stone won his twenty-third game, raising his record to twenty-three and six, by handcuffing the Toronto Blue Jays 6-1. He scattered eight hits, struck out seven and pitched his ninth complete game of the campaign.

Nine days later, Steve notched his twenty-fourth triumph — and thus matched the Oriole club record held by McNally and Cueller. Oddly, the opponent and the score were the same as in his last win: a six to one victory over Toronto. Only a ninth-inning home run by Toronto's John Mayberry spoiled Steve's shutout bid.

Before the season ended, Steve got a final opportunity to break the club record for victories that he had just equalled — and he did it, with a four to three win over the Boston Red Sox. Finally, the Yankees edged Baltimore for the Division title by playing superb winning baseball through the September stretch drive. But if Baltimore came up slightly short in the end, it was through no fault of Stone's; it was only because of their pitching ace's superlative season that the Orioles were able to make as gallant a run as they did. Stone ended his season with twenty-five wins — more than any other pitcher in the major leagues — against only seven losses. He started thirty-seven games, more than any other leading hurler in the league (Rudy May of the Yankees appeared in forty-one, but some of those were in relief).He pitched two hundred fifty innings, yielding two hundred twenty-four hits and striking out one hundred forty-nine, and compiling an E.R.A. of 3.23.

On November 12, Steve Stone was awarded the Cy Young Award as the American League's best pitcher. The vote was taken of twenty-eight reporters, two from each of the fourteen American League cities. Only seven hurlers in the entire league got any votes at all. Stone was the only pitcher who was named on every single ballot. With thirteen first-place votes, ten second-place tallies, and five for third place, he was the clear winner over Oakland's ace Mike Norris, who came in second, and Yankee stars Tommy John and Rich Gossage, who finished third and fourth, respectively.

"He deserved it," said John graciously. "He pitched well all year and won twenty-five ballgames. And when a guy wins twenty-five games, it's hard not to give it to him."

Steve accepted the award with delight, gratitude and deep appreciation. He was quick to give credit to his teammates for the slick defense, sturdy relief pitching and clutch hitting that had contributed so much to each of his victories. "It's a great way to end the year," he said happily.

"I've been written off a lot of times," he noted. "I guess because I wasn't six-five and two hundred pounds. But the most important thing was, I didn't believe them. I was taken from the ranks of journeyman and lifted to the pinnacle of my profession," added the star who would never again be called a journeyman. "I think it means if you don't quit, you always have the chance to turn it around. If you see something out there, go after it."

"If I were to write a script for the 1980 season," he concluded, "I don't think I could have possibly written one any better than what happened."

Indeed not. The major leagues' biggest winner, with twenty-five victories. Starting pitcher in the All-Star game, and star of that game with a flawless three-inning stint. Winner of the American League awards for both Player of the Week and then Pitcher of the Month. Named by his peers, in the *Sporting News* poll, as the Pitcher of the Year. And finally, what Steve himself called "the final accolade" — the Cy Young Award.

Steve Stone had emerged as an exciting new star in the

galaxy of American sports, and reporters from the media rushed to chronicle his interestingly varied background and pastimes. Much was made of the various stuffed animals and good-luck charms he kept in his locker; the superstitious rituals of eating the same meal in the same town which he had had before his last victory there; his visits to psychics, hypnotists or anyone else who might be able to contribute something useful, if only psychologically, to his career; his excellently schooled taste in vintage wines, and his success as a restauranteur. It was worth noting that when Steve did decide to own and manage a number of restaurants, he applied himself to the job with the same dedication and seriousness that marked his pitching. He worked as a waiter, bartender, bookkeeper and maitre d'. "Lots of ballplayers have invested money in restaurants and lost their shirts because they didn't learn the business," he remarked, "and I was determined that wasn't going to happen to me."

In addition to his business acumen, the reporters discovered, Steve offered credentials in their own field — writing — as well. His poetry, short stories and book reviews had been published in various periodicals, including *The National Jewish Monthly,* and newspapers in Los Angeles, San Francisco and Chicago. "I write in spurts," Steve told *The Baltimore Jewish Times.* "I haven't written too much lately." He began writing poetry in 1970 while he was pitching for Amarillo in the Texas League.

"I was warming up in the bullpen for a game in Little Rock," he explained, "and I had overwhelming stuff. I thought I was going to pitch a no-hitter. But then I walked seven guys in one and a third innings and got knocked out of the game. I got real depressed and I walked around all night." At about five in the morning, he returned to his hotel, picked up pen and paper, and began to write. "I had never written anything before and I don't know what possessed me, but I started writing," he said. What emerged was a poem he titled "Today's Hero," which includes the lines:

> Your supreme effort of yesterday may
>   fall short of winning tomorrow — then what? . . .
> You have to go out tomorrow and win
>   again because the people like their heroes
>   a day at a time.
> The top of the world and the bottom aren't
>   really that far apart — now are they?

Clearly, this was not a man who was going to be taken in by passing adulation. But he certainly relished what he jokingly referred to as his "overnight success after nine years." Speaking to Michael Elkin of *The Jewish Exponent* of Philadelphia, Stone candidly and cheerfully conceded: "I enjoy the publicity. It's tremendous, especially the way it benefits my social life," he added with a grin. "Life outside the field is fun for me."

He had a desire to "settle down," and this feeling may well have come from Steve's closeness to his own family. "Family is very important to me and I see my parents and sister whenever I can." Whenever the Orioles visit Cleveland, he regularly visits his mother, an avid baseball fan who Steve insists makes "the best matzoh-ball soup this side of Tel-Aviv."

Steve told Michael Elkin that he had had "a regular Jewish upbringing" while growing up in Cleveland. "We were affiliated with a Conservative Temple, but as I got older I became more Reform." He joked that at Passover, his grandfather "conducted the longest seders in the history of Judaism." His evident fondness for his parents and grandparents has clearly affected his regard for his elders. "I was raised with a good feeling about the elderly," he said. "My parents impressed me with the fact that the elderly are not to be discarded in life. You know, I was a history major in college, and I learned that every great civilization had a council of elders on whom they relied. Old people are to be revered for what they can offer."

"Everyone in this game," he reflected of his baseball career, "has the opportunity to set a fine example for youngsters. I always want to set a good role model, just like Sandy Koufax did for me." Obviously honored to be compared to the great Koufax, Steve has remarked — with his tongue firmly in his cheek — that "I can say honestly and unequivocally that I'm the best right-handed Jewish pitcher to come into the majors in the past twenty years — mainly because I don't know of any others."

Committed Jew as he is, Steve has never found that his Jewishness has hampered his progress in baseball. "Being Jewish in this sport has never been a drawback," he told Elkin. "Those who claim anti-Semitism has held them back are looking for an easy excuse. They're not doing well simply because they're not good enough. In this business, talent will out. If you can do it, you'll play, and it doesn't matter if you're white, black, green, Jewish or whatever."

Still, the subject has arisen occasionally, such as the day that Garry Maddox, a black outfielder for the Philadelphia Phillies, asked Steve if he was Jewish.

"Yes, I am," the pitcher responded.

"You people own all the ghettos and don't fix them up," the black man accused the Jew.

"Yeah," said Stone dryly, "and you people all eat watermelon."

The two of them began discussing racial issues and stereotypes, and eventually, Stone told Murray Chass, Maddox had a deeper understanding of Jews in general and Stone in particular. "We got to be such good friends," Steve concluded, "that he invited me to his wedding."

What Stone accomplished in his remarkable 1980 season, though, was to be not merely the best Jewish pitcher in baseball, but to be the best pitcher in his league, period, of any color, race or creed. Asked by Jacobson to explain his amazing season, Steve answered: "I didn't sell my soul to the devil — but I'm having a hard time convincing my parents." More seriously, he pondered the various factors that contributed to his incredible turnaround and ended up simply concluding: "It just doesn't get any better than this."

"Vince Scully said it best at the All-Star banquet," Stone told Henry Hecht of The New York Post, referring to the Dodger announcer. "He said, 'Boys, in the twinkling of an eye you go from the All-Star game to the Old-Timers' game, so drink it all in now, and feel it, and enjoy every second of it while you can.' "

Steve paused, then said, "Sometimes, in the middle of the game — even when my concentration is so intense — I step off the mound, and I look around at the fans in the stands — at everything — and I say to myself: this is nice." Steve Stone smiled the smile of a man who has found his dream and lived it, and repeated simply, "This is nice."